Memory's Stories

Interdisciplinary Readings of Multicultual Life Narratives

Thomas V. McGovern

UNIVERSITY PRESS OF AMERICA,® INC.
Lanham • Boulder • New York • Toronto • Plymouth, UK

Copyright © 2007 by
University Press of America,® Inc.
4501 Forbes Boulevard
Suite 200
Lanham, Maryland 20706
UPA Acquisitions Department (301) 459-3366

Estover Road
Plymouth PL6 7PY
United Kingdom

Library of Congress Control Number: 2007924041
ISBN-13: 978-0-7618-3764-0 (clothbound : alk. paper)
ISBN-10: 0-7618-3764-7 (clothbound : alk. paper)
ISBN-13: 978-0-7618-3763-3 (paperback : alk. paper)
ISBN-10: 0-7618-3763-9 (paperback : alk. paper)

To
John Patrick and Peggy McGovern
Patricia Pausha McGovern
Maureen, Beth, and Matthew McGovern

Contents

1 Listening to Memory's Stories   1
Composing and Reading Life Narratives   3
Saint Augustine's Testimony   10

2 Mapping the Examining Conscience   25
Unifying Literary Metaphors   27
Psychobiography as Cross-Disciplinary Map   28
Erik Erikson and the Architecture of Identity   29
Thomas Merton's Storied Mountains   36

3 Revealing Prophetic Voices   54
Spiritual Turning Points   56
Maps and Metaphors   61
Roots of Two Collaborative Composition Strategies   67
Fruits of Collaborative Authorship   68
Memory's Episodes   78
Prophetic Voices   86

4 Coloring Women's Stories   94
Scholarship by and about Women Authors   96
Commentaries by Sidonie Smith and Colleagues   99
Maxine Hong Kingston's Talking Stories   108
Remembering Continued   119

5 Continuing Anthologies of the Self   127
Personality Psychology   130
Dan McAdams and the Life Story Model of Identity   131
Assessing Richard Rodriguez   143

6 Transforming Chaos into Hope   168
   Redemption Stories   170
   Composing Relationships   174
   Episodes   178
   James McBride and the Coloring of Identity   183

Preface

This book is an anthology of stories about how multicultural authors composed texts of their lives. There are stories about how scholars created theoretical perspectives to interpret lives and texts. The book invites you to listen with empathy to lives and perspectives different from your own, to expect and to respect differences. You may learn more about your own stories.

I examined life narratives that scholars regard as classics: *The Confessions* by Saint Augustine, *The Seven Storey Mountain* by Thomas Merton, *Black Elk Speaks*, and *The Autobiography of Malcolm X*. I included recent texts that are emerging classics, thanks to the wider canon of multicultural authors: *The Woman Warrior: Memoirs of a Girlhood among Ghosts* by Maxine Hong Kingston and *Hunger of Memory: The Education of Richard Rodriguez, Days of Obligation: An Argument with My Mexican Father*, and *Brown: The Last Discovery of America*, by Richard Rodriguez, and *The Color of Water: A Black Man's Tribute to His White Mother* by James McBride.

We will begin with what one scholar called life narratives' *ur-book*, composed more than sixteen hundred years ago. The last chapter synthesizes scholars' new analytical tools with a commentary on a text composed at the end of the twentieth century.

I hope you will be challenged to think in interdisciplinary ways about the texts of others' lives and about your own.

Acknowledgements

My book grew out of fifteen years of conversations and classes in the Department of Integrative Studies at Arizona State University at the West Campus. Linda Stryker and Arthur Sabatini were constant explorers with me of the uncharted terrain between the disciplines, with Joe Buenker's maps.

Several undergraduate students were especially helpful in working on specific authors and chapters. Beth McGovern created the very first bibliography for my Multicultural Autobiographies course. Samantha Burkhardt assisted me with Chapter Three and using Erik Erikson's theory to examine Malcolm X's story. Michelle Martin brought her interdisciplinary talents to Chapter Four for Sidonie Smith's feminist literary theory and Maxine Hong Kingston's stories. Rebeca Lopez Pollack evaluated contemporary Latina texts and all the criticism on the three memoirs by Richard Rodriguez covered in Chapter Five. Samantha Leigh Miller read everything from cover to cover and worked on the Endnotes, as well.

Reverend Robert Krajicek is a Roman Catholic priest and a psychologist. I am indebted to him for his feisty readings of my interpretations of Saint Augustine and Thomas Merton, now Chapters One and Two. He helped me to re-learn Augustine and to truly discover the powerful voice of his mother, Monica.

Dan McAdams, about whose theory you will learn much more in this book, read early drafts of this manuscript. Without his candid feedback and the continuing insights I drew from his scholarly work, the interdisciplinary quality of this book may have never been achieved. He was there at the final stages, as well, to challenge me on Chapter Six and its synthesis material.

Allan Brawley read my whole manuscript while composing his own biographical study of a socialist philanthropist. Both of us hesitantly explored methodologies and subject matter outside of our original academic fields. We kept each other encouraged and resolved and smiling. Allan epitomizes the richness of collegiality and the continuing grace of friendship.

My wife, Pat, is the co-author of the most important episodes of my life narrative for more than forty years, now. She was happy that I started this project. She was very happy when I finished it.

Thomas V. McGovern
ASU at the West Campus
Phoenix, Arizona
December 2006

Chapter One

Listening to Memory's Stories

PRECIS

Composing a life narrative requires three overlapping tasks. Writers gather memory's episodes. They decide on a composition strategy to communicate events and meanings to particular audiences. Finally, they provide their readers with maps and metaphors as compasses to navigate their narratives. Listening to or reading a story requires our empathy. We can retrace authors' processes in constructing stories by first examining the maps and metaphors they used; second, by evaluating their unique composition strategies; and third, by analyzing each episode in relation to the whole text and in the context of the authors' lives.

In this chapter, I will introduce you to these three activities and weave together the interdisciplinary work on life narratives done by literary theorists and by psychologists. The former have always been interested in stories, but became more attentive to the psychological characteristics of authors in the last half of the 20th century. Psychologists investigate human behavior using scientific methods; they became more attentive to the rich qualities of narratives and diversified their traditional methods during the same period.

The chapter begins with an historical synthesis of theoretical tools to evaluate a life narrative text more critically and to appreciate authors' stories. In this first chapter, we will use these tools to examine what many scholars consider the first autobiography–Saint Augustine's The Confessions.

In 1771, Benjamin Franklin introduced his *Autobiography* with some thoughts to his son. He had gathered pithy anecdotes from his ancestors, doing so while on various trips abroad. He felt it only appropriate to tell his son all about these family tales, and could do so during his leisure time, writing while in retirement from his public life and worldly affairs. Two hundred years later, Maxine Hong Kingston began *The Woman Warrior: Memoirs of a Girlhood among Ghosts* quite differently. Her mother issued a stern prohibition that Maxine used to launch her narrative. The prohibition was to tell no one about her aunt who committed suicide in China. The family had been shamed and erased all memory of her from their collective story. To this day, they act as if her father only had brothers, denying she had ever been born.

Fathers and sons. Mothers and daughters. Heroines and heroes. Saints and sinners. What do I remember? What should (not) be told? Who will listen to my story and what will they make of it? About whom am I writing? Why did I do the things that I did? How do I make sense of all these memories of my life?

From after World War II to the turn of the new millennium, there was a heightened interest in writing, reading, and commentary on the literary form of autobiography, defined more generically now as life narratives or life writing. America always has been captivated by autobiographical texts. Sayre called them the Song of Ourselves, the quintessential American literature.[1]

How and why do persons compose such stories? They may arrive at a moment in their lives when there are so many episodic fragments that a story is required to hold them together. It may be when an adolescent shares private diary entries with a peer or when an older person probes their soul-searching prose. A story may begin when a parent fills in the blanks about family history while sitting on a couch with a son or daughter at a funeral home, and in that accounting, connections take shape that were neither fully understood nor stated. The story's composition may come when private experiences thrust an individual into public light by choice or circumstance. Articulating a justification of one's choices becomes more important than any one event or sequence ever seemed when they originally took place. This composition may follow the survival of a horrific medical episode. After reflecting on its parts, extracting some meaning from all that happened, an inspirational story takes shape about how the author cobbled together the resources to live through it.

In writing a life narrative, authors progress from the kernel of an idea and an inchoate motivation to tell a story, through choices about how to structure a text, and eventually compose their personal tale as a public one. The term, "text", came from the Latin words for "tissue" and "weave". Composing the text of a story and creating the character of a self is thus a psychological and a literary process. It requires three activities that overlap: gathering memory's episodes and plumbing one's motivations and intentions for remembering or forgetting them; fashioning composition strategies to weave the episodes into a text; and creating maps and metaphors for audiences to understand the whole story as more than the sum of many parts.

I use these activities as guideposts in my university classes to examine autobiographical texts. First, we identify the maps or metaphors of a life story, revealed in the author's title and chapter headings. Second, literary scholars offer powerful lenses for us to critique authors' writing strategies and their creative approaches to their narratives. Third, a close reading and discussion of passages help us examine memory's episodes. I use theories from developmental and personality psychology to explore authors' possible motivations and intentions culled from the data of their constructed episodes.

Scholars interpret texts by using different theoretical lenses and interdisciplinary perspectives. Anthropology, communications, cultural studies, ethnic studies, feminist studies, history, literary criticism, media studies, and religious studies are all viewpoints that enable us to understand authors, their texts, and the contexts in which they lived and wrote. New research on memory in neuroscience and cognitive psychology also inform our understanding of the construction of life narratives and autobiographical memories.

In the next section, I amplify some ideas about writing a life narrative and introduce the interdisciplinary perspectives and the autobiographical texts examined in subsequent chapters.

COMPOSING AND READING LIFE NARRATIVES

Gathering Memory's Episodes

The author's first task is similar to assembling an album from shoeboxes filled with old photographs, or scanning images from disparate sources and burning them onto a compact disk. In the opening pages of *Storyteller*, Leslie Marmon Silko recalled a Hopi basket filled with family photographs from the Laguna Pueblo and how each one evoked distinct, yet intersecting memories. I sometimes ask students to gather a collage of images from their personal shoe-boxes and then to write short descriptions, walking a reader along the path of their lives. My faculty colleagues ask students to create videotaped interviews of family members and friends' oral histories. Biography and autobiography blend.

One snapshot, image, or anecdote leads to another, then to another, and then to questions about the times, places, and people in between. The end-result is a bundle of episodes that will remain disconnected without editing and the creation of an explicit story line. There are frequent surprises in this early gathering task. Happy moments and quite painful memories come to the surface. They had been forgotten, consciously or unconsciously. Looking directly at these episodes has unintended consequences. Why did I (not) remember some times, places, or people? Are there folks with whom I must finish what is unfinished? How will I look behind the reflecting glass, beyond the episodes to my motivations and intentions? Writing about episodes can be seductive. It also arouses anxiety.

The definition of "autobiography" is: "the writing of one's own history; a story of a person's life written by himself or herself".[2] Breaking down this definition into its component parts reveal three distinct elements. "Autos" (self) means one's own, of or by oneself, independent, self-produced, spontaneous, automatic. "Bios" (life) means course or way of living. "Graphe" (writing) means something written or drawn in a specific way. The literary scholar, James Olney [3], used these three root elements to examine texts, describing how different authors added to the richness and variations of this genre in the twentieth century. His insightful commentaries oriented later scholars about the complex interactions between the three "I's" of an autobiographical text: the self who remembered the memories, the self whose experiences were publicly observable and sometimes were the object of biographical review by others, and the self revealed by the author and composed into a character for the text.

Autobiographies are self-critical works-in-progress, always needing our skeptical scrutiny. They deserve our deep and probing empathy. John Barbour, writing about the conscience of the autobiographer, described a host of quandaries to be resolved as authors gather memory's episodes and figure out their intentions and motivations.[4] His thought-provoking analyses of the ethical and religious intentions of autobiography suggested a number of questions that I ask my students to consider.

What does it mean to be truthful?
What are my boundaries for truthful disclosure?
Are my moral values evident in what I did, and in how I write about it?
How can I communicate genuine moral conflict without appearing self-serving?
How accurate are my memories or are they distorted?

The last question leads directly to cognitive psychology and the research on autobiographical memory. Scientists investigate how memories are encoded, stored, retrieved (or forgotten), and communicated to others. Researchers now distinguish among those memories that define our core selves, those that we can remember because of the heightened affect associated with them, and those we continually work and re-work. Cognitive scientists are just scratching the surface of how intentions, values, and neural communication systems influence memory processes. Social scientists examine our remembered episodes for traces of family, gender, ethnicity, class experiences, and the larger culture and society in which we live, as well as the historical epochs in which all of these factors come together in unique ways.

When the autobiographer's accumulated basket of memories becomes too heavy or a critical incident calls for a synthesis to solve an immediate problem, a sorting process then begins. Sorting and prioritization require some standard by which one episode will be considered more important or evocative than another. To use composition teachers' rhetoric, the "free-writing" time is over and deliberately chosen composition strategies need to be developed.

Composition Strategies

The well-read, 21st century author has many structures and strategies from which to sample. Smith and Watson [5] described fifty-two different forms of what they termed "life narratives". I will describe several of these forms and preview some of the texts examined in subsequent chapters of this book.

Conversion Narratives

St. Augustine wrote *The Confessions* at the end of the fourth century and it remains a vibrant prototype. Thomas Merton's *The Seven Storey Mountain* was a twentieth century conversion narrative that drew inspiration from Augustine's maps for life experiences and his composition strategies. Merton's *The Seven Storey Mountain* had its fiftieth anniversary in 1996. At about the same time, his private, secular journals were released so that a reader could study the layers of an evolving consciousness in a man who once noted that when he seemed to be revealing the most about himself, he was actually hiding the most. [6] Merton's work will be examined in Chapter Two, "Mapping the Examining Conscience".

Collaborative Life Narratives

Among the most celebrated collaborative life narratives are *Black Elk Speaks. As told through John G. Neihardt (Flaming Rainbow)* and *The Autobiography of Malcolm X as told to Alex Haley*. These texts are mediated narratives. The collaboration can become a source of controversy and ambiguity, especially when it is a bicultural effort involving the translation of complex languages and customs. However, these texts' continuing value comes from what they may teach readers about contemporary constructions of the self. They appeal to the thirst for redemption, present in most adults as they age. Moreover, their often-prophetic messages motivate younger generations to follow the rugged path of public commitment to a personal calling. These two texts will be examined in Chapter Three, "Revealing Prophetic Voices".

Feminist and Ethnic Autobiographies

The immigration or ethnic autobiography merges with "autogynography" when women of color compose their stories.[7] In Chapter Four, "Coloring Women's Stories", I use the historical and feminist analyses developed by Smith and Watson [8] to explore women's voices, characterized by richly nuanced understandings of subjectivity, strength, empathy, and discontinuity. With their lens, we will examine the deftly crafted stories of Maxine Hong Kingston in *The Woman Warrior: Memoirs of a Girlhood among Ghosts*.

Serial Autobiographies

Some stories were just too big to tell in one installment or volume. Serial autobiographies are multiple texts published over a longer period of time by the same author to describe the evolving chapters of their lives.[9] They provide an excellent opportunity to synthesize psychological and literary theory. Dan McAdams's life story model of identity will be the theoretical perspective used in Chapter Five, "Continuing Anthologies of the Self". In that chapter, we will examine the serial texts of Richard Rodriguez: *Hunger of Memory: The Education of Richard Rodriguez*, *Days of Obligation: An Argument with My Mexican Father*, and *Brown: The Last Discovery of America*, published when the author was thirty-eight, forty-eight, and fifty-eight years old.

Therapeutic and Survivor Narratives

Overcoming cultural, economic, physical, psychological, and social adversity became an increasingly popular theme in the last quarter of the twentieth century.[10] After World War II, psychoanalysis and clinical psychology inspired a vocabulary and conceptual principles for the increased emphasis on the *autos* characteristics of life writing. Generativity and redemption have become, once again, critical ingredients in adult lives. These issues have historical, psychological, and spiritual roots as unique responses that some individuals are able to make to incredibly difficult life circumstances. In Chapter Six, "Transforming Chaos into Hope", we will explore narratives about postmodern vagaries and their redemptive possibilities, in particular, James McBride's *The Color of Water: A Black Man's Tribute to his White Mother*.

There are so many exemplary texts and theoretical perspectives to which an author can turn for inspiration and guidance in arriving at a composition strategy. Discovering one's own voice requires responses to additional questions.

To what stories does my contemporary reading public respond?
Who is my audience?
How do I construct my autobiographical "I"?

What always should remain private in my life?
What are the ethical consequences of making my private life, public?

When authors wrestle with such questions, trying to compose episodes, to connect them in some effective way, they discover that devising a composition strategy alternates with ongoing psychological reflection. And that brings us to the final stage of the process. With so many factors at work inside and outside of authors' control and even consciousness, they must figure out how to communicate the meanings inherent in their episodes, to give their readers a compass with which to navigate the landscape of their whole story.

Maps and Metaphors

After authors gather a cornucopia of episodes, describing them with alternating vivid imagery and dispassionate details, they construct rhetorical bridges from one memory to another, from one period of their lives to another. Passages expand and some get deleted. Authors come to terms with the goodness and evil woven into the tissue of their stories. Perhaps the text in this early form was ready for review by a potential publisher. Perhaps a trusted and plain-speaking friend offered to read it, or a partner listened patiently during the months and years of composition's trials and tribulations. Perhaps the author had the luxury to put it away for awhile–to compost it–then to return for another fresh look.

Authors now find themselves, whether they realize it or not, in the middle of one of the major philosophical-psychological-literary debates of the last century. Is there some principle of continuity and unity in all our lives? Why do we constantly search for some cohering theme with which the sum of all of our episodes becomes meaningful? Or–are our selves saturated, discontinuous, fragmented, multiple, and non-linear? The search for a unifying theme may be illusory, a Sisyphean task. Is there really any continuity and coherence in our lives? There are varied maps and metaphors to communicate authors' conclusions about these vexing questions.

Before World War II, American literary criticism about autobiographies focused on the historical and biographical characteristics—*bios*—of exemplary lives as portrayed in texts. Public figures like Benjamin Franklin or Henry Adams or Henry Ford were considered representatives of a period's character and they transcended time, culture, and society as "men for all seasons". Sayre [11] suggested that a life was distinctive if its narrative connected to some great American virtue or ideal. The heroic story moved the imagination from abstractions to specific pathways for how to be the best that we all should hope to become.

Construing our lives as a spiritual pilgrimage from sin to grace, a journey from tragic circumstances and bad choices to redemption and moral clarity has been another inspirational map for the autobiography. All individuals get lost, but some get found. Others believe that they have been born again. The unity of such a story is in the circular journey, returning via our memory to where we began, and understanding for the first time a place we believe is where we ought to be. This understanding of unity rests often on a faith in some powerful guiding force that brought us to particular moments of epiphany. Such a narrative makes direct contact with audiences filled with sinners and born-again saints and those who live mostly vanilla lives somewhere in between.

Sigmund Freud and Erik Erikson believed that we understand lives by plumbing the psychologically unifying principles. Moving beyond Freud's psychosexual explanations for human behavior, Erik Erikson mapped what he believed were universal and cross-cultural ages and stages of psychosocial development. With his concept of *epigenesis*, he proposed the optimistic possibility that we are able to get better and better at understanding our selves. By dealing with the predictable crises associated with growing older, our stories and lives become richer.[12] Like Erikson, the literary scholar Georges Gusdorf focused on the continuity within authors' lives and their stories, but he recognized earlier than most that "the original sin of autobiography is first one of logical coherence and rationalization".[13] He asserted that the production of inspiring texts was only possible when a particular society was sophisticated enough to produce distinguished, representative selves. Unity and continuity were not only possible, but became the standard by which we judged all others, influencing authors to extract an underlying coherence out of their lives' episodes.

What if the episodes do not reveal easy linkages? What if daily events or the chronological brackets of one's life are replete with disconnected experiences? Some women's stories written in the twentieth century seemed quite similar, in actuality or composition, to those written by men.[14] However, as more and more such texts were published after the Civil Rights and Women's Movements of the 1960s and 1970s, differences in the metaphors and maps employed by women versus men became evident. Feminist scholarship published after the 1970s resurrected earlier texts with different voices and ultimately prompted the production of more texts by and about women. First the similarities and then the far-reaching differences among women's composition styles and understandings of their lives' patterns were celebrated. Scholarship by African Americans, Asian Americans, Latinas, and Native Americans resurrected, and then illuminated more brightly the distinct and heterogeneous constructions of selves in ALL American life.

Class, sexual orientation, and multi-ethnic identities informed autobiographies and its scholarship in ways not possible before.

Even scientists who based their work on the predictability and reliability of human behavior were left at loose ends to explain contemporary metaphors and maps of the self. Kenneth Gergen [15] proposed a "saturated self" for which "the center fails to hold"; his alternative to unity was a constant coping with a state of "multiphrenia".

Narratives of unity from religious sources abound, but authors must create new metaphors for a time when the old, predictable maps have less common value. David Leigh [16] argued that many twentieth century spiritual autobiographies were sagas of individuals who lost confidence in finding any unity in life. Theirs was a post-Holocaust, post-Hiroshima world that left persons of faith alienated, seeking a personal autonomy that too often yielded less than it promised. Individuality revealed the limitations of a freedom with few shared visions; loneliness became the natural consequence of psychological agency and choices became anchored by fewer and fewer common assumptions. The philosopher and psychologist, William James [17], noted at the beginning of the twentieth century that a common state of individuals was that of the "divided self"; alternative responses found in life narratives were many and difficult.

In short, the maps and metaphors used to title many pre-World War II texts were simple and descriptive, such as "The Life of John X: My Experiences in Corporate America." In contrast, contemporary autobiographers' choices of titles like *I Know Why the Caged Bird Sings, The Color of Water, The Woman Warrior, The Latin Deli, Storyteller, Hunger of Memory, Days of Obligation,* and *Brown,* appear deceptively simple as maps for their readers to follow or metaphors for their readers to identify with. All these texts were about coming of age—a timeless and universal challenge—but they emphasized the unique experiences of specific gendered, family, cultural, and geographical contexts. The power of their metaphors, and their composition strategies, as we shall see in coming chapters, makes them authors to be read with our deepest reservoirs of empathy. As our own reading journey, we must push ourselves to listen to their stories and to have our assumptions stretched beyond previous imaginings.

Before meeting these contemporary authors in subsequent chapters, it will be beneficial to consider the person who created memoirs. I first read St. Augustine's *The Confessions* when I was studying philosophy in my junior year in college. I read him again, thirty-five years later, as an academic psychologist teaching interdisciplinary courses on life narratives. My second reading was a profoundly different experience. I hope to convey why in the following pages.

SAINT AUGUSTINE'S TESTIMONY

Biographical Notes

Aurelius Augustinus was born on November 13, 354 CE, in Northern Africa, son of a pagan father, Patricius, and a Christian mother, Monica. He had two brothers and a sister. His father was a town government official with tax collecting duties, who placed high value on a classical Latin education for his son and made financial sacrifices to accomplish that goal. A classical education was a passport out of a life lived in one impoverished locality and into the larger world of the Roman Empire. Augustine was fond of Latin literature, but hated the rote learning coupled with corporal punishment in his Greek and arithmetic classes. He began his study of classical rhetoric at age eleven, described by Peter Brown, in his biography.

> The aim was to measure up to the timeless perfection of an ancient classic.
> Vergil, for such people, had 'not only never made a mistake, but had never
> written a line that was not admirable'. Every word, every turn of
> phrase of these few classics, therefore, was significant. The writer
> did not merely write: he 'wove' his discourse; he was a man who had
> 'weighed the precise meaning of every word'. . . .Above all, this education
> would have taught Augustine to express himself. He was encouraged
> to weep, and to make others weep.[18]

By the age of fifteen, such an education had already established the platform for his amazing memory of other texts, his close readings of rhetorical styles, and most of all his capacity to use words to reveal his heart and to urge his readers to discover their own.[19]

At sixteen, during a financially required hiatus in his education, Augustine began the adolescent sexual adventures described in Books II and III of *The Confessions*. When he went to Carthage to resume his studies by day, his nightly exploits were shameful and lusty, in the company of a group he called "the wreckers". He remembered how he was more in love with the idea of being in love than genuinely experiencing it. Augustine began a fifteen-year, loving relationship with an unnamed woman who bore him a son, Adeodatus ("God-given") in 372. In that same year, his father was baptized on his deathbed as a Christian.

At nineteen, the Latin scholar Cicero inspired a devotion to philosophy and the pursuit of knowledge only to be attained by suppressing sensual urges. Augustine came to terms with his conflicts between mind and body via Manicheanism with its lightness and darkness dualism. Redemption in this popular cult-religion was accomplished by a combination of intuitive knowledge and abstinence from food, wine, and sex. Career demands temporarily supplanted his singular pursuit of a life of the mind, however, and from 374 to 383, Augustine taught grammar and rhetoric, first in his hometown and then back in Carthage where he opened a school. He became a respected scholar and orator.

In 384, Augustine went to Rome to study philosophy, taking Adeodatus' mother and his son, but deceiving his mother, Monica, and leaving her behind in Africa. He explored Neo-Platonism and the skeptical views of the New Academy. Skepticism seemed a good fit for Augustine's traits and characterized his life even after he left their particular tenets behind—virtue rested in suspending final judgments whereas danger followed from a too quick and total adherence to any one point of view. At age thirty, he was appointed as a professor of rhetoric in Milan, and was captivated by listening to the sermons of Saint Ambrose. The bishop's provocative interpretations of the scriptures blended with a mysticism that offered Augustine some antidote to the gnawing experiences of evil and sin in his life. Monica arrived in Italy the following year and arranged for him to marry a woman more appropriate to a future career and his increasingly Christian religious pursuits. Augustine left his lover and the mother of his son. She returned to Africa vowing not to give herself to another man. Augustine took another lover to stave off his desires while he waited on a proper marriage partner.

Brown's interpretation of Augustine's relationship with the mother of Adeodatus is an unflattering one.

> Our curiosity about her is a very modern preoccupation, which Augustine
> and his cultivated friends would have found strange. . . .As a provincial
> professor 'on the make', Augustine had no wish for anything but a
> 'second-class' marriage with a concubine. He had little inclination to
> tie himself, by a premature match, to some family of impoverished
> gentlefolk at Tagaste. . .it was not moral scruples that led Augustine
> to abandon his concubine. It was ambition.[20]

In a more sympathetic analysis, O'Donnell [21] reminded us of the common practices of the age and suggested that this relationship collapsed due to the absolute restrictions of the Roman caste system. Augustine wrote of her departure, passionately describing the bonds he felt with her, now rent asunder and bloodied by the experience. He turned to his friends and rationalized her loss by a discussion with them about good and evil; to satisfy his sexual self, he turned to another woman. The closing passage of Book VI construed the episode as part of the larger unity of his life's map leading from sin to grace.

In the summer of 386, Augustine adopted the work of Plotinus as his new intellectual standard. Brown suggested that this exercise was a turning point for him as he changed his sights from a career as a rhetorician to that of a philosopher.[22] His biographer suggests that he was attempting to synthesize so many strands of thought, trying to apply them directly to his own life, integrating into some coherent whole the works of philosophy, early readings of Saint Paul, and most of all the relentless piety and influence of his mother Monica's faith in Christianity. [23]

This restless intellectual pilgrimage was the platform for Augustine's conversion experience. In the famous scene in the garden, he captures readers with vivid prose about how his head and his heart were being rent asunder because he did not have the wherewithal to make a final commitment although his very bones knew what he should be doing. In one moment of epiphany he read from Saint Paul's letter to the Romans (13:13–14): "Not in dissipation and drunkenness, nor in debauchery and lewdness, nor in arguing and jealousy; but put on the Lord Jesus Christ, and make no provision for the flesh or the gratification of your desires", and therein his conversion of mind and heart came together. The first person he told was Monica, who felt affirmed immediately in her long-suffering vision for her son's future.

Ambrose baptized him into Christianity at the Easter Vigil ceremonies on April 24, 387. His time in Italy ended with Monica's death, after the two of them shared a mystical vision. He returned to Africa with Adeodatus, hoping to establish a monastic community and to live out his life as a contemplative and teacher. The first nine books of *The Confessions* chronicled this story of continuing intellectual pursuits, of plumbing the depths of his own human nature and its sinful concomitants, his conversion and baptism, and the restless pursuit of unity with God through grace.[24]

In 390, Augustine plunged into a deep sorrow with the death of his son, only seventeen, as well as from the too-young death of a dear friend, Nebridius. He wandered for awhile, but was recruited by the Christian community at Hippo to be ordained as their priest. In 397, they installed him as their bishop and he began to write *The Confessions*. In 427, Augustine catalogued all his works in a book translated as the *Reconsiderations*. This was not just an inventory, but a careful (and final) evaluation of his intellectual and spiritual development. When he reviewed *The Confessions*, he judged that he would not change anything. Thirty years had passed since its composition and first readings by the Christian community at Hippo. Correcting past memories in revisionist fashion was deemed unnecessary; the text continued to inspire him and his community.

Until his death in 430 in Hippo, Augustine nurtured and educated his flock through sermons that remain rhetorical works of art; he must have been a spellbinding preacher. As bishop, he brokered all of the civil and religious disputes of his flock. In his spare time, he composed theological, philosophical, and political texts in response to the wild array of belief systems of that era. When the Vandals plundered North Africa, his library was spared, leaving a legacy of one hundred books, two hundred and forty letters, and more than five hundred sermons. His texts shaped the Christian faith for centuries to come. Unfortunately, this legacy was often negative inasmuch as his theological interpretations about the Genesis story and about original sin and its consequences cast a long, relentless shadow over women's identities and aborted the legitimate roles of ministry and leadership they held in the early Christian community.

It remains for modern readers to reflect on the ideas developed over Augustine's lifetime, and to respond critically and with empathy to his texts and their author. James O'Donnell [25] described his own 1992 three-volume translation and commentary on *The Confessions* as "a new set of grappling hooks, meaning-extractors, and nuance detectors", inviting readers to Augustine with fresh eyes and to be captured as he had been throughout his scholarly life.

Confession as Metaphor and Map

I defined map and metaphor earlier as authors' overarching statements about the unifying principle they identified for their life narratives and its text. Cartographers and scientists make choices about how fine-grained the detail of their topographies, depending on function and purpose. Poets and storytellers use language to suggest more than what is said, inviting their audiences to become engaged with them as they imagine their worlds. Augustine's title can be appreciated as both a map and a metaphor.

> *Confiteri* is a verb of speaking, and *confessio* is speech that is made
> possible, and hence authorized by God. . . .Depending on the subject,
> the effect may be that of praise (*confessio laudis*), self-blame (*confessio
> peccatorum*), or (least common in A. and in *conf.*) determined avowal
> (*confessio fidei*). . . .His business is with his God, for the edification of those
> who are chosen by his God to benefit from the text; other readers are left
> to shift for themselves.[26]

In his biography of Augustine, Garry Wills pushed O'Donnell's analysis of confession as praise, sin, and faith further. Addressing the interpretations heaped by supporters onto Augustine from immediately after his death, through more antagonistic Reformation writers, and into the facile readings from our contemporary *True Confessions* culture, Wills asserted that "*confiteri* means, etymologically, to *cor*roborate, to *con*firm testimony".[27] Wills argued that a more apt translated title should be *The Testimony*.

Augustine's story is a testimony, a written prayer addressed to God, and all the while he is thinking out loud about what he and God are doing in his life and why. His text weaves the Hebrew Scriptures (especially Genesis and the Psalms) and Christian Scriptures (especially Paul's epistles) into his life's fabric.[28] Augustine's famous introit that I remembered so well, returning to the text after more than thirty years, spoke of the stirring of God in one's soul and the restlessness and disruption we feel in our hearts as we pursue its origins. The relentless question that guides his whole story becomes: how will the God who created all things possibly see fit to enter my mind and heart and soul? Moreover, Brown described *The Confessions* as a truly psychological work, a probing portrait of an individual who is able to communicate his story by counter-pointing his certainty of God's plan with a genuine humility about whether he is worthy or will choose that plan.[29]

As a baptized Christian for ten years and a bishop for two, Augustine most probably composed his autobiography over the calendar 397 year, in the midst of all his pastoral duties. Writing *The Confessions* was therapeutic. Its motivation and its lasting inspiration for us readers derive from his being able to come to terms with the myriad of experiences and motivations in his life, to arrive at a compelling synthesis, and to communicate that mid-life understanding with such sincerity.[30] He was at Erikson's psychosocial stage of generativity and fully appreciating the psychological powers of redemption illuminated by McAdams.[31] O'Donnell concluded:

> The,Confessions then, present themselves to us as a book about
> God, and about Augustine: more Augustine at the beginning, more
> God at the end. But Augustine does not disappear in this work. Properly
> speaking, Augustine is redeemed, and in so far as he is redeemed and
> reformed according to the image and likeness of God, he becomes
> representative of all humankind.[32]

In contemporary and more humanistic narratives, this acknowledged blending of voices remains paramount. Maxine Hong Kingston observed in *The Woman Warrior's* last chapter that the story belonged to her mother at the beginning but became hers at the end. Both were always there and neither needed to get lost for the other to emerge so strongly.[33]

> The *Confessions* are, quite succinctly, the story of Augustine's 'heart'
> or his 'feelings'. . . .The emotional tone of the *Confessions* strikes any
> modern reader. The book owes its lasting appeal to the way in which
> Augustine, in his middle age, had dared to open himself up to the feelings
> of his youth. Yet, such a tone was not inevitable. Augustine's intense
> awareness of the vital role of 'feeling' in his past life had come to grow
> upon him.[34]

Genesis of Composition Strategies

Audience, text structure, relationships among significant characters, and narrative plots and patterns are common ingredients to consider when evaluating a text's composition strategies.

The Confessions is a record of a mind thinking out-loud. Augustine had several audiences for his meditation on life's journey. His first and foremost audience, motivation, and inspiration were his Creator. Like the Psalmist, he addressed his Lord with joy, but the response was always silence.[35] Augustine's audience was more than himself and his God.

> It is not surprising that the *Confessions*, suffused as they are with a dramatic sense of God's interventions in Augustine's life, are studded with the language of the Psalms. This was, in itself, a startling literary innovation: for the first time, a work of self-conscious literary art had incorporated (and most beautifully), the exotic jargon of the Christian communities.[36]

Augustine, with his scribes, composed this first life narrative text by hand and circulated it to his flock as separate books for reading aloud, in public. Like Ambrose's sermons that brought Augustine to the faith, *The Confessions* are about teaching. He is the narrating guide for all who would listen, as well as the central protagonist in the story. His text is replete with direct quotations and allusions to the scriptures, evoking from reader audiences across the centuries and listener audiences at that time and place, connections that were familiar and persuasive. In the late twentieth century, literary scholars interpreted life narratives as performance. The same could be said about Augustine. Imagine him dictating his life story to his scribes—the first performance—knowing full well that his congregation will listen as episodes and their gloss are read to them—the second performance. For centuries thereafter, there will be the continuing performances as readers listen to him "tell all".[37]

Structurally, he composed his text as nine books that traverse his life's events in a linear chronology from 354 to 387:

Infancy and Boyhood (Book I)
Adolescence (Book II)
Student Years at Carthage (Book III)
Augustine the Manichee (Book IV)
From Carthage to Rome and Milan (Book V)
Milan, 385: Progress, Friends, and Perplexities (Book VI)
Neoplatonism Frees Augustine's Mind (Book VII)
Conversion (Book VIII) and
Death and Rebirth (Book IX).

Book X is a treatise on Memory. Books XI, XII, and XIII are the theological and philosophical foundations that defined his and other believers' future Christian lives.

The story is filled with vivid descriptions of his relationships with a cast of earthy characters. Augustine's responses to his mother Monica at different stages of their lives were described in ways that might still educate sons and psychologists. She was the pious figure early in his life, drawing him to her Christianity that he was not yet ready to embrace, and away from profligate adventures. She was her son's worldly advocate, urging not only his professional pursuits, but urging romantic commitments to only the right kind of woman of proper social status. She was his confidante as his religious motivations turned towards hers, finally departing earthly life but only after a mystical experience in union with her son. He tenderly described his love for his son Adeodatus and the woman who birthed him and loved Augustine. He wrote with affection about friends like Alypius and Nebridius. His scorn bristled about Faustus, on whom he set high expectations for learning, but was terribly disappointed by his lack of even the most basic knowledge in the liberal arts. In contrast to this fallen Manichean hero, Augustine described Ambrose, Bishop of Milan, with admiration for his preaching in both its style and intoxicating substance. Ideas and books and their authors also are among the memorable characters in this story. Augustine's philosophical and rhetorical touchstones evolved from Cicero to Manicheanism to Academic Skepticism, and to Neoplatonism. These intellectual challengers remained in memory, but eventually were overshadowed by the new guiding lights of the Psalmist and Saint Paul.

The narrative plots and patterns of Thomas Merton's and Malcolm X's spiritual journeys become so much more evident after reading Augustine. He established a three-stage narrative pattern for subsequent spiritual autobiographies: ". . . childhood events (stage one) raise questions that drive the author on a negative journey of wandering in a desert of illusory answers (stage two) before he or she discovers a transforming world in which the original questions can be resolved (stage three)".[38] I shall describe in later chapters how some human experiences at the end of the second millennium did not resonate with Augustine's faith that providence is always at work in our lives or that all our experiences conspire together unto some good. The narrative patterns for these later twentieth century stories, especially by women and people of color, departed from the linearity and the unity of life to which Augustine gave eloquent witness.

Understanding Memory's Episodes

Augustine foreshadowed the living of one's life in multiple temporal layers at the same time—a practice that permeates our current consciousness and has been injected into life narratives. He believed that we are conscious, in the present, of past events, present experiences, and even future stirrings, and all in a very real way. He called our consciousness of past things, memory, of present things, attention, and of future things, expectations.[39]

For Augustine, a spiritual knowledge of God became possible via a psychological knowledge of one's self, quoting Saint Paul—"then shall I know even as I am known." Augustine's insight on this dimension was echoed by many autobiographers over the years. He ardently believed that he was doing truth in order to discover truth by coming to the Light. Merton would describe his efforts in a similar way, but never accomplish the same quality in his young man's narrative for *The Seven Storey Mountain*. Gandhi actually titled his autobiography, *The Story of my Experiments with Truth*. These will be two personalities and discovery and composition processes that we will examine in detail in the next chapter.[40]

Augustine's theory of memory in Book X began with a description of how our senses produced myriad images that become food for constant thought. Constructing one's self from memory's episodes and then composing a story became a 20th century art form. The study of memory also became the important scientific task for cognitive psychologists and neuroscientists. In early research, Atkinson and Shiffrin [41] proposed a three-stage processing model of memory, still found in almost every Introductory Psychology textbook at the turn of the 21st century. We record information as sensory memory, subsequently processing or encoding it into short-term memory, with further encoding then taking place for long-term memory and its retrieval. After two decades of investigations on general neurological mechanisms involved in memory processes, psychological researchers began to look deeper into autobiographical recollections [42] and how we can recall some events from as early as age three.[43] In studies on adolescents, adults, and older adults, other researchers discovered the phenomenon they termed the "reminiscence bump"; fewer memories were recalled prior to age three, but a disproportionately higher number came from ages 10 to 30.[44]

Olney's literary interpretations of Augustine merge with such scientific investigations. He acknowledged the saint's "archaeological model" and "processual model" of memory. Augustine asserted that he could form imaginary pictures that resembled what he had experienced. With those pictures, he could weave a roadmap for future actions from his memory's episodes, reflecting on them in the here and now in very real terms. Olney spotlighted the activity of weaving in this passage: "the weaver's shuttle and loom constantly produce new and different patterns, designs, and forms, and if the operation of memory is, like weaving, not archaeological but processual, then it will bring forth ever different memorial configurations and an ever newly shaped self".[45]

Beyond memory's lively residues, the contemporary examiner of life narratives wants to know about the author's motives and intentions that prompted the construction of these episodes. O'Donnell understood Augustine and his *Confessions* when he recognized that the text should not be misunderstood as the territory it tried to illuminate. [46] He was circumspect about the possibility of any contemporary analysis of Augustine's psychological make-up and history. I believe, however, that we can safely evaluate the critical importance of relationships of every kind and stripe in his life. He explores their meanings, and then describes their effects with passion. Whether it is his early ruminations on the presence of others as a motivation to steal pears, to his thrills and regrets with sins of the flesh, to being captured by one after another philosophical mentor–relationships reveal Augustine to himself and then his text communicates those insights to us. The two religious climaxes of this story, first the conversion episode in the garden and then the mystical union in prayer with Monica, are both experienced with and through others. [47]

O'Donnell said this about Augustine's continuing relationships with us across the centuries: "Charity, the substance of grace at work in the world, becomes the means by which barriers of suspicion and detachment are eradicated, and readers come to share the experience of a writer. This is not a book to be read so much as a prayer in which the reader is to share." [48]

Conclusion

I have come full circle from examining the maps and metaphors of Augustine's life narrative, to his gathering of memory's episodes, the unity of which he discovered anew, transformed, and brought them forward into all of our reading futures. In the following chapters, I hope to illuminate the life narratives of other fathers and mothers, daughters and sons, heroines and heroes, sinners and saints. In different ways, their stories shed light on the human conflicts that Augustine experienced and captured for our imaginations. There is the more lofty hope embedded in composing a story of the self—that anyone who does truth' comes to the light.

In the next chapter, we will look at Thomas Merton using Erik Erikson's psychosocial theory of life development. From Augustine's *Confessions* to Dante's *Purgatorio* to *The Seven Storey Mountain* was not such a long journey—dancing with the poetics of sin and searching for grace's light make for great life narratives.

NOTES

1. Robert F. Sayre, "Autobiography and the Making of America," in *Autobiography: Essays Theoretical and Critical*, ed. James Olney (Princeton, NJ: Princeton Uni-

versity Press, 1980), 146–168. Another literary scholar, Stone, wrote that "*Life* is the more inclusive sign—not *Literature*—which deserves to be placed above the gateway to the house of autobiography." In Albert E. Stone, *Autobiographical Occasions and Original Acts* (Philadelphia: University of Pennsylvania Press, 1982), 19.

2. *Shorter Oxford English Dictionary* (Oxford, UK: Oxford University Press, 2002), 154.

3. ". . .the heart of the explanation for the special appeal of autobiography to students of literature in recent times: it is a fascination with the self and its profound, its endless mysteries and, accompanying that fascination, an anxiety about the self, an anxiety about the dimness and vulnerability of that entity that no one has ever seen or touched or tasted. . ." In Olney, *Autobiography: Essays*, 23.

4. John Barbour, *The Conscience of the Autobiographer: Ethical and Religious Dimensions of Autobiography* (Hampshire, UK: MacMillan, 1992).

5. Sidonie Smith and Julia Watson, *Reading Autobiography: A Guide for Interpreting Life Narratives* (Minneapolis: University of Minnesota Press, 2001).

6. Michael Mott, *The Seven Mountains of Thomas Merton* (New York: Harvest, 1993), xvii.

7. "Immigration or ethnic autobiographies" were standard fare in the twentieth century, chronicling different groups' struggles. W.E.B. DuBois identified a common denominator for these stories—double consciousness—that was used as a psychological and literary theme across the century by many scholars. Whatever the nature of a person's hyphenated identity, the construction of self was characterized by the personal, sociocultural, and historical conflicts between assimilation and separation. Henry Louis Gates, Jr. gathered many Black voices (e.g., Baldwin, Brown, Cleaver, Davis, hooks, Hughes, Hurston, Staples, Walker, and Wright) on this topic in his *Bearing Witness: Selections from African-American Autobiography in the Twentieth Century* (New York: Pantheon, 1991).

"Autobiographics", "autogynography", "captivity narratives", "diaries", and "letters" were variations developed by women authors and examined by scholars especially in the last two decades of the twentieth century. Carolyn Heilbrun's *Writing a Woman's Life* (New York: Ballantine Books, 1988) analyzed the distinctive contributions made by women to this American genre. Jill Ker Conway's anthology, *Written by Herself. Autobiographies of American Women: An Anthology* (New York: Vintage, 1992) was a sampler with historical and contextual material for each excerpt.

8. Sidonie Smith and Julia Watson, eds. *Women, Autobiography, Theory: A Reader* (Madison: University of Wisconsin Press, 1998).

9. For example, Frederick Douglas published a trilogy of such works in the 1800s. Maya Angelou published seven installments from 1969 to 2002. After publishing *Souls of Black Folk* in 1903, a collection of literary, political, and autobiographical essays, W.E.B. Dubois composed three autobiographical texts as social-political histories of his times and struggles. John Edgar Wideman continued this multi-volume approach among African American authors. Richard Rodriguez's trilogy and Judith Ortiz Cofer's two-volume work explored the bilingual and bicultural experiences of two contemporary Latina/o authors as they declared their ethnic identity and voice.

10. Smith and Watson used the terms "autopathography", "scriptotherapy" and "self-help and trauma narratives" to describe variations on autobiographical compositions. The appeal comes from the vividly described and widely experienced problems or the unique tragedies of a widely known public figure. Surviving a stroke or neurological illness, major depression and its treatment, and even consensual incest are recent examples of this type of life narrative. In her commentary on the genre, Jill Ker Conway labeled these recent accounts, especially those about surviving dysfunctional family situations as "grim tales"; autobiographical texts often merged with an explicit biography of the family members involved in the survivors' experiences. In Jill Ker Conway, *When Memory Speaks: Exploring the Art of Autobiography* (New York: Knopf, 1999).

11. Sayre, "Making of America".

12 Erik Erikson & Joan Serson Erikson, *The Life Cycle Completed: Extended Version with New Chapters on the Ninth Stage of Development* (New York: Norton, 1997). Erikson's psychohistorical analyses of Luther's and Gandhi's lives were blueprints for the journey of 'homo religiosus'. See Erik Erikson, *Young Man Luther: A Study in Psychoanalysis and History* (New York: Norton, 1958) and *Gandhi's Truth: On the Origins of Militant Nonviolence* (New York: Norton, 1969).

13. Georges Gusdorf, "Conditions and Limits of Autobiography," in *Autobiography: Essays*, 41.

14. The social activist, Jane Addams, the academic psychologist, Margaret Floy Washburn, the women's health political activist, Margaret Sanger, the photojournalist, Margaret Bourke White, and the professional golfer, Babe Didrikson Zaharias— all published their life stories, composing them within the traditional structure of the linearly unfolding life.

15. Kenneth Gergen, *The Saturated Self: Dilemmas of Identity in Modern Life* (New York: Basic Books, 1992), 71. Gergen's postmodern perspective (See "Psychological Science in a Postmodern Context," *American Psychologist* 56, 2001: 803–813) has been met often with harsh criticism by scientific colleagues. One psychologist characterized it as "anthrax of the intellect, if allowed into mainstream psychology, postmodernism will poison the field" (E. A. Locke, "The Dead End of Postmodernism", *American Psychologist* 57, 2002: 458). Their vitriolic protests suggest some anxiety about the plausibility of Gergen's point of view.

16. David J. Leigh, *Circuitous Journeys: Modern Spiritual Autobiography* (New York: Fordham University Press, 2000).

17. William James, *The Varieties of Religious Experience* (New York: Penguin Classics, 1982, original published in 1902). Recent commentaries on James's touchstone volume can be found in *William James and a Science of Religions: Reexperiencing the Varieties of Religious Experience*, ed. Wayne Proudfoot (New York: Columbia University Press, 2004) and Charles Taylor, *Varieties of Religion Today* (Cambridge, MA: Harvard University Press, 2002).

18. Peter Brown, *Augustine of Hippo: A Biography* (Berkeley, CA: University of California Press, 2000), 25.

19. Brown, *Augustine*, 26.

20. Brown, *Augustine*, 50–52.

21. James J. O'Donnell, "Introduction", in *Augustine "Confessions": Introduction and Text, Volume I*. (Oxford, U.K.: Clarendon Press, 1992).

22. Brown, *Augustine*, 93–94.

23. Brown, *Augustine*, 97.

24. Augustine's reflections on memory informed the narrative theory of James Olney who, 1600 years later, would characterize this text as: ". . . the great *ur*-book of life writing, the initiator and progenitor of a literary (and more than literary) tradition that, in however altered form (sometimes altered almost out of all recognition), continues alive and well—very, very alive and, depending on one's view, very well or very sick—in our time." In James Olney, *Memory & Narrative: The Weave of Life-Writing* (Chicago: University of Chicago Press, 1998), 29.

In Book X, Augustine performed an examination of conscience as he began to write his long discussion on the nature of memory. The trinity of Books XI, XII, and XIII are theological statements, titled "Time and Eternity", "Heaven and Earth", and "The Days of Creation, Prophecy of the Church". As I will make the case in the next two chapters, discussing *homo religiosus* and its manifestations in the lives of Thomas Merton, Black Elk, and Malcolm X, Augustine's last three books are the theological grounds for his unifying principle. For Merton and Malcolm, like Augustine, that principle was a monotheistic faith, discovered in adulthood, and then re-examined relentlessly throughout life. For the Native American visionary, Black Elk, the vocation of *homo religious* manifested itself first in a vision at age 9, then in the healing powers of a tribal shaman, later as a Catholic catechist on a reservation, and finally as a latter day prophet to multicultural audiences.

25. O'Donnell introduced the first volume of his magisterial commentary in this way. "All of us who read Augustine fail him in many ways. . .(1) we choose to ignore some of what he says that we deny but find non-threatening; (2) we grow heatedly indignant at some of what he says that we deny and find threatening; (3) we ignore rafts of things he says that we find naïve, or uninteresting, or conventional (thereby displaying that in our taste which is itself naïve, uninteresting, and conventional); (4) we patronize what we find interesting but flawed and primitive (e.g., on time and memory); (5) we admire superficially the odd purple patch; (6) we assimilate whatever pleases us to the minimalist religion of our own time, finding in him ironies he never intended; (7) we extract and highlight whatever he says that we find useful for a predetermined thesis (which may be historical, psychological, philosophical, or doctrinal). . ." O'Donnell, *Augustine "Confessions": Volume I, xix*.

26. James J. O'Donnell, *Augustine "Confessions": Commentary on Books 1–7. Volume II* (Oxford, U.K.: Clarendon Press, 1992), 4–5.

27. Garry Wills, *Saint Augustine* (New York: Viking, 1999), (italics in original), *xiv*.

28. Jean-Francois Lyotard mused that *The Confessions* was sublimely infused with the tone of prayer and praise, so fitting by its constant appeal to the Psalms for inspiration. One can feel from Augustine, just like from the Psalmist, that a person's life and their writing in such texts are inseparable. Jean-Francois Lyotard, *The Confession of Augustine*, trans. Richard Beardsworth (Palo Alto: Stanford University Press, 2000).

29. Brown, *Augustine*, 173.

30. Brown, *Augustine*, 158.

31. Dan McAdams, *The Redemptive Self: Stories Americans Live By* (New York: Oxford University Press, 2006).

32. O'Donnell, *Augustine "Confessions", Volume I, xl–xli*.

33. In an interesting parallel, certainly without intending any comparison to Hong Kingston's work, Brown interpreted *The Confessions* in a way that suggested its future elevation to master narrative status in this genre. "Augustine allows his past self to grow to the dimensions of a 'classic' hero: for these experiences summed up for him, 'the condition of my race, the human race'. Every incident in the book, therefore, is charged with the poignancy of a Chinese landscape—a vivid detail perched against infinite distances". Brown, *Augustine*, 161.

34 Brown, *Augustine*, 163.

35. Lyotard described such encounters with silence as representative of all our quests to bring to language what language cannot express. We struggle to put into words our understandings of what has never been said, both about ourselves and about our God. Making an allusion to contemporary psychotherapy processes, he suggests that Saint Augustine was "working through" that which has yet to be expressed or grasped, even in a most primitive way. Lyotard, *Confession*, 26–27.

36. Brown, *Augustine*, 168.

37. In his recent biography of the saint, O'Donnell made this interpretation about *The Confessions*: "The book is marked by a mannered self-revelation, almost self-betrayal, that comes from the Augustine who would continually return to, and often carefully display, anxiety and self-mistrust in the midst of his most self-assertive and overbearing of public displays. Wherever he wrote, the people who saw him day by day very likely suspected little of the subterranean seething that bubbles through on these pages". James J. O'Donnell, *Augustine: A New Biography* (New York: Harper-Collins, 2005), 37.

38. Leigh, *Circuitous Journeys*, 5.

39. Olney compared this passage from Augustine with two from Samuel Beckett's work: "The individual is the seat of a constant process of decantation, decantation from the vessel containing the fluid of future time, sluggish, pale and monochrome, to the vessel containing the fluid of past time, agitated and multicoloured by the phenomena of its hours". Olney, *Memory & Narrative*, 4.

In *Krapp's Last Tape*, at age 69, Krapp reviews a tape he made at age 39. Olney described Beckett's understanding of the narrative self in this way: "Krapp, in order to assist himself in extending expectation over the whole period of his life, listens to the narrated episodes of his life pass from the spool of expectation on the left across the head of the tape player, which corresponds to the present of narration, to be taken up by the spool of memory on the right—which, when rewound, becomes once again the spool of expectation". Olney, *Memory & Narrative*, 8.

40. Brown described this consciousness in this way, weaving together passages from Books III, V, and X: "*The Confessions* are a manifesto of the inner world: 'Men go to gape at mountain peaks, at the boundless tides of the sea, the broad sweep of rivers, the encircling ocean and the motions of the stars: and yet they leave themselves unnoticed; they do not marvel at themselves.' A man cannot hope to find God unless he first finds himself: for this God is 'deeper than my inmost being', experience of

him becomes 'better' the more 'inward'. Above all, it is man's tragedy that he should be driven to flee 'outwards', to lose touch with himself, to 'wander far' from his 'own heart': 'You were right before me: but I had moved away from myself. I could not find myself: how much less, then, could I find You'". Brown, *Augustine*, 162.

41. Richard Atkinson and Richard Shiffrin, "Human Memory: A Proposed System and its Control Processes" in *The Psychology of Learning and Motivation*, eds. Kenneth W. Spence and Janet T. Spence (New York: Academic Press, 1968).

42. Conway distinguished between autobiographical memories where the experience of remembering, personal interpretations, and context-specific sensory attributes are important features versus autobiographical facts that are truthful and self-referential but have fewer process features. Martin A. Conway, *Autobiographical Memory: An Introduction* (Philadelphia: Open University Press, 1990).

Baddeley elaborated on short-term memory and described a more complex working memory with visual and verbal components that are highly interactive with already stored material. He defined autobiographical memory as the capacity of people to recollect their lives. Alan Baddeley, "Working Memory", *Science* 255, (1992): 556–559.

43. In his studies of childhood amnesia, Howe concluded that much of the biological hardware for the Atkinson and Shiffrin memory processes is present from birth. Memory is capable of being updated and recoded at every turn; at age 18 to 24 months, the cognitive self emerges (and the linguistic self that can say "I", "me", and "you") and with it the capacity for personalized memories for events. With continuing development of more sophisticated cognitive software, the longevity, complexity, organization, and meaningfulness of memories is significantly enhanced. Howe addressed the thorny problem of the accuracy of autobiographical memories—an important issue in the examination of any oral or written text that reports them—with a scientific proposal for continuing study that: ". . .takes into account (a) the event itself (the nominal situation); (b) the initial encoding and storage of that event with its attendant interpretation and bias (the functional memory trace); (c) changes in what was originally stored due to corresponding alterations in knowledge, additional experience, and so on; and (d) the current context (including motivations) in which autobiographical events are being recollected". Mark L. Howe, *The Fate of Early Memories: Developmental Science and the Retention of Childhood Experiences* (Washington, D.C.: American Psychological Association, 2000), 130.

44. In his review of research studies, Rubin found this reminiscence bump for not only autobiographical memories, but for autobiographical facts as well. In David C. Rubin, "Beginnings of a Theory of Autobiographical Remembering," in *Autobiographical Memory: Theoretical and Applied Perspectives,* eds. Charles P. Thompson, et al. (Mahwah, NJ: Erlbaum, 1998), 47–67.

Habermas and Bluck's review of this literature suggested that adolescence is the ripe time for using new cognitive tools to construct the elements of a life story. It is a time when young people have the social and motivational reasons to make that story personally meaningful as part of an overall identity formation process. In Tilman Habermas & Susan Bluck, "Getting a Life: The Emergence of the Life Story in Adolescence," *Psychological Bulletin* 126, (2000): 748–769.

In Pillemer's view, autobiographical memories serve three critical functions for the self: to communicate to others the vividness of our stories, to probe and understand, for ourselves, the emotional meaningfulness of life's events, and to use that information to direct our future behavior. David Pillemer, "Momentous Events and the Life Story", *Review of General Psychology* 5, (2001): 123–134.

45. Olney, *Memory & Narrative*, 20.

46. "A text is not a life: so far so good. To narrate one's past life and deeds is to put a pattern of words next to a life (by nature patternless, full of event and incident) and to declare that the words and the life have something to do with each other. . . .But the life of this particular act of 'confession', the writing of this text by a man self-consciously turning from youth to middle age, is as present to us on the page as our own lives—indeed, becomes as we read it a part of our own lives. It is that fragment of the 'life' of Augustine that is most accessible to us." O'Donnell, *Augustine "Confessions", Volume I, xxx.*

47. Brown, *Augustine*, 174.

48. O'Donnell, *Augustine "Confessions", Volume II*, 14.

Chapter Two

Mapping the Examining Conscience

PRECIS

In this chapter, I use perspectives from literary criticism and psychological theory that emphasize the unity and continuity of the self over time, and evaluate Thomas Merton's The Seven Storey Mountain. *Literature uses metaphors to capture this unity, whereas psychological science stresses paradigmatic maps to articulate the common denominators of human behavior.*

Erik Erikson's psychosocial development theory helps us understand authors' gatherings of memory's episodes and the search for unifying principles in the midst of intrapersonal conflicts and social changes. The literary theorist, Georges Gusdorf, discovered new ways to understand the composition strategies authors use to bring their remembered meanings to a public audience.

The "seven storey mountain" was an allusion to Dante Alighieri and his Renaissance pilgrim's story of life's journey from ignorance and the slavery of sin to the freedom of grace and knowledge. Merton's examined life was a theological geography. Although the abiding metaphor for The Seven Storey Mountain *was Dante's* Purgatorio, *Saint Augustine's* The Confessions *was thoroughly woven into Merton's composition strategies.*

In this chapter, we will use Erikson's life cycle theory of conflicts and acquired virtues, especially about identity, to explore Merton's life narrative—its maps, metaphors, composition strategies, and reconstructed episodes. He examined his conscience, like Augustine, in a classic spiritual autobiography as well as in private journals published after his untimely death. The vocations of monk and writer were evident in both sources.

Examining stories of the self requires multi-disciplinary lenses. Literary criticism and psychology went down a life narrative track from 1900 to 1980, but on separate rails. By this chapter's title, "Mapping the Examining Conscience", I want to signal how story tellers use metaphors and psychologists construct maps to understand the evolving self portrayed in autobiographical texts. In both disciplines, there were similar assumptions about how stories were lived and composed by their authors. Before the 1970s, we celebrated mostly men, few women, as the primary authors and objects of study in this genre. The articulation of a singular life theme was of paramount concern in the pursuit of a unifying metaphor for life or in sketching an organizing map for seemingly disparate behaviors.

The linear structures and common themes of men's narratives demonstrated the unity they perceived in their lives. In psychology, unity was the basis for a spate of studies about life's developmental progression through ages and stages. Religion was understood as another unifying principle via its capacity to organize a life as the progression from sin to grace, from ignorance to awareness, from emptiness to fullness, from being all too human to becoming a little closer to the divine. Saint Augustine's *The Confessions* was the story of a man restlessly seeking a unifying principle for his life and conflicted behaviors. Thomas Merton's *The Seven Storey Mountain*, Malcolm X's *The Autobiography of Malcolm X* (as told to Alex Haley), and Nicholas Black Elk's *Black Elk Speaks* (as told through John Neihardt [Flaming Rainbow]) were grounded in comparable pilgrim metaphors. Colored and more fragmented variations on religious themes were evident in recently published works by Richard Rodriguez's *Days of Obligation: An Argument with my Mexican Father*, in Maya Angelou's *I Know Why the Caged Bird Sings*, Elie Wiesel's *Night*, or in James McBride's *The Color of Water: A Black Man's Tribute to His White Mother.*

Scholars in literature or psychology now borrow from each other with gusto. Literary scholars like James Olney[1] and Paul John Eakin[2] incorporated findings from neuroscience and cognitive psychology research on autobiographical memory in their recent analyses of the life narrative genre. Literary scholars examined texts and the complex nuances of characters and their authors who use metaphors to capture lives' meanings. Psychologists are cartographers of behavior and personality theorists like Dan McAdams[3] borrowed from literary models to examine adults' stories. Most scientists rely on paradigmatic maps or models, using quantitative analyses to understand persons' lives in aggregate terms. They appreciate narrative (a.k.a. anecdotal) data, but too much admiration for case studies may be suspect and lead to skeptical responses from their scientific discourse communities.[4]

In this chapter, I focus specifically on theories from the two disciplines that emphasize the unity and continuity of the self. In subsequent chapters, we will explore how diverse authors challenged such assumptions with rainbow colorings in their maps and metaphors.

UNIFYING LITERARY METAPHORS

Smith and Watson[5] saw the history of autobiographical genre criticism as unfolding in waves. The first wave began with George Misch's multivolume text, *History of Autobiography in Antiquity*, when he advanced the notion that Western history was the product of great public figures whose lives were representative of a distinctive time, place, and culture.[6] Such a standard muted women; although they had been producing autobiographical texts for a long time, no one chose to notice. A canon of representative texts was identified and the characteristics of its authors were defined using a great men or master narrative standard. First wave critics emphasized the *bios* (life history) elements of autobiography. The focus shifted to *autos* (self) in the second wave.

Smith and Watson placed Georges Gusdorf at the heart of the second wave in their historical review.[7] Gusdorf's criteria became the touchstone for subsequent analyses, although Mary Mason[8] noted the absence of women authors in lists of the "classics" and challenged his assumptions about the construction of a unified identity. As I will describe in Chapter Four, Mason's chapter and those by other scholars in the last two decades of the millennium opened the doors for many critical works by and about women.

For Gusdorf, Saint Augustine, Rousseau, Goethe, Chateaubriand, Newman, and Gide wrote the masterpieces. Augustine's *The Confessions* exemplified the Christian principle that every life was important because of grace. After Augustine, the classic spiritual autobiography re-created Christianity's redemptive story by chronicling authors' sins and their acceptance of grace. The converted life became exemplary; we ascend life's mountains and our missions become spiritually motivating forces. The texts demonstrated that exemplary self-awareness comes to us when we initiate heroic actions and take responsibility for the consequences.

A heightened self-awareness prompts the autobiographical act. By the 1950s, psychology and psychoanalysis already had given us robust tools for introspection and a language to communicate interpretive insights. Personal history came to be understood as a linear progression to be read (written) forward or backward. Thus, Gusdorf proposed that ". . . autobiography properly speaking assumes the task of reconstructing the unity of a life across time." [9] In Book X of *The Confessions*, Augustine first described how this exploration continually creates and re-creates memory. Gusdorf saw it similarly: ". . . autobiography is a second reading of experience, and it is truer than the first because it adds to

experience itself consciousness of it. . . .The passage from immediate experience to consciousness in memory, which affects a sort of repetition of that experience, also serves to modify its significance."[10] He emphasized individuals'
capacities to compose narratives, rich in meanings, from memories that are subject to alternative interpretations by writers and their readers. Contemporary
ethnic and women authors' emphases on widening the genre's forms seem
equally legitimate within his framework. In the same essay, Gusdorf wrote that
". . . the prerogative of autobiography consists in this: that it shows us not the
objective stages of a career—to discern these is the task of the historian—but
that it reveals instead the effort of a creator to give the meaning of his own
mythic tale."[11]

Having sketched some lines of literary commentary, I want to re-trace the
same period and to describe maps used by psychological scholars for stories
of the self.

PSYCHOBIOGRAPHY AS CROSS-DISCIPLINARY MAP

"Psychobiography, born in the primeval blue-green seas of Freud's Vienna
Psychoanalytic Society, clumsily struggles up onto the beach, and the story
begins."[12] After Freud's case study of Leonardo da Vinci was published in
1910, psychoanalysts examined the lives of Luther, Shakespeare, Socrates,
and Wagner. By the end of the 1930s, psycho-biographical studies were published on Alexander the Great, Caesar, Coleridge, Darwin, Dostoevsky,
Goethe, Moliere, Nietszche, Rousseau, and Sand. Authors of these works
were educated in psychoanalysis, history, and political science; they were
psychologists and literary scholars, as well as those trained in a specific field
and writing about one of their founding heroes or heroines.

Reading about the early days of psychobiography reminded me of Henry
Murray's fourth primary proposition in his 1938 theory of personality. The
following quote was one of psychology's early statements about how to study
individual lives.

> The organism consists of an infinitely complex series of
> temporally related activities extending from birth to death.
> Because of the meaningful connection of sequences, the life
> cycle of a single individual should be taken as a unit, the *long
> unit* of psychology. It is feasible to study the organism during
> one episode of its existence, but it should be recognized that
> this is but an arbitrarily selected part of the whole. This history
> of the organism is the organism.[13]

Dan McAdams, who followed in the Murray tradition, studied complex motives using research participants' responses to projective tests and then their autobiographical stories. The biographical strategy, however, always had tough going in the scientific community.[14] Psychology staked its scientific reputation on the analyses of aggregated responses given by groups specifically designed for comparative purposes. While the case study offered fascinating details to inform clinical practice or to advance research method development, the paragon for the discipline was to generate conclusions drawn from representative samples that were administered rigorously standardized protocols.

Psychobiography is the systematic application of psychological theory to enhance the understanding of an individual life. The orienting premise of psychobiography was that a single person could represent many men's lives. The intensive focus enabled the researcher to fashion questions for further study. Using a single theory to analyze a single life provided a unifying framework within which to interpret myriad personal data.

In the next section of this chapter, I explore the work of Erik Erikson, an interdisciplinary artist-scholar, once described by George Goethals as "Freud in sonnet form."[15] He listened to the stories told to him by undergraduate students, clinical patients, colleagues in many disciplines, historical figures, and African American and Native American young people and their parents. From these stories, he constructed an integrative framework used across many disciplines. His psychosocial theory of development is an excellent map for men's life narratives.[16]

ERIK ERIKSON AND THE ARCHITECTURE OF IDENTITY

Erikson was a psychotherapist and essayist. His map of the human experience was the life cycle model of development; its centerpiece was the concept of identity. One biographer[17] summarized his 92-year lifework as being "identity's architect". He stressed the universal potential for unity in a life, despite tumultuous internal crises and external events. Erikson's own story illuminates his interdisciplinary theory.

Erikson's Psychosocial Development

Erik Homburger (his adoptive stepfather's name) and his young family left Europe, his mentor Anna Freud, and the Viennese psychoanalytic circle in 1933. He journeyed to America where he became a practicing therapist and a researcher on one of Henry Murray's projects at Harvard. There, he was exposed to multi-disciplinary colleagues, students, and a daily synergy of ideas that characterized his psychoanalytic training days in Vienna. He had a short stint at Yale, with periodic trips to Columbia University's personality and culture seminars taught by the anthropologists Margaret Mead and Ruth Benedict, and a summer visit to the Pine Ridge reservation of the Oglala Sioux in South Dakota. In 1939, the family moved to Berkeley's Institute of Child Welfare so that he could study normal children, doing more summer anthropological fieldwork projects with the Yurok Indians and the anthropologist, Alfred Kroeber. Active in psychoanalytic practice, he continued to construct his own version of psychoanalytic theory, using cross-cultural stories and to converge on the theme of identity.

In 1950, he and his wife, Joan Serson Erikson, collaborated on a presentation for the Mid-Century White House Conference on Infancy and Childhood. *Childhood and Society* was his first book and became his most popular theoretical statement. It was a collection of previously published essays written in California in the 1940s, and revised after his World War II experiences. He gathered disparate ideas from clinical case studies, trips to Native American reservations, studies of Hitler's effects on German youth, and created a life cycle theory of human development. The book was the product of his psyche's development fashioned in the crucible of socio-cultural and historical events.[18]

Joan remembered 1950 in this way. They were driving to the train station so Erik could preview the White House paper with a group of psychologists and psychiatrists. "With the life cycle chart on my lap while Erik drove, I began to feel uneasy. Shakespeare had seven stages as did we, and he had omitted an important one. Had we too left one out? In a shocking moment of clarity I saw what was wrong: "We" were missing, and so were the children in Erik's new book <u>Children [sic] and Society</u>".[19] That epiphany produced the sixth stage, defined as generativity versus stagnation. Fifty years later, Joan at age 93 added material on another stage of life that she and Erik had just passed through, poignantly describing wisdom and an "existential identity" whereby some elders can integrate past, present, and an ever-shortening future.

The Eight Stages of Man from *Childhood and Society* can be found in almost every introductory or developmental psychology textbook. A "stage" describes how normal children develop in families and grow into adolescents and adults, and how society, culture, and the historical moment intersect with that development. The visual map of the eight stages, presented at the White House conference and in the 1950 book, was displayed as a diagonal sequence. Despite Erikson's original description and continuing commentaries, the ages and stages get translated in popular understanding into a linear hierarchy of discrete conflicts; he always intended a fluid and circular wholeness. Joan and Erik's stages echoed Jaques' speech in Shakespeare's play, *As You Like It* .

The Eriksons' eight stages were neither discrete nor linear:
Trust versus Mistrust
Autonomy versus Shame, Doubt
Initiative versus Guilt
Industry versus Inferiority
Identity versus Role Diffusion
Intimacy versus Isolation
Generativity versus Stagnation
Integrity versus Disgust, Despair.[20]

The stages were iterative; each incorporated aspects of the prior stage, beginning with the very first crisis of trust versus mistrust solved by the infant's being-in-the-world. Trust is accomplished when the infant experiences a consistency, continuity, and sameness in the environment of caretakers, learning to expect similar patterns of responses early in one's psychosocial life. Trust reflects a naiveté in its reliance on others, but this stage's life lesson is that seeking and finding mutuality is very important as the first task of the ego. Parents next must foster autonomy and prevent shame in the two-year old by their consistent encouragement, being firm in preventing potential anarchy because the child cannot discriminate when to hold on and when to let go. With increasing motor skills, the pre-school child goes places and does things. Initiative enables the youngster to use toys and tools in meaningful ways; the alternative is guilt, produced by receiving harsh consequences for having gone too far, too often. Industry is observed in the elementary school child's successful completion of tasks, demonstrating emerging skills of daily living, versus alternative feelings of inferiority. The platform is thus built for the most important stage and task of all—adolescence and identity. The following lengthy quote is one of those passages about unity and continuity and its disruptions that any parent or twenty-plus person will recognize.

> With the establishment of a good relationship to the world of skills
> and tools, and with the advent of sexual maturity, childhood proper
> comes to an end. Youth begins. But in puberty and adolescence all
> sameness and continuities relied on earlier are questioned again. . .faced
> with this physiological revolution within them, [they] are now
> primarily concerned with what they appear to be in the eyes of others
> as compared with what they feel they are, and with the question of how
> to connect the roles and skills cultivated earlier with the occupational
> prototypes of the day.

In their search for a new sense of continuity and sameness, adolescents
have to re-fight many of the battles of earlier years, even though to do
so they must artificially appoint perfectly well-meaning people to play
the roles of enemies; and they are ever ready to install lasting idols and
ideals as guardians of a final identity: here puberty rites "confirm"
the inner design for life.[21]

Ego identity in adolescence is the capacity, via accrued experiences, to understand one's passions and skills and effectively implement them in social interactions; the opposite result is role diffusion. Intimacy recapitulates all of the prior stages' conflicts and successes to manage Freud's *lieben und arbeiten* (i.e., to love and to work) lifelong challenge; failure to do so leads to isolation, something that the person has been struggling against since the very first stage when they found trust in mutuality. The seventh and eighth stages of generativity versus stagnation and ego integrity versus despair received only brief coverage in the 1950 model.

Friedman made persuasive connections between the life cycle theory of human (identity) development and Erikson's biography—his childhood, passages to and in America, and working with Joan to raise three healthy adolescents as well as their struggles with a Down Syndrome youngster. The multiple turning points, transitions, uncertainties about his original and adopted cultures, coupled with the Nazi Germany and World War II events, were a motivational subtext for his recurring emphasis on the sameness and continuity in ego development. "The study of identity, then, becomes as strategic in our time as the study of sexuality was in Freud's time."[22] Erikson's two psycho-biographical studies elaborated on this theme, exploring identity in different historical and socio-cultural circumstances. Moreover, they serve as a platform for our examination of the autobiographical works of Thomas Merton in this chapter and of Black Elk and Malcolm X in Chapter Three.

Mapping Luther and Gandhi

Erikson's *Young Man Luther: A Study in Psychoanalysis and History* and the Pulitzer Prize and National Book Award winning *Gandhi's Truth: On the Origins of Militant Nonviolence* demonstrated a methodology he called "triple bookkeeping".[23] Erikson interpreted human behavior in complex, interdisciplinary ways, and revised the orthodox psychoanalysis in which he was trained. He borrowed ideas and methods from anthropology, literature, history, religion, and psychology; academic colleagues from all these fields were drawn into reviewing his manuscripts, simulating the roundtable give-and-takes of clinical staffings.

Erikson plunged into the life of Martin Luther, the 16th century religious reformer, focusing on seven years in his life (1505–1512; from ages 22 to 29) to illuminate how one individual's identity crisis should be understood in its historical context, as well as demonstrating the interactive play of religious ideology and human development. Erikson understood this identity crisis as a critical transition point in the life cycle. The youth looks backward to discover some sense of unity among the disparate experiences of childhood and tries to weave them into hopeful expectations for adulthood. This discovery process also brings into focus how an internal sense of self may not be the same as what others have been judging and voicing their expectations to be for the individual.

Understanding the concept of crisis is essential to understanding the motivating forces of the life cycle model of human development. Adolescents' accumulated physical, emotional, cognitive and social experiences make them ready to move beyond childhood concerns and their social environments expect them to do so. Turning points become evident as new tasks must be addressed. Erikson's life cycle model enables individuals to recycle their experiences in achieving an adult personality by resolving crises or conflicts across their whole lifespan.

Using a stack of historical sources (Margaret Mead prepared a bibliography prior to the Eriksons' departure to a village in Mexico to write this book), Erikson unpackaged Luther's life and its expressions as theological tenets. He did so using his continually crystallizing understanding of psychosocial development as a metabolism of the crises of trust, autonomy, initiative, industry, identity, and then on to intimacy, generativity, and ego integrity. Religion was an ideological compass with which individuals explored their identities. It was a unifying principle that guided judgments and actions, and framed the social and cultural boundaries for one's behavior. All the developmental issues and their polar conflicts converged in Luther's religious commitments of late adolescence and early adulthood. In one poignant scene, Erikson described the tensions Luther experienced while celebrating his first Mass. Donning the new identity as God's representative to his people on earth, the young priest either had to look to the future and trust in the Eucharist's uncertain grace or go back to established patterns from his youth and re-experience his earthly father's very certain wrath.

We are all someone's child, seeking compasses by which to navigate our lives, building skills to become workers and lovers, and, at every stage, we return to the issues of basic trust versus mistrust. This dynamic is poignant in late adolescence. In the epilogue to *Young Man Luther,* Erikson described what sets great historical figures like Luther apart. He labeled such individuals, *homo religiosus.* They are older (but not necessarily wiser) before their time, and thus mature on this dimension before the peers with whom they have to compare. Moral scruples invade their consciousness long before others and their sense of life's meaning and death's judgments concern them at much earlier stages in their development, going beyond even their parents and teachers. The integrity crisis came last in Erikson's ages and stages theory, but for the *homo religiosus*, it is layered right on top of the identity questions of young adulthood.

Erikson saw similar dynamics in Gandhi's life. He read the Mahatma's autobiography and visited India three times for interviews with those who remembered one critical event in 1918. Erikson interpreted Gandhi as a *homo religiosus,* focusing as he had done with Luther on his identity choices as individual, socio-cultural, and historical in nature. Whereas this crisis took place when Luther was in his twenties, Erikson interpreted Gandhi's critical turning point as an event that took place when he was forty-nine. Moreover, he grouped historical figures like St. Augustine, Gandhi, and Freud by their common tendencies to write their great introspective works—*The Confessions, My Experiments with Truth, The Interpretation of Dreams*, respectively—as mid-life projects when they were approaching, not looking back and savoring, the times of their greatest accomplishments.

As Erikson composed *Gandhi's Truth*, the psycho-historical backdrop of his own life permeated its evolving story. Malcolm X's life and violent death, Martin Luther King's nonviolent strategies for social change and his assassination, the conflicts over strategy within various camps of the American Civil Rights Movement—all evoked opposing public responses. The book's composition required his rediscovery of psychoanalysis as its own truth-force, a path of self-suffering and especially one that used nonviolent methods and strategies. Erikson's biographer, Friedman, observed the parallel processes of fusing individual personality with political ideology and powerful spirituality with powerful social activism. The text was about the life of one individual, Gandhi, but Erikson was constructing his own narrative interpretations of history, gender, race, and global relationships in the twentieth century.[24]

Gandhi's Truth made Erikson a celebrity and pieces written in the *New York Times*, *Newsweek*, *Saturday Review*, and especially Robert Coles' feature story for the *New Yorker* catapulted him into the role of public intellectual. "Beyond Freud" and "The Quest for Identity" with its "crises" became a permanent part of American public discourse.

Erikson's Final Statement on the Life Cycle

The Life Cycle Completed was Erik Erikson's last book, published in 1982 when he was in his 80s, then expanded in 1997 with a new introduction and three new chapters on a ninth stage of development by Joan Erikson. Their explanation of the concept of epigenesis as a continually evolving differentiation and synthesis of life experiences was especially lucid in this final statement.[25] The diagonal sequence, first proposed in 1950, was depicted some three decades later as a dense chart of the eight original stages, with psychosexual stages and modes, psychosocial crises, radii of significant relations, basic strengths or virtues, core pathology and basic antipathies, principles of social order, binding ritualizations, and ritualisms.

For example, during adolescence, puberty is the biological or psychosexual stage and identity versus identity confusion is the psychosocial crisis. This crisis is worked out via peer groups and out-groups, with contemporary models of leadership serving as exemplars after which adolescents can pattern their lives. Fidelity is the consequent virtue and a repudiation of others is a potential antipathy. Constructing an ideological worldview replete with principles and adaptations are central. In epigenetic fashion, fidelity foreshadows love, care, and wisdom; establishing an ideological framework prompts a deeper understanding of the needs for affiliation, generational respect, and a philosophical stance in one's old age. Fidelity is a renewal of one's discovery of trust at an early age; looking forward it becomes the capacity to commit oneself to others and to what they espouse as an ideology. The 1997 text with Joan Erikson's additions had a deeply optimistic tone, celebrating the two nonagenarians' experiences.

Erikson and Mapping Memory's Episodes

Erikson's 1975 essay, "On the nature of psycho-historical evidence", recalled the methods he used in writing *Gandhi's Truth*, in particular his close reading and interpretations of Gandhi's autobiography. Erikson used the disciplined subjectivity of the clinical psychoanalyst and the academic historian. Taking a clinical history always means composing a narrative. In reading Gandhi's autobiography, he was aware of how the English translation from the original Gujarati robbed the text of its humor and passion. Erikson mused that authors of autobiographies do not make the contract of free association's "tell everything" that is necessary for any therapy's success. Borrowing Kierkegaard's insight, "all confessions seek to settle a (big or small) curse", psychohistorians must explore the stated and unstated consequences.[26]

I pose a series of questions to my students when they step back from a text and try to understand an autobiographer's intentions in gathering and composing memory's episodes.

At what stage of life was the autobiographer when writing this text?
How did its composition fit the author's other tasks and accomplishments?

How is an episode compatible (or not) with events expected in others' lives?
How plausible is an episode as a developmental continuity with prior
  episodes?

Erikson questioned each textual episode in and of itself, then in its developmental sequence, and finally for its meanings within a particular socio-his-
torical community. The same questions must be asked by readers about the
author of the text, about themselves, about the audiences to whom the author
was writing, and about how comparable individuals might portray similar
episodes.[27]

Erikson knew these complexities; he was taken aback by Gandhi's genuine
fear that his autobiography and how he composed his own life's episodes
might not be able to sustain a critical examination by smart readers. Nevertheless, the Mahatma continued to write, not to please his critics or to justify
his actions, but as an experiment with truth. Erikson interrupted his composition of *Gandhi's Truth* by writing his own letter to the Mahatma, disclosing
his genuine biases and limits as he explored the life of this historical giant.
Recall Saint Augustine's similar reflection on "doing truth" when writing *The
Confessions* that I spotlighted in Chapter One.

Thomas Merton's adolescence unfolded as World War II engulfed Europe
and America. Erikson's theory helps us to understand his memory's episodes,
his epigenetic search for unifying principles and a religious faith in the midst
of a chaotic family and world conflicts. Literary theorists help us to understand the composition strategies he used. In my analysis of Merton, I will use
the three activities of reading/writing a life narrative that I introduced in the
first chapter: maps and metaphors, composition strategies, and gathering
memory's episodes.

THOMAS MERTON'S STORIED MOUNTAINS

Thomas Merton was born in France on January 31, 1915. His mother died
when he was six years old and his father when he was fifteen. He was supported until early adulthood by his grandparents and a trust fund executed by
his London physician-godfather, enabling him to study in private boys
schools, at Cambridge, and then to complete his baccalaureate and master's
degrees in literature at Columbia University. After years of reading philosophy and religion, at the age of twenty-three, Merton went to his first Roman
Catholic mass. On November 16, 1938, he was baptized and received his first
Holy Communion. Merton entered a Trappist monastery in December of
1941, having just received a call from his draft board to be conscripted for
World War II military service. With the encouragement of his abbot to pursue

the careers of both monk and author, he wrote *The Seven Storey Mountain* in his first years at Gethsemani, Kentucky, and published it in 1948 at the age of thirty-three. The text maps the first three decades of his journey and a young adult's black and white understanding about a spiritual mission. His private journals, published according to his wishes twenty-five years after he died in 1968, probed the myriad conflicts between the sacred and the secular motivations in his life.

Thomas Merton used a mountain metaphor to capture his relentless ascents and assents. With a dual vocation as monk and writer, he construed his narrative's autobiographical "I" as being a representative person to inspire others. Saint Augustine's *The Confessions* and *The Seven Storey Mountain* used several similar composition strategies. Both employed a linear, chronological plot line. Both authors described their memory's episodes as unfolding with a predetermined purpose. They believed that their life scripts had been written before they eventually discovered them. The narrative was their attempt to capture the coming-to-awareness processes that they judged should be a common human quest. The intended audience for Augustine was the fourth century Christian community and his pastoral flock at Hippo. For Merton, the audience was a multi-faith public, asking questions about personal meaning and values in the midst of profound socio-cultural changes in post-World War II America.

Merton in the 1940s, like Black Elk in 1930 and Malcolm X in the 1960s, genuinely felt he had discovered significant answers for his life and for the people of his times. All three emphasized *bios* and their religious journey's place in the history of significant global and local events. Deeply steeped in literature by virtue of his days in prep school, at Cambridge, and from his baccalaureate and master's degrees at Columbia, Merton's opening lines trumpet a reckoning of his own life's significance, akin to Dickens' "best of times, worst of times" statement from the *Tale of Two Cities.* Merton's book (certainly Augustine's and Black Elk's) was written before psychology became America's secular religion; in fact, he often wrote skeptically about its early attempts to evaluate individuals and their stories. Although his *autos* was replete with complex motives and intentions, he subsumed them under the greater powers of Jesus Christ and the Trappist community to which he pledged lifelong fidelity. The episodes and all of the richly described players in Merton's story, as it was for his inspirational fathers, Saint Augustine and Dante, can be illuminated by the stages and turning points of Erikson's *homo religious.*

The Columbia scholar and Merton's literary mentor, Mark Van Doren, once noted that the definition of a great book is one that survived fifty years in print. I hope to describe why Merton's narrative deserved affirmation, beyond just the longevity of its global reading publics.

Merton's Metaphors & Maps

The "seven storey mountain" is an allusion to Dante Alighieri and *The Divine Comedy*, a Renaissance pilgrim's story of life's journey from ignorance and the slavery of sin to the freedom of grace and knowledge. This universal journey echoes Exodus themes of the Hebrew Scriptures, with Dante and his two guides, Virgil and Beatrix, navigating the three regions of the *Inferno, Purgatorio,* and *Paradiso.* In the *Inferno*, a reader encounters grim figures and forms, men who can only look backward or who have lost their heads, grouped into circles and condemned to an eternal death. Leaving this place that cannot entertain any hope, Dante enters Purgatory. Purgatory was Dante's island mountain where light and darkness alternate and pilgrims ascend a series of spiral circles to explore the roots of our sins.[28] In this didactic book, Dante's sermons about earthly life begin—homilies about love, about free will, about liberty and the importance of making count each breath in our temporal lives. The ascent up the mountain is a corrective discipline, enabling individuals to work through the causes of the seven capital sins: the misdirected love manifested in pride, envy, and wrath, the deficient love revealed in sloth, and the excesses of love seen in avarice, gluttony, and lust.

Dante instructs pilgrims and readers to examine their lives and work out the answers for themselves, facilitated by meditations, prayers, and benedictions along the way. At each stage, the purged soul encounters a caretaker angel, a sign of sin removed, and the upward journey continues. Dante believed in an instinctive love that draws us back to our Creator, but that our freedom also allows the same love to lead us sometimes into evil and its consequent punishments. Life's earthly journey ought to be a return to innocence, during which we store in our memories for later use an abundance of physical, spiritual, and intellectual images. This spiraling journey is one of hope, a continuing re-discovery of the possibilities and limits of love and freedom. (Recall how in Erikson's first stage conflict, trust versus mistrust, hope is the strength or virtue that results.) *The Seven Storey Mountain* unfolds as the stages of Merton's path to Gethsemani. He takes the reader on a journey from Europe to America and the many tribulations of his personal Purgatory to reach his temporal Paradise in a Trappist monastery.

Merton's chapter and section titles are his maps for readers who take the journey with him as their guide. The opening section, "Prisoner's Base", begins with an epic-quality first line in which he declares his life began on the last day of January 1915, with a great war as its historical backdrop, but in an out of the way place near French mountains on the borders of Spain. He concludes Part One with an account of life at twenty-two in 1937. His spirit had descended into a blind alley where he felt helpless, yet hopeful that his defeats would establish some base for his eventual rescue.

Part Two, a chronicle of the events immediately around his conversion to Catholicism and decision to become a priest, has an opening section titled, "With a Great Price", that Merton began with a homily about a paradox of human existence that we must probe and arrive at some understanding if we are to be happy. The paradox is that our human nature does not give us the tools, by itself, to solve life's challenges. With a pessimism that permeates this narrative, he asserts that to follow only our personal talents, philosophies, or ethical standards will lead us directly to hell. This stark realization leaves Merton, at the end of Part Two, on his knees and asking God that if it be His will, let him become a priest.

Part Three continues this theological and geographical trek with an opening section, "Magnetic North", on to "True North", then past the "Sleeping Volcano", and finally to arrive at Gethsemani and "The Sweet Savor of Liberty".

Merton made his way through *Purgatorio*, returning to a place of earthly innocence, Gethsemani, and discovering, like Dante, the love and freedom for which he had been destined. The book's formal narrative ends in April, 1943 when Merton was twenty-eight years old. His only brother and last surviving immediate family member, John Paul, died after his bomber was shot down over the English Channel. In Dante's book, the poet's companion, Virgil, departs with no notice. Merton's narrative ends in similar fashion; his only brother departs and there was no opportunity to say good-bye; only memory could keep him alive.[29]

In the Epilogue, Merton mused about his dual vocation as Trappist monk and writer. The reader is brought back to the opening pages and the "Prisoner's Base"—that children's game of running free but always yearning to return to the stability of a home. We have walked with Merton through life's contradictory choices about which Dante and he had to learn. His examined life is a theological history and geography. Merton finished the story with the cartography of what he was just starting to understand. His old self died to live anew in God's mercy and love, having been led on a complex journey from Prades to Bermuda to St. Antonin to Oakham to London to Cambridge to Rome to New York to Columbia to Corpus Christi to St. Bonaventure to the Cistercian monastery of Gethsemani. Thus the book ends, but Merton knows that his journey will continue.

Merton's Composition Strategies

If the map and the dominant metaphor for *The Seven Storey Mountain* was the *Purgatorio*, then Saint Augustine's *Confessions* is thoroughly woven into Merton's composition strategies. In the summer of 1938, a Hindu monk visited Merton and his Columbia University buddies in New York City. Merton asked him what he should read to understand spirituality and mysticism. Bramachari surprised him when he suggested two Christian books: St. Augustine's *Confessions* and *The Imitation of Christ* by Thomas a Kempis. While studying Thomas Aquinas's philosophy, Merton had an important discussion with an influential teacher, Dan Walsh, who told him that his thinking had an Augustinian quality to it. Several months later, Merton was baptized and formally entered the Catholic Church, and, over the following summer of 1939, he finally got to read *The Confessions*.

That summer he composed a fictional and autobiographical text, *The Labyrinth*.[30] Michael Mott, in his official biography, saw James Joyce's *Finnegan's Wake* as the literary seed for Merton's autobiographical project and supported this view with persuasive documentation from the journal entries that he alone had been able to read, prior to 1993. Mott's analyses of these journals and the interviews he conducted with Merton's friends and colleagues balanced the motivations of Merton to be writer and to be a Catholic. From my own readings of the private journals that began being published in 1995, I believe that the zeal of the recent convert, coupled with the power of Augustine's *ur*-book as a spiritual and literary model, should also be linked to the narrative.

The journal entries after *The Labyrinth's* composition and his reading of *The Confessions* were suggestive.[31] The entry on November 20, 1939 [32] is a commentary on autobiographical writing, providing support for Mott's argument that Merton wanted to compose his text as an "anti-autobiography". He disdained the spate of autobiographical texts being published after World War II in both their substance that revealed lives not worth reading about and their belief that they were just the opposite. In the same entry, Merton described telling the undergraduate students he was teaching in a night school class to write out of their own experience (Mark Van Doren first taught him to read out of his own experience), and then he critiqued recent autobiographical works by Joyce, Lawrence, Thurber, Saroyan, Auden, and Gertrude Stein.

In 1946, five years after entering the monastery, Merton received permission from his abbot for a writing project that would be autobiographical, but not solely. He saw it as a cross between the *Purgatorio*, Kafka, and a medieval miracle play, called *The Seven Storey Mountain*. [33] He originally intended this work to be one hundred and fifty pages; it grew to six hundred and fifty pages. Mott asserted that with the growth of this manuscript also came the growing realization of his being someone special and that fate intended him to write something extraordinary and of lasting value. The difficulty was how to reconcile that sense of special destiny with self-examination worthy of the consciousness of a Trappist monk.[34] In March, 1947, he took his Solemn Vows, renounced all of his worldly possessions, then signed the publisher's contract for *The Seven Storey Mountain*.

Chastity was Augustine's demon; Merton's conscience preferred pride. The final editing process for the manuscript's publication is part of the folklore of this book's destiny. A Trappist censor refused to grant the Catholic Church's *nihil obstat* (i.e., nothing herein is contrary to faith and morals) with a stinging critique of the author's candor about his pagan past, but he also scorned the young monk's amateurish writing style.[35] Yet, it became a best-seller the very first month after its publication.

On its fiftieth anniversary, Robert Giroux, the original publisher, reported total sales of multiple millions and in many languages, continuing to sell year after year. Reviewers in 1948 suggested that Merton's story touched his era's American audience, adrift in the aftermath of World War II, reflecting on both the victory of Allied Forces perceived to represent freedom and the defeat of Axis Forces and their totalitarian regimes. A national consciousness had not yet been raised about the depth and breadth of evil in the Holocaust and the seeds of future destructiveness sown at Hiroshima and Nagasaki. Examinations of conscience used religious and historical, not psychological standards of justification.

In the following section, I suggest that the salience of Merton's continuing message can be understood from the newly emerging psychological formulations at that time, of which Erikson was a popular spokesperson. Moreover, the author's identity as a 1940s monk in seclusion grew to become one of bearing witness as a very public spokesperson for peace and justice in the 1960s. Erikson's life cycle concept of epigenesis helps us to understand Merton, the *homo religious*, and his role models Augustine and Dante, as well.

Merton's Episodes and the Examining Conscience

The Seven Storey Mountain can be evaluated using Erikson's developmental cycle with its conflicts, virtues, and epigenetic progression of episodes and their resolutions. We can pose questions about the developmental stage at which Merton composed the narrative, that stage's typical conflicts, and its linkages to what came before and after. He composed *The Labyrinth* in his early twenties and completed *The Seven Storey Mountain* as a young adult. This age aligns with Erikson's psychosocial stage when the critical issues are intimacy versus isolation, and the core strength or virtue is love. Merton had committed to his vocation, had taken vows to make public that commitment, and declared Gethsemani his lifelong home where he would deepen his holiness and advance his writing every day.

For the monastic life in general and Merton's life in particular, there is a daily paradox in the issues of intimacy versus isolation as preparation for the adulthood crisis of generativity versus stagnation and growing into the virtue of care. Intimacy is pursued, sometimes found, as a spiritual connectedness with a transcendent "Other". Earthly intimacy is manifested in living with one's priestly brothers, celebrating communal rituals of prayer and liturgical worship, and in laboring daily on an individual task that contributes to the social and economic welfare of the monastery. At this stage, according to Erikson's theory and the historical ethos of America in the 1950s and early 1960s, most individuals were working through the challenges of heterosexual relationships based on earlier trial and error romantic encounters and short-lived commitments. They were making decisions about a lifelong partner who matched up well with all of the personal characteristics that crystallized during the prior identity stage. Isolation was a failure to achieve this intimacy and could be linked to unresolved conflicts and unrealized virtues. For example, one could hypothesize that isolation derived from the individual's role diffusion with no virtue of fidelity established during adolescence, or to feelings of inferiority and a lack of competence from school age experiences, or the roots may be found all the way back in a basic mistrust and lack of hope from a person's infancy. When Merton confronted isolation AND intimacy, he was developmentally grounded in a history of a supportive and extended family life, close male friendships, and the experiences of both healthy and not so healthy interactions with women.

Merton's identity as a writer and saint-in-progress is best understood by wending through the text of his story beginning with his childhood. His adolescent and young adulthood formulation was consistent with how he first recorded and then was allowed to publish his memory's episodes in *The Seven Storey Mountain*. His private journals suggested that this identity, the episodes, and examining them in writing had complexities that would have left Erikson, the detective-analyst, smiling, indeed.

In the opening chapter, Merton reported that he could read, write, and draw by age five. Ruth, his mother, wanted him to be independent and not to go along with the crowd. He wrote about her dreams for him in the first part of his life narrative. Her image of Tom was someone who did not come off the assembly line, someone with a strong character and who stood for definite ideals. Ruth kept a journal about Tom for his first three and a half years and was his ever-present teacher. Despite such attentiveness, this Quaker woman evoked harsh memories in Merton. Tom remembered both that the family always spoke of her as gay and very light-hearted, but that photographs of her at that time revealed a stern visage, even an anxiety. These external images reflected his mother's inner qualities and Tom also remembered her critical nature, especially towards him.

Mott's interpretation of these memories was twofold. First, Ruth's attention shifted in November, 1918, to her younger son, John Paul. Second, in letters Merton wrote to a close theologian friend, Rosemary Reuther, in 1967, he confessed that he was frightened by their interaction and that he understood his negative adult reactions to her as projections of lingering resentments about his mother's constant intellectual demands of him.[36] With Erikson's epigenetic model, early difficulties and unresolved issues can be worked through at later stages as individuals mature and relationships may mature with them. Merton did not get that chance with his mother. In the summer of 1921, Ruth Merton was diagnosed with stomach cancer and hospitalized. Owen Merton brought home a letter from Ruth to Tom, who was only six at the time. She had never before written a letter to the young boy and although he knew what was happening, he still was very confused. What became evident, perhaps from the safety of the monastery where he wrote his narrative, was that his mother was telling him that she was going to die, soon, and forever be gone from his life. He recalled taking the letter outside, sitting under a tree, and trying to make sense of the words and their deeper meaning. A sadness and depression weighed him down, and the adult writer recalled his emotions, not those of a child expressed with tears aplenty, but more like the gloom that adults who grieve allow the world to see. Tom felt so unnatural. Why was his mother dying so young, and why was he responding the way he did?

Merton's mother died on October 3, 1921. Memories never finish. As Augustine understood, we may believe that they have been filed away, but they continue their work of re-collection and revision long after, in response to the sensory and cognitive stimuli of new episodes. Tom began elementary school and was promoted quickly to the second grade. His father, Owen, left, returned, and then took Tom, but not John Paul, with him as a companion to the artist's community in Provincetown, Cape Cod. One year later, having returned only briefly to the site of his mother's death in New York, Owen and Tom went off to Bermuda so his father could paint. In 1923, Tom came back to live with his grandparents and Owen was off to France leaving Tom behind. In 1925, at age ten, Tom went back to France with his father, and would stay in Europe for the second decade of his life. These are the times in Erikson's two developmental stages when initiative and industry are the critical issues, when family, neighborhood, and school are the sites of significant relationships, and when the strengths of purposefulness and competence are to be achieved.

While writing *The Seven Storey Mountain* during the developmental stage of intimacy versus isolation, Merton evaluated his childhood as a time of one change after another. He recalled that each time Owen and his two sons landed somewhere and settled, they were off again in fairly short order. For Tom, leaving the home base most recently established became as predictable as the changing of the seasons, but with as stormy upheavals as the weather at its worst. He judged the freedom to be without boundaries as exhilarating, and couldn't even imagine that this state of affairs was not how every other family lived their lives. In 1966, at the age of fifty-one, having been a Trappist for two decades, and in the developmental stage when generativity is the issue and care is the primary virtue, Merton was wiser about his memories of that earlier time. He described the last years of his first decade of life as desperate and despairing. His mother was dead and his father was on the move. When Owen finally retrieved him, he felt saved when they moved to France.

"Prisoner's Base" thus became a defining theme for all his journeys. Memories about the loss of his mother and the changing geographies with his father kept working within his psyche. I believe it was why France, Cambridge schooling, and the development of a dual identity—writer and monk-saint—became so important to the adult who composed *The Seven Storey Mountain*. But more threads need to be sewn into this tapestry before arriving at that conclusion.

The reader can review Merton's passages about his adolescent years when he talks about his positive and negative traits, role models who possessed idealized characteristics, about considering various occupational roles, values and ideology, and how all of these were nurtured (or not) by significant others in the family or in schools and society. I will map in finer detail Merton's identity period as between 1928 (age thirteen) and 1937 (age twenty-two).

He remembered a conversation at age thirteen with his beloved Aunt Maud. Occupational roles and ideal characteristics of the self were already emerging. He asked her what she thought of his becoming a novelist or a writer. Her response was immediate and very affirming. She added an observation that sometimes writers had a hard time, economically. Tom had taken that into account already and re-assured her that such considerations were in his plan. In the actual text, all of this conversation is wrapped in quotation marks. Because it was about talking with Maud, Merton had vividly precise memories of it. The use of verbatim quotes for the extended interaction punctuates how the author, when composing this passage eighteen years later, wanted to tell the reader how this identity script for one of the two critical elements of his adult vocation was already being drafted in early adolescence.

His mother's early and high expectations for Tom's individuality were evident at age fifteen. He read Plato and Descartes at prep school in England, and reported that such intellectual feats established his platform for independence and for rebellion. Like any adolescent, egoism inflated his realistic appraisal of genuine accomplishments. Acknowledging that this tendency was hard-wired into his personality at a very young age, Tom let himself be governed, even gladly, by the authority of good teachers and those willing to challenge his ideas and attitudes.

One of those individuals was Tom, his physician godfather, who treated him as intelligent and mature, but perhaps more than he deserved and less than he really wanted. Merton's Augustinian mind was at work when he wrote his memory's episodes about his boundary-setting godfather, recalling and certainly revising them while in the monastery at age thirty. Although acknowledging all of his parental and career support, he criticized Tom for his seemingly contradictory stances of loving D.H. Lawrence's art, but finding reprehensible that author's ideas about how a man should live his life.

In these recollections, *The Seven Storey Mountain* is a good example of the revisionist history that Gusdorf described as the authorial strategy of all autobiography and that Erikson understood as the psychological recycling of human experience. Using such a strategy, firmly believing in the unfolding of yet-to-be meaning in one's life, the continuity and unity in the text of one's story is quite predictable. The autobiographical "I", whether judged by literary or psychological standards, read history backwards during Merton's era.

In 1930, Owen Merton died when Tom was fifteen. He was depressed for a couple of months, but the feelings passed. He felt free and eager to pursue his will's desires and appetites, becoming his own man of the world. In a bleak commentary, Merton described that world and his era as distinguished by poison gas, atomic bombs, and images of the Apocalypse. The last traces of religion and God were squeezed out of him—at least for the next four or five years.

During a medical crisis from an abscessed tooth and blood poisoning at age seventeen, Merton had an apparition of death. Remembering the episode, he described at length how no inklings or leanings toward God struck him at the time. He described his mouth and soul as equally gangrenous. Saving grace alone allowed him to survive because his heart was cold and indifferent to what bad spiritual shape he was in. A year later, and suffering from another tooth infection, there came another apparition. While traveling in Rome, wandering through its churches and vivid images and religious art, Merton sensed Jesus Christ all around him, bought a copy of the New Testament and began to read it, putting aside the D.H. Lawrence novels he brought as favorite traveling companions. One evening, while in his hotel room, he felt the presence of his deceased father, now dead for more than a year. He was overcome by a newfound insight into his misery, of his soul longing for escape and freedom, with an urgency that he had never felt before. He reported praying, possibly, for the very first time in his entire life. Despite the magnitude of such an epiphany, his prose was uncharacteristically uninspiring. For several pages, Merton continued to not talk about this incident, to not label it as important in his life, and to not try to explain it. All he could recall was that as an eighteen-year old he was convinced that he would get better.

There was some healthy sinning yet to be done. Mott made an insightful comparison between Augustine's episodes and those that Merton disclosed. He judged the former as plain speaking; the latter always seemed camouflaged. Mott, the biographer, was not persuaded that this was an erasure by either the Church's censors or Merton's literary editors. Based on the sources I've read, and as a psychologist, I agree. At age thirty one, identity and intimacy issues seemed unresolved. Mott reported a comment made in one of the earlier typescripts that Merton edited out before the final draft, and he chastised Merton, adding, "this comment was itself censored, or edited out, but one could bear to be more often embarrassed in the printed text, and less often teased." [37] For example, there is evidence that Merton participated in a rowdy party while at Cambridge, where the group reenacted the crucifixion scene, and on the next day he had to go and bury his beloved Aunt Maud. Mott found the following sentence in an earlier draft of the manuscript. "It was embarrassing to receive on my cheek the chaste kiss of one of my aunts, my Father's sister, when my mouth still burned with the contrast of the night before."[38] From that passage, Mott introduced another feature of adolescence and the stormy identity stage. Thomas Merton probably was a virgin when he arrived, but not when he left Cambridge.

Like Augustine, Merton explored his sexuality and ruminated about its meanings. Unlike Augustine's *Confessions*, however, candor about these explorations and evidence of any commitment to a relationship are not to be found in Merton's episodes. Tom's adolescent Carthage was Cambridge. This period's best thing was reading Dante, but he chastised himself in the text for never applying the poet's ideas to his own life. He may have been a sensitive and appreciative reader of the *Inferno, Purgatorio,* and *Paradiso,* but his moral fiber had seven layers of obtuse and resistant sinew. There are hefty abstractions and moralizations in his passages about Cambridge, but few details. The available biographical facts are that Merton probably impregnated a young woman and that his godfather, Tom Bennett, worked out a legal settlement with her, for many of the same motivations as Augustine's mother. Bennett then summoned Tom to his offices for a verbal dressing-down. Dejected and guilty, Merton finished the term, took his exams, and sailed to America to be with his grandparents on Long Island. Shortly thereafter, a letter arrived from his godfather urging him to stay in America and never return to Cambridge. Mott suggested that this passage was another example of the censoring Merton. His pride had been stung by the chastising interviews; his hopes had been devastated by being told never to return. In *The Seven Storey Mountain*, he rambles on for several pages using *Inferno* images to describe England and Europe, punctuating all that depravity with an account of a friend's suicide.

In 1935, he enrolled at Columbia University to finish his undergraduate degree, and he met Mark Van Doren. More important than the literature they read together or the pedagogical approach of his classes, about which Merton raved for several pages, Van Doren became his mentor. Recall the classical origin of this often-used term. The goddess of wisdom, Athena, came to earth in the form of a crusty older man named Mentor. His task was to be the guide for the gifted young man in his journey, but more importantly to affirm that his was a special life. Such a relationship can be at the heart of resolving the identity crisis stage and often has deep importance for one's future. Merton was twenty years old when he took his first class with Van Doren. He ended the first book in *The Seven Storey Mountain* juxtaposing this discovery with an account of his grandparents' deaths in 1936 and 1937. Merton attributed to Van Doren's intellect, his honesty, and his integrity, the important task of preparing his mind to study philosophy, and ultimately to his religious conversion.

In college, identity issues are typically receding and intimacy issues advancing to the foreground (at least during the historical era in which this narrative took place). For the writer in preparation, Columbia and Van Doren and other mentors would continue to inspire Merton's intellectual identity work. His text echoes Augustine's intellectual journey to Christianity through Ambrose's thought-provoking sermons and philosophical syntheses of the ideas of his time. For the spiritual Merton, the Catholic monk in preparation, the second and third parts of *The Seven Storey Mountain* rendered an account of a conversion predetermined by Providence. I will return for a fuller look at the conversion process in the next chapter, using William James's *The Varieties of Religious Experience* to explore Black Elk's and Malcolm X's extended religious epiphanies.

Intimacy issues were being addressed within his circle of literary friends at Columbia with whom he maintained warm and close relationships even after entering the monastery, much like Augustine's communal companions, Nebridus and Alypius. Intimacy was also addressed in his deepening love and commitment to Jesus Christ. In confronting intimacy conflicts, however, Merton never had a Monica at his side nor did he have a woman who loved him, or who had birthed a son named Adeodatus, or "God-given".

Mott treats Merton's relationships with women while at Columbia in a curious manner. Friends sometimes reported that Merton often was surrounded by women in casual company; close friends told the biographer that Merton too often rushed at women, thereby insuring that he never had to get close to any. All except Sylvia at Cambridge and an unnamed woman about whom he wrote in coldly clinical terms on the eve of his fiftieth birthday, January 30, 1965. He described having sex on his mind as he recalled the immaturities of his youth, now twenty-five years since what he labeled as an adulterous affair. Their night's passion in a summer heat became the next morning's vapid conversation, and he judged that there was no meaning in it for either.[39] Merton's passion in his early twenties was invested in his writing and not in his sexuality. Even conversations about becoming a priest, forsaking marriage and family, and entering a religious community were attached to a proviso—he must be allowed to write or the deal was off!

The personality psychologist, Dan McAdams, describes identity as a continuing life story beyond the chronological period and the developmental stage in which its issues are first addressed. Identity concerns are always at the center of the self after adolescence. We become an anthology of stories and we constantly revise these stories throughout our lives, as we will explore in more detail in Chapter Five. In the third section of *The Seven Storey Mountain*, chapters are titled: "Magnetic North", "True North", "The Sleeping Volcano", and "The Sweet Savor of Liberty", before the closing Epilogue. Merton narrated various episodes in his life after his conversion. They could be described in secular psychological language as occupational, decision-making events—graduation from Columbia, teaching literature to adult students in an evening college, teaching literature at Saint Bonaventure University, and whether to do charitable community work in Harlem. The episodes are about Dante's spiritual circling also—a trip to Cuba and a transcendent experience at the Church of Saint Francis, rejections by various orders of priests, and a retreat to the Trappist monastery during Easter season. Read backward, he saw all these secular and spiritual episodes as leading him inexorably to be admitted as a postulant at Gethsemani on December 13, 1941. Whatever the geography being explored or the religious commitment being considered, the writer's vocation and its centrality to Merton's identity never stopped evolving. He was truly blessed to be under the direction of an abbot who nurtured his writer's instincts from the very first day he entered the Trappist community.

The last of memory's episodes in *The Seven Storey Mountain* is about John Paul's death on April 17, 1943. Merton had been at Gethsemani for a year and he was twenty-eight. The very "last word" is particularly striking. He brings the reader up to date on his friends' and teachers' lives. Merton professed his solemn vows on Saint Joseph's Day in 1948. Around a simple description of this milestone, he wove an Augustinian-like recollection of learning the power of solitude and concluded the entire book with the spiritual geography sites over which he had trekked. Yet, there was a still-struggling secular heart revealed in the epilogue, and Merton finished this installment of his story in the throes of ambiguity about his identity.

Readers of *The Seven Storey Mountain* made him a celebrity, a spiritually romantic hero, a worldly author who had the courage to give up everything and retreat into the monastery where the world could not encroach, where the grimy, ordinary, and baser motivations of human nature could not prevail. The autobiographical "I" composed for this text became mythic. The autobiographical "I" of the secular journals displayed a less confident, more sober self. It is another rendering of the identity life story as Gusdorf and McAdams would have predicted. For example, Merton wrote on May 7, 1951 that the character who so confidently voiced his beliefs on the pages of *The Seven Storey Mountain* was dead, and the story was the work of someone whom he never knew.[40] This is the same rhetoric that infused the original tale with black and white certainties. Like Augustine, a different consciousness needed to emerge; for Merton, it would take longer than the publication of this first examination. Re-working memory can foster humility.

By reading the journals composed after *The Seven Storey Mountain*, we discover how Merton's identity left behind its need to dominate with the virtues of will, purpose, and competence associated with the struggles of Erikson's autonomy, initiative, and industry phases. Spiritually and psychologically, Merton returned to the virtue of hope and to the stage dynamics where basic trust is paramount. It was a continuing discovery of trust in others and in his God. Merton progressed through the developmental conflicts of intimacy and generativity, discovering an increased capacity for Erikson's virtues of love and caring. An interdisciplinary eye can examine both *The Seven Storey Mountain* and the seven volumes of his secular journals using Henry Murray's personology, Dan McAdams' life story model of identity, or Erik Erikson's epigenetic theory and its applications to the lives of *homo religious* figures like Luther, or Gandhi, or Thomas Merton. Augustine's descriptions of memory processes in Book X of *The Confessions* can also be a powerful lens for the analysis of this text.

By the end of his life, Merton's identities as monk and writer had grown into that of a mystic, public intellectual, and political advocate. Like Augustine and like Dante's pilgrim, he had done so by responding to grace. He wrote an examination of an existential conscience on April 14, 1966, approximately two years before his untimely death in Southeast Asia. Writing, for him, had become a way of being, an activity of the intellect and the heart. Very much echoing Augustine, he described his writing as testimony and praise, as inquiry and truth-telling, as loving when at its best and insecurely authoritarian when at its worst. He felt best about his work when he was able to truly confess and witness to something larger than the self. [41]

In the next chapter, we explore how Black Elk and Malcolm X contributed to the life narrative genre via similar unity stories of conversion and redemption, and ultimately were transformed after their deaths into prophetic witnesses.

NOTES

1. James Olney, *Memory & Narrative: The Weave of Life-Writing* (Chicago: University of Chicago Press, 1998).

2. Paul John Eakin, *How Our Lives Became Stories: Making Selves* (Ithaca, NY: Cornell University Press, 1999).

3. Dan P. McAdams, *The Stories We Live By* (New York: Guilford, 1997c) and "The Psychology of Life Stories," *Review of General Psychology* 5, (2001c): 100–122.

4. Evaluating American undergraduate education in psychology, McGovern and Brewer suggested that we live in a post-disciplinary and pluralistic world and will need to attend to both paradigms and narratives if psychology is to continue to be regarded as one of the contemporary liberal arts. See Thomas V. McGovern and Charles L. Brewer, "Paradigms, Narratives, and Pluralism in Undergraduate Psychology" in *Unity in Psychology: Possibility or Pipedream?* ed. Robert J. Sternberg (Washington, DC: American Psychological Association, 2005), 125–143; and Thomas V. McGovern and Charles L. Brewer, "Undergraduate Psychology" in *History of Psychology, Volume 1*, ed. Donald K. Freedheim in *Handbook of Psychology*, Editor-in-Chief Irving B. Weiner (New York: Wiley, 2003), 465–481.

5. Sidonie Smith and Julia Watson, *Reading Autobiography: A Guide for Interpreting Life Narratives* (Minneapolis: University of Minnesota Press, 2001).

6. ". . . Misch's notion of autobiography as the record of a representative life of the great man had long served as a norm, a 'master narrative' about the meaning and role of a particular model of life narrative in western civilization." Smith & Watson, *Reading Autobiography*, 117.

7. Georges Gusdorf, "Conditions and Limits of Autobiography." In *Autobiography: Essays Theoretical and Critical*, ed. trans. James Olney (Princeton, NJ: Princeton University Press, 1980), 28–48.

8. Mary Mason, "The Other Voice: Autobiographies of Women Writers" in *Autobiography: Essays*, 207–235.

9. Gusdorf, "Conditions", 37. He recognized the limits of constructing this narrative self as well. ". . .the original sin of autobiography is first one of logical coherence and rationalization. The narrative is conscious, and since the narrator's consciousness directs the narrative, it seems to him incontestable that it has also directed his life", Gusdorf, "Conditions", 41. "The illusion begins from the moment that the narrative *confers a meaning* on the event which, when it actually occurred, no doubt had several meanings or perhaps none", Gusdorf, "Conditions," 42 (emphasis in the original).

10. Gusdorf, "Conditions," 38. Michael Mott prefaced his biography of Merton with a characterization of his subject's life as a "continuing conversion, continuing autobiography". Michael Mott, *The Seven Mountains of Thomas Merton* (New York: Harvest, 1993), *xvii*.

11. Gusdorf, "Conditions", 48. Spengemann also wrote a history of the first wave of autobiographical writing beginning with 1900. He attributed the ever increasing readership to three factors: popular market texts, acceptance by literary journals of

scholarly criticism of these texts, and Wilhelm Dilthey's theory of history that encouraged the reading of autobiographies as primary source material. Autobiography was considered a subset of biographical writing, but, over the 20th century, the texts and their critics moved away from the history/biography emphasis to include more psychological interpretations and then to an analysis of the actual composition process. Whereas Olney defined this evolution as the movement from *bios* to *autos* to *graphe*, Spengemann labeled it as a shift from life to mind to text, with Gusdorf's essay as the work that oriented subsequent discussion of the governing conditions of autobiography. He concluded his historical analysis of the genre with an evaluative comment that remains current: ". . . the recent upsurge of critical interest in autobiography coincides, on the one side, with a feeling that the genre is ubiquitous and, on the other, with a doubt that it exists at all." William C. Spengemann, *The Forms of Autobiography: Episodes in the History of a Literary Genre* (New Haven, CT: Yale University Press, 1980), 245.

12. William M. Runyan, "Progress in Psychobiography." In *Psychobiography and Life Narratives,* eds. Dan P. McAdams & Richard L. Ochberg (Durham, NC: Duke University Press, 1988), 295.

13. Henry Murray, *Explorations in Personality: A Clinical and Experimental Study of Fifty Men of College Age* (New York: Oxford University Press, 1938), 39 (emphases in original).

14. Rosenwald acknowledged his discipline's prejudices thus: "Psychologists' ambivalence about the study of lives is well-known. Lives, their own in particular, may have been the engrossing enigma that first teased them into the discipline. But it was only a tease. . .their teachers pledged them to the austere and self-denying mandate of generalization: Lives in general were to be the object of investigation. . .This is how the case study has come to be regarded as the scholar's trap". George C. Rosenwald, "A Theory of Multiple-Case Research," in *Psychobiography and Life Narratives*, eds. Dan P. McAdams & Richard L. Ochberg (Durham, NC: Duke University Press, 1988), 239.

15. Quoted in J. Roy Hopkins, "Erik Homburger Erikson (1902–1994)," *American Psychologist* 50 (1995): 786.

16. Gergen wrote: "Erikson is also a master of the well-turned phrase—the phrase that prompts sudden recognition that borne to lofty flight is a thought previously dwelling only in the quagmire of the preconscious. . .not the types of statements that send one scurrying for his data in defense of theoretical premise; they do on the other hand, invite a warm and admiring 'yes'". Kenneth Gergen, "Flight from the Quagmire," Review of Erik H. Erikson's *Identity, Youth and Crisis. Contemporary Psychology* 14(2, 1969): 49–50.

17. Lawrence Friedman, *Identity's Architect: A Biography of Erik H. Erikson* (New York: Scribner, 1999).

18. He wrote that this work "must be a subjective book, a conceptual itinerary", "a psychoanalytic book on the relation of the ego to society," "at the same time it throws some light on the fact that the history of humanity is a gigantic metabolism of individual life cycles." Erik Erikson, *Childhood and Society* (New York: Norton, 1950), 13–14.

19. Erik H. Erikson and Joan M. Erikson. *The Life Cycle Completed: Extended Version with New Chapters on the Ninth Stage of Development* (New York: Norton, 1997), 3.

20. Erikson, *Childhood and Society*, 234.

21. Erikson, *Childhood and Society,* 227–228.

22. Erikson, *Childhood and Society*, 242.

23. The psychological biographer examines lives at three levels: (a) inherited biological characteristics, (b) ego characteristics that reveal how individuals respond to experience and adapt to adversity, and (c) the family, social, cultural, and historical contexts that shape those responses and adaptive qualities.

24. Friedman, *Identity's Architect*, 388.

25. Erikson and Erikson, *Life Cycle Completed,* 29.

26. Erik H. Erikson, *Life History and the Historical Moment* (New York: Norton, 1975), 124. Mott's prefatory epigraph for his biography is a similarly telling quote by Merton: "When I reveal most, I hide most". Mott, *Seven Mountains, xvii.*

27. In developmental theory, such questioning reflects the concept of cohort differences. For example, the biological changes of puberty may be relatively universal across time and geography, but the cultural rituals around these changes get constructed in a variety of ways. The emotional and cognitive changes in adolescence may yield different consequences based on history, gender, ethnicity, class, geography, and a myriad of other identity-shaping parameters.

28. William James wrote in *The Varieties of Religious Experience* that scientists can only evaluate the fruits of religious experience, because its roots need be left to literature and religion.

29. In the last Canto of the *Purgatorio*, Beatrix leads Dante through the waters of oblivion; he will remember all his past, but with forgiveness accepted, he can do so without shame or pain.

30. In his June 20, 1948 private journal entry, Merton mused about how *The Seven Storey Mountain* was all part of God's plan for its author. It had taken nine years to see it published after the summer's drafting of *The Labyrinth* at Olean, and then being unable to sell that version. Jonathan Montaldo, ed. *Entering the Silence: The Journals of Thomas Merton. Volume Two (1941–1952)* (San Francisco: Harper Collins, 1997), 212–213.

31. On September 13, 1939, Merton wrote about his experiences with keeping a diary. He would identify a specific date and then compare his entries over the last several years on that date. He made a number of negative comments about the style of journal that seems self-confessional but that is actually more self-serving and rife with personal ambition. Rousseau's confessions appeared to be the latter, whereas Augustine's were the former. The important difference was that Rousseau exalted himself and Augustine exalted God. Patrick Hart, O.C.S.O., ed. *Run to the Mountain: The Journals of Thomas Merton. Volume One* (1939–1941) (San Francisco: Harper Collins, 1996), 20–21.

He followed up on this affirmation of Augustine's motivations and text on November 2, 1939, when he wrote how the saint was writing to Christians and doing so as a skillful rhetorician. Augustine did not need to either overstate his case or to appeal to philosophical persuasive strategies. The truth was in revelation and Augustine wrote to move others' will toward God's faith and love. Hart, *Run to the Mountain,* 83.

32. Hart, *Run to the Mountain,* 91.

33. Quoted from a letter, in Mott, *Seven Mountains,* 226.

34. Mott, *Seven Mountains,* 229.

35. Merton wrote in his journal on April 16, 1947 that sometimes he just wanted to put his pen down and to stop all his writing, Yet, he realized that his road to sanctity included learning how to write while being a monk, writing for the glory of God and denying himself, and abating his immature need to hastily get this text into print. Montaldo, *Entering the Silence,* 63.

After another round of suggestions from the censor, he wrote on May 29 how he was trying to be obedient and to tone down his rhetoric. He could only imagine the responses of his future audiences—men reading the book while riding to work on the railroad, monks and nuns in European monasteries and convents, non-Catholics, Jews, communists, and American priests. These were people he could only imagine as his readers but his censor, Father Gabriel, could and did not want to offend anyone. Montaldo, *Entering the Silence,* 78.

And then in July, 1948, after receiving the first hardbound copy from his abbot, Merton found himself wondering whether Gary Cooper might play him as the hero when they made his book into a movie. What began as a writer's lark in Olean ten years earlier, now might become a whopping success and a moneymaker for the monastery at Gethsemani, and at a time when his spiritual community could really use the funds. Montaldo, *Entering the Silence,* 218.

36. Mott, *Seven Mountains,* 17.

37. Mott, *Seven Mountains,* 77.

38. Mott, *Seven Mountains,* 80.

39. R. E. Daggy, ed., *Dancing in the Water of Life: The Journals of Thomas Merton, Volume Five (1963–1965)* (San Francisco: Harper Collins, 1998), 198.

40. Montaldo, *Entering the Silence,* 458.

41. Bochen, *Learning to Love,* 371.

Chapter Three

Revealing Prophetic Voices

PRECIS

In Chapter One, we explored how literary scholars interpreted Saint Augustine's The Confessions *as the* ur-*book of life narrative writing. In Chapter Two, I reviewed literary criticism and used Erik Erikson's psychosocial development theory to examine Thomas Merton's identity constructions. Saint Augustine and Thomas Merton wrote their memoirs as recent converts to Christianity. Their memory's episodes reflected the cultural values of the epochs in which they lived. Their texts employed the composition strategy of the linear chronology, replete with adolescent triumphs and setbacks, as they discovered their identities, and concluded with their early adulthood insights about spirituality and generativity.*

In this chapter, we will listen to two prophetic lives and texts—Black Elk and Malcolm X. The titles of The Confessions *and* The Seven Storey Mountain *were metaphors about the experience of grace in everyman's journey. In contrast, the titles of* Black Elk Speaks *and* The Autobiography of Malcolm X *established the authors and not their pilgrimages as the central focus of the narrative. Both texts' episodes are woven into the fabric of tumultuous periods in American history. Their stories were exemplary because the authors became icons for their peoples and for the ideas to which they gave witness. Gathering memory's episodes was accomplished as a collaborative dialogue and mediated by another person. That collaboration became the center of ongoing literary analyses.*

These are texts about one tradition in American autobiographical writing, conversion narratives. I illuminate them via William James's psychology of religion. They are also texts about generativity, redemption, and prophecy. The publication of these works established a ground for other ethnic voices and narratives. In the next chapter, I will turn to women's narratives as part of the continuing diversification of lives and texts.

Saint Augustine and Thomas Merton construed their stories as the movement from sin, a fundamental element of human nature, to grace, an unmerited gift that transforms individuals. Their explanatory metaphors derived from Christian faith. Theirs was a spiritual map to examine the psychological progression to mature adult life.

Christian faith is one set of guiding principles used to find meaning in pluralistic America's society. Examining Black Elk and Malcolm X broadens our understanding of the interrelationships of conversion, redemption, and prophecy. My viewpoint is grounded in William James's classic, *The Varieties of Religious Experience*. James, the philosopher-artist striving to be a scientist, argued that we can observe and then describe with nuanced detail the *fruits* of transformative moments; their *roots* are better interpreted by theologians and writers. In this chapter, I weave together viewpoints from psychology, literary theory, and religion to evaluate two influential life narratives of the twentieth century.

Conversion can be a sudden or gradual phenomenon. Individuals realize that an alternatively powerful way of seeing and being in the world is possible, and better. They are captured in heart and mind by this realization and it infuses all their subsequent behavior.

Redemption, as a secular phenomenon, is the sense of heightened optimism after encountering adversity and coming to terms with "what might have been". Embracing a social justice ethic or one of empathic caring is a natural consequence of redemption. As a sacred phenomenon, it inspires believers that someone sacrificed greatly for them; they were saved and will continue to be graced by that timeless action.

Prophecy is grounded in the experiences of conversion and redemption. Individuals, captured by a new way of seeing themselves and their destinies, who have faced demons and prevailed, now go public and portray personal experience as representative of a community's or people's needs. It is an arrogant stance if misguided or self-serving. History regards such an individual more favorably when the messenger captured a consciousness beyond themselves or the era in which they wrote. As Henry Louis Gates, Jr. titled his anthology of African American autobiographies, some lives and texts signal the prophetic experiences of *Bearing Witness*.

' SPIRITUAL TURNING POINTS

Conversion

In the springs of 1901 and 1902, William James gave the Gifford Lectures in Scotland after teaching his fall semester course, "The Psychological Elements of Religious Life", at Harvard University. The twenty lectures were published as *The Varieties of Religious Experience: A Study in Human Nature*. In contrast to other scholars of the time who used questionnaires, James's data were pious and dramatic accounts of transcendent experiences. He distilled principles and conclusions from affect-laden, highly subjective, and eccentric, even abnormal individuals. His lecture topics included: Religion and Neurology, Religion of Healthy Mindedness, Sick Souls, Conversion, Saintliness, and Mysticism.

The American religious historian, Martin Marty, wrote in his Introduction to the 1982 imprint that *Varieties* "was a hybrid of disciplinary conscientiousness and interdisciplinary risk, of high-culture analysis and low-culture examples, of connections that James liked to make but with which his critics then and ever after felt uneasy."[1] Psychologists regarded the work as too religious; religious studies scholars felt it was too psychological and represented too narrowly the historical and social forms in America. Niebuhr quoted from James's letter (April 12, 1900) about his vision for *Varieties*, predicting how it would be received by skeptics:

> . . .to make the hearer or reader believe, what I myself invincibly
> do believe, that, although all the special manifestations of religions may
> have been absurd (I mean its creeds and theories), yet the life of it as a
> whole is mankind's most important function. A task well-nigh impossible,
> I fear, and in which I shall fail, but to attempt it is *my* religious act.[2]

James defined religion as "the feelings, acts, and experiences of individual men in their solitude, insofar as they apprehend themselves to stand in relation to whatever they may consider to be divine."[3] This is a pluralistic understanding of private religion, not focusing on ritual practices or dogmatic statements. He articulated common denominators that lay beneath religious moments. James's healthy minded individuals, though rare, believed religion provided the way to see all things as good, and to deliberately exclude evil from their day to day living. Most individuals, however, were sick souls, in need of being twice-born, and Christianity exemplified this universal human need to be delivered and born again.[4]

The pathway leads through the conversion experience that James defined in this way:

To be converted, to be regenerated, to receive grace, to experience
religion, to gain an assurance, are so many phrases which denote
the process, gradual or sudden, by which a self, hitherto divided,
and consciously wrong inferior and unhappy, becomes unified and
consciously right superior and happy, in consequence of its
firmer hold upon religious realities.[5]

He understood conversion as a movement away from sinfulness versus a conscious and deliberate advancement to holiness. James admitted that both psychology and religion appeal to forces outside of our conscious selves to explain what impels this movement. Anecdotal testimonials about this
experience are the richest data we can obtain. Ultimately, the fruits of conversion remain the most persuasive evidence for its efficacy. We experience
the peace that comes from grace, perceive whole new truths, shift our per-
ceptions of the world around us, and know a previously unknown ecstasy.
Thinking about religion, heretofore peripheral to the person's life, now becomes a source of resolving the divided self, while still accepting that tragedy
and loss are woven through life's fabric. Summing up this deliverance, James
was led to exclaim:

Let us be saints then, if we can, whether or not we succeed visibly or
temporally. But in our Father's house are many mansions and each of
us must discover for himself the kind of religion and the amount of
saintship which best comports with what he believes his powers and feels
his truest mission and vocation.[6]

Re-reading *The Varieties of Religious Experience* every year before I teach
it in my classes, I find myself substituting passages from Saint Augustine,
Thomas Merton, Black Elk, Malcolm X, and other spiritual autobiographies,
for the testimonies gathered by James. He would support substitutions because the "divine can mean no single quality, it must mean a group of qualities, by being champions of which in alternation, different men may all find
worthy missions. Each attitude being a syllable in human nature's total message, it takes the whole of us to spell the meaning out completely."[7]

John Barbour wrote that "the moment of truth is a paradigmatic event in an
autobiography, when a writer dramatizes how his conscience first made significant moral judgments and presents this moment as a key to understanding
later experience."[8] Such turning points inform subsequent events, but also
guide the author to evaluate them honestly and report them with as much veracity as their moral consciousness permits. This was illustrated often in Malcolm X's descriptions of moments of truth as he completed an intensive ethical reflection on his life's choices in dialogue with Alex Haley. Both

Augustine and Gandhi saw the autobiographical act as doing truth, galvanized by the earlier moment when it was first realized.

Peter Dorsey saw the rhetoric of conversion as a central theme in American autobiography; it informed idiosyncratic understandings of a commonly experienced "sacred estrangement".

> As a trope for self-definition, conversion was widely available
> at different times and under different circumstances to conservatives
> and radicals, traditionalists and innovators, and those in between.
> Not confined to any single theological or ideological system,
> conversion experiences have been described by feminists, communists,
> television-evangelists, alcoholics, psychoanalysts, and scientists,
> by men, women, atheists, believers, whites, and peoples of color.[9]

There is a danger in such an expansive definition of this life-altering phenomenon and Dorsey understood that there were important variations. Change, especially dramatic ones in a life, makes for good characters and good plot lines in a literary text; conversion becomes a marker scene amidst the chaos of memory's gathered episodes.

Redemption

The root of the word, "redemption", is from the Latin and French, *emere*, "to buy back; make payment for (a thing held or claimed by another)." Its meaning also includes: "free or recover (property)"; "free (a person) from captivity or punishment, esp. by paying a ransom"; "save, rescue (of God or Christ), deliver (a person) from sin and damnation."[10] Accrued meanings derive from its usage in the Hebrew and Christian Scriptures. In Genesis, Joseph was sold and then redeemed from slavery. The stories of Ruth and Boaz and Hosea and his wife are about reclaiming that which needed to be recovered. The Psalmist portrayed the human condition as the story of the innocent man, "born guilty, a sinner from the moment of conception" (Psalms 51:5) and therefore in need of being freed by Yahweh. Beginning with Job, Yahweh also takes on the powerful role of avenger when he redeems the innocent. Man's smallness is made obvious over against Yahweh's greatness. For Isaiah, He is avenger and liberator, but there is a *quid pro quo* for the display of favorable divine power—the people must turn from sinful ways.

The Hebrew prophets' statements were given apocalyptic value by Saint Paul who interpreted passages about a Redeemer as being fulfilled in the person of the Christ. The evangelist John pushes Paul's theological interpretations of Hebrew avenging, redeeming, and covenant further with symbolic descriptions of Jesus as Lamb of God. The book of *Revelations* author appealed to believers to maintain their commitments and hopes, writing at a time when the nascent Christian community was under siege. The Lamb will come with the faithful multitudes, singing a new hymn that transcends all concerns and human conditions. Centuries of theologically-based reflection fashioned specific doctrinal statements about sin and grace, about the Hebrew understandings of covenant and their prophecies, and about the redemptive power of Jesus, a historical person, who became for the faithful the Christ who died, rose from the dead, and will come again. Literature portrays redemption as one of the quintessential human struggles, with some of its most memorable characters and plots.

McAdams and Logan summarized redemption from an adult development research perspective in the context of Erikson's generativity stage of middle adulthood. They described the psychological construct of generativity as a "concern for and commitment to the well-being of future generations."[11] Individuals vary in the strengths and expressions of generativity; attending to this internal demand and cultural support for generative behavior produces enhanced psychological well-being and a range of social involvements. McAdams and his colleagues discovered that generativity has a rich texture with meanings manifested in what and how respondents articulated their life narratives. In analyzing these texts, McAdams discovered a common theme — "the life stories of highly generative adults affirm the power of human redemption and renewal."[12]

At first glance, this description may seem intuitive. A more interpretive perspective might link this way of construing life's episodes as evidence for James's dichotomization of people into those who are healthy-minded versus the sick souls in need of being twice-born. Redemption, for James, was linked to the conversion experience whereby the person discovered a new center of being, a new compass out of their melancholic hell. In earlier research, McAdams identified that some individuals' narratives had more optimistic tones than others, and linked this pattern in their recollected memories to developmental adaptations from earlier periods in life.[13]

The concepts of conversion and redemption are especially salient as guideposts for reading and interpreting life narrative texts. After gathering life's episodes and spending time to appreciate their connections, authors must explore how they construe these events. Redemption, whether religious or psychological, accepts life as fraught with adversity, pain, and suffering, yet potentially transformed by bestowed graces and the rugged virtue of hope. Conversions foster this awareness, as we saw in Saint Augustine and Thomas Merton. The compelling power of grace in their lives captured mind and heart and changed how they saw their world and how they wanted to live in it — with hope. Writing one's life narrative is a generative act. The life and its text sometimes transcend the individual's place and time. Then, they become prophetic.

Prophecy

A prophet is "one who speaks for God or a god; a divinely inspired teacher or interpreter of the will of God"; "an innovative proclaimer or advocate of a cause, principle; a visionary leader or representative."[14] Prophets' messages and their callings never seem to allow for saying no, and they must endure the consequences of being a messenger. Prophets are threats and consolations to a community; they appeal to their group's belief that their collective story is special. Prophets rely on the persuasive hope that this prized status, once lost, can be re-gained, but that sacrifice and the return to core values will be required. The more difficult the times, the more ready an audience will be to respond; the cost-benefit calculus is apparent during periods of the collective melancholy of sick souls.

G. Thomas Couser wrote about the prophetic mode in American autobiography and traced its literary roots to the Puritans who

> . . .tended to blur the distinctions between secular and ecclesiastical
> history, between political and spiritual exhortation, between private
> and public welfare, and between history and allegory. By virtue of a
> set of interlocking covenants joining them with God, the individual,
> the Church, and the colony were assumed to share a special role
> in the scheme of redemption. . . .The Puritan imagination tended and
> intended to create a "colony in the image of a saint" and vice versa. . .
> the conflation of individual and communal history derived from the
> persistent notion that American history had redemptive meaning.[15]

This fusion of self and society wrapped in religious metaphors is a recurring theme in American narrative. The Augustinian platform of a life narrative as a chronicle from sin to grace was enlarged by an American scaffolding where the self (*autos*) written and read out loud (*graphe*) became important as history (*bios*). Spiritual autobiography was linked inextricably to American history with its emphasis on transcendent values informing practical and political affairs. Couser included texts by Mather, Edwards, Franklin, Douglass, Thoreau, Whitman, Henry Adams, Stein, Malcolm X, and Mailer among his exemplars.

The messenger dies; the message survives; the text becomes prophetic. We now evaluate how *Black Elk Speaks* and *The Autobiography of Malcolm X* came to be prophetic for their people's communities and wider audiences in America.

MAPS AND METAPHORS

Black Elk Speaks

The title of this memoir evoked different images and responses since it was first published. The Indian as "noble warrior" or "tragic hero", portrayed in movies and television for most of the twentieth century, was a man of few, but always wise, words. That changed with more Native American writers, actors, directors, and producers, especially in independent cinema circles. In academic circles, scholarship by and about American Indian authors contested the warrior and tragedy stereotypes. We now appreciate that tribes spoke many different languages, but not using European high-culture vocabularies, and thus we labeled them as "primitive". (The roots and definition of this word are about being first, earliest, and uncontaminated. Much lower in its hierarchy of meanings is as a comparative adjective.) When an Indian spoke, we came to attention and listened closely to what was said, but then interpreted wildly what was not being said.

The title, *Black Elk Speaks*, signals an oral tradition that is at the heart of American Indian literature. Telling stories is revered, a means of discovering one's identity, finding a unique voice, rediscovering one's place among past generations, and resisting the forces of assimilation and acculturation that diminish contemporary lives. In the next chapter, the oral tradition will guide our analyses of Maxine Hong Kingston, demonstrating how women authors and scholars celebrated storytelling. When Black Elk spoke, it was his honored turn to do so in the circle; he illuminated the interdependent relationships between the individual and his tribe, and between him and nature that had been entrusted to his care. These narratives may carry the name of a primary voice, but they must be understood as polyphonic testimonies, different from autonomous self-statements of the Western psychological and Judeo-Christian religious traditions.

The complex authorship of "as told through John G. Neihardt (Flaming Rainbow)" is all about the collaborative process which birthed this text. The preposition, "through", is defined: "From one end, side, or surface of (a body or space) to the other, by passing within it; into one end, side, or surface of, and out at the other. Between, among; along within."[16] Arnold Krupat noted that Neihardt requested a change in the original phrasing from "to" to "through" when the work was reprinted by Bison Press at the University of Nebraska in 1961.[17]

Neihardt was an historian of Indian and Western America culture; his credibility for attempting this project was advanced by the name given him by Black Elk—Flaming Rainbow—at a ceremony in their second summer meeting in 1931. Black Elk and his friends gave special names to Neihardt and his two daughters who also took part in receiving this oral history.[18] A flaming rainbow guarded the entrance to the home of the Six Grandfathers. Black Elk wrapped Neihardt into his sacred vision as the portal for listeners for as long as the story would be told.

In his Preface to the 1932 edition, Neihardt described Black Elk as a saint and rare genius, inviting readers to drink deeply his wisdom and history. The 1961 Preface reads like a methods section in a cultural anthropology chapter, filled with details about their meetings, oral testimonies by Black Elk and his tribal friends, composing from the transcriptions, and listing the collaborators on the project. Neihardt reiterated this methodological statement in the 1972 Preface, but added another note about their special relationship. His task was not only to translate the elder's story, but to re-create in the English language the powerful mood and senses of what he was told. He felt convinced that he and Black Elk were destined to communicate with each other on an almost mystical plane, and he was obliged to do so in a sacred way.[19]

The revised preface had a precipitating inspiration. In 1972, Sally Mc-Cluskey published a scholarly article in *Western American Literature*, based on an interview in which Neihardt described his more expansive writing role than was earlier assumed for him as simply a recorder of the original work. The article was intended to celebrate Neihardt's respect for what he heard and his virtuosity as a poet-writer, evident from her title, "*Black Elk Speaks:* And so does John Neihardt". However, elsewhere in literary criticism circles, what Neihardt was reported to have said during the McCluskey interview began to raise questions about truthfulness in memoir-writing. By 1989, the life narrative literary scholar, G. Thomas Couser, would characterize this bicultural relationship and authorial statement as: "Black Elk Speaks with Forked Tongue", arguing that despite his best intentions, Neihardt re-enacted the cultural oppression of acculturation and appropriation that Black Elk's story witnessed against.

The controversy about authorship continued and in *Black Elk Lives: Conversations with the Black Elk Family*, Hilda Neihardt summarized a 70-year history thus:

> The process that took place seemed straightforward enough at the time—
> Black Elk spoke, his son Ben translated, my sister Enid took notes, and
> my father edited and shaped the material. With each passing year, however,
> the relationship between Neihardt and Black Elk has been increasingly
> clouded by speculation, assumption, and interpretation. Those interested
> in exploring how the book came to be have asked questions regarding
> authorship, appropriation, material selection, and other important issues.[20]

Malcolm X's collaborative voice, Alex Haley, wrote an extended Epilogue in that autobiography addressing many of these same issues that I will explore in the next section.

What additional maps for this story are found in the chapter titles? Chapter 2 of *Black Elk Speaks*, "Early Boyhood", situates the story in its family, tribe, and historical setting.[21] The last installment, Chapter 24, "The End of the Dream", described his recollections of the Battle of Wounded Knee when he was turning twenty seven years of age. There are twenty three episodes, each labeled with a central event in Black Elk's learning to be a warrior, e.g., "The Bison Hunt" (4), "The Rubbing Out of Long Hair" (i.e., Custer) (9), "The Killing of Crazy Horse" (11), or about his discovering his mission as a healer and seer, e.g., "The First Cure" (17), and "The Messiah" (21). The important messages that Black Elk wanted to transmit for the ages can be found in "The Great Vision" (3) that came to him at age nine, and grew in his understanding and his public disclosures thereafter: "The Horse Dance" (14) at age seventeen, "The Dog Vision" (15) and "The Heyoka Ceremony" (16) at age eighteen, "The Spirit Journey" (20) when he was in Europe at age twenty six, and finally while taking part in the Ghost Dance on the eve of the Wounded Knee battle in 1890,"Visions of the Other World" (22).

His father and his father's father were medicine men and part of traditional Lakota culture with its deep respect for natural spirituality. At age nine, Black Elk received a vision from the Thunder-beings; it was a foreshadowing of his powers as a warrior, a healer, and prophetic seer. At age eighteen, he told this vision to Black Road and other medicine men and they immediately recognized its depth and breadth and power. They led him through the ceremony of the horse dance, and Black Elk established his spiritual calling to all his people. At nineteen, he was favored with another vision and accomplished his first cure. Black Elk signed on with Buffalo Bill's Wild West Show in 1886 and toured New York City, England, and stayed in Europe. When he returned to America and the Pine Ridge Reservation in 1889, relationships with the *Wasichus* (white man, but not as a reference to the biological color of one's skin) had deteriorated. He explored the new religion of the Ghost Dance, seeing in its teachings parallels to his own vision, and re-committed to his identity and vocation. The Ghost Dance was perceived by United States government officials as a dangerous war assembly and ultimately led to the slaughter of three hundred at Wounded Knee in 1890—literally and symbolically "The End of the Dream" (25) in American Indian history. The Neihardt book ended with this tragic episode; in Black Elk's longer story, however, Wounded Knee was just another turning point at age twenty- seven.

Black Elk married Katie War Bonnet in 1892 and they had three sons, all of whom were baptized as Catholics. The Jesuits, who set up a mission on the Pine Ridge Reservation in response to an invitation from Chief Red Cloud, were less than pleased with Black Elk's traditional healing practices, especially because of their successes and his acknowledged leadership position. Black Elk probably converted to Roman Catholicism in about 1904. His

wife's death, followed by a confrontation with a Jesuit priest over whose healing rites took precedence, and finally instruction in the faith, all came together in this decision. For Black Elk, conversion was a passport into a sanc-
tioned community of like-minded peoples. The Jesuits used elders as
catechists and Black Elk's talents and respect among his people made him a
natural recruit. He became one of their star preachers of the Good News beyond his own reservation, and the source of material as well as spiritual resources and counsel for his people during the first three decades of the new
century. His life changed with the arrival of John Neihardt and the publication in 1932 of his Great Vision.

Neihardt's original intent was to write another chapter in his epic history of
the West and to develop a more nuanced understanding of the Ghost Dance. De-
Mallie captured the historical intersection of the two men's agendas in this way:

> Black Elk, for his part, was tying together the ends of his life. Now,
> at age sixty-seven, he was returning to the days of his youth to tell
> about his great vision, and the sacred power from the six grandfathers,
> which he had put behind him when he converted to Roman Catholicism.
> Surely the decision to disclose the sacred teachings and to preserve them
> for the benefit of posterity—rather than to let them die, completely replaced
> by the white man's religion—had not been made lightly. Black Elk sensed
> an interest and a power in Neihardt that was kindred to his own, and he
> felt compelled to respond to it.[22]

When they met by chance in 1930, Black Elk told Neihardt that he knew that
he was coming. The former was a healer and the latter was a poet, both moved
by deeply spiritual commitments, expressed in rich metaphors; their kinship
in telling the story and having it told became a bond that their extended family members have affirmed without qualification since that first summer.

When Neihardt asked Black Elk why he left his old religion to embrace
Christianity, the elder said his children had to live in this world. After copies
of *Black Elk Speaks* appeared on the reservation, the Jesuits were not pleased
that their influential catechist still harbored pagan inclinations. Black Elk declared his acceptance of the one, true faith, despite the book's passionate description of past native beliefs. Catechists on other reservations were also of-
fended by the book's appeal to older spiritualities, blaming Neihardt for not
including a more accurate portrayal of Black Elk's Catholic life after
Wounded Knee. Amidst these reactions, Black Elk made several public appearances at the newly sculpted Mount Rushmore, demonstrating rituals to
primarily white audiences in the interests of mutual education and understanding. DeMallie noted that in Black Elk's day, the concept of ecumenical
synthesis or the sharing of faith practices in public was a radical idea and the

elder received continuing criticism. Several years later, when he was seriously injured in a wagon accident, the priests withheld giving him their last rites until he assured them yet again of his unwavering Catholic faith. Joseph Epes Brown, a young college student, lived with Black Elk during the winter of 1948–49 enabling the sickly healer to give a final testament about the sacred rituals of his traditional tribal religion. *The Sacred Pipe: Black Elk's Account of the Seven Rites of the Oglala Sioux* was the resulting "synthesis of Lakota and Christian beliefs, for in them he structures Lakota rituals in parallel fashion to the Catholic sacraments."[23]

Nicholas Black Elk died in 1950. More and more visitors to Black Elk in the final years of his life discovered that he had returned to reflections on his original vision and little mention was ever made of the Catholic catechist period of his life. As in many Native American stories, he had come full circle — a sacred hoop drawing to a close. Black Elk died on August 19, 1950 after receiving Holy Communion and the Catholic sacrament of Last Rights.

The Autobiography of Malcolm X

This title is a map about one man's story whose life and reputation were already matters of public record. Malcolm X, not Malcolm Little at the beginning of his life or El-Hajj Malik El-Shabazz at the end, was the heart of this story. Such a title situates the text in a longer historical lineage of representative men and their American texts — from *The Autobiography of Benjamin Franklin* to the classic Black texts of *Narrative of the Life of Frederick Douglas, An American Slave* published in 1845, *My Bondage and Freedom* in 1855, and *Life and Times of Frederick Douglas* in 1893.

The chapter titles are more metaphoric. The first, "Nightmare", opens with a family story told about Malcolm, his mother, a light-skinned woman from Grenada, and his brothers, being threatened with death by the Ku Klux Klan in Omaha, Nebraska where he was born on May 19, 1925. His Baptist minister father and his mother were followers of Marcus Garvey and advocated black-race purity and the return to ancestral Africa. The family moved to Lansing, Michigan where Malcolm's earliest memory was at age four, in 1929, when their house was burned to the ground. Two years later his father was killed mysteriously, and the family unraveled until his mother suffered a mental breakdown and was committed to the state mental hospital in 1937. She remained there for twenty-six years. When he was twelve, Malcolm and his siblings were distributed to different foster families.

In the next eight chapters — "Mascot", "Homeboy", "Laura", "Harlemite", "Detroit Red", "Hustler", "Trapped", and " Caught" — Malcolm chronicled his descent into a life of drugs and crime, finally convicted of burglary and

sentenced to serve ten years in the Charlestown State Prison in Massachusetts. It was February, 1946 and he had not yet turned twenty-one. The final
passages in Chapter 9 are important maps for the reader. He confessed that he
had never before disclosed his sordid choices in such detail, and his motivation was not to celebrate evil, but to acknowledge that his present story rested
on all that had gone before. Malcolm was not fashioning his own theory of
developmental psychology here; this was not case study material for Murray's personality proposition that "the history of the organism is the organism". This was the preface of a religious conversion narrative. In telling his
whole story, he felt that he could capture how he plunged to the very bottom
of the White man's world, but in prison, found the religion of Islam and how
Allah transformed his life.[24]

"Satan" (10) described his prison entry and discovery of Elijah Muhammad
and the religion of the Nation of Islam. "Saved" (11) chronicled how the hustler finally was brought by family and Allah to fall to his knees and pray. After being switched to the Norfolk Prison Colony, he began a self-designed education, first copying the pages of a dictionary to expand his vocabulary, and
then a voracious reading program of books on history, philosophy, and religion that were given to the prison by a philanthropist-benefactor. Malcolm
synthesized an encyclopedic knowledge base with his new agenda to articulate the causes and consequences of black-white relations in the world. A new
man—educated in Black history and the English language and converted to
the Nation of Islam—left prison in 1952 and embraced his "Savior" (12).

In "Minister Malcolm X" (13) and "Black Muslims" (14), Malcolm recalled his meteoric rise within the Nation of Islam from 1952 to 1963. He was
a brilliant orator and became the head of the New York Mosque # 7, establishing himself in the religion's leadership. He became the most public
spokesperson of a new force for social change in the Black community and to
the white media. An intense father-son relationship between Malcolm and
Elijah Muhammad pulses in these chapters, until like the Greek "Icarus" (15),
he flew too high and had his wings melted. He recalled this mythic story
while delivering a speech at the Harvard Law School Forum.

The moral, filial, and political rift between Malcolm and Elijah Muhammad grew wider until he was "Out" (16), with the assassination of John
Fitzgerald Kennedy in November, 1963 and his "chickens come home to
roost" comment. Malcolm was about to be "thrice-born." During a trip to
"Mecca" (17), his radical separation beliefs shifted to a traditional Islamic
faith that unites peoples of all classes and colors. He described the personal
consequences of this religious epiphany and the new political identity in "El
Hajj Malik El Shabazz" (18). The terse "1965" (19) closed the text and an unfinished life at age thirty-nine. Alex Haley's "Epilogue" concluded the book

with his reminiscence of their first meeting and the complex relationship that they fashioned; the journalist's description of the events that followed Malcolm's assassination at the Audubon Ballroom in Harlem on February 21, 1965 completed the life narrative.

In 1992 and 1994, two films appeared which re-kindled the nation's interest in the life of Malcolm X. Spike Lee based the script of his production on *The Autobiography of Malcolm X*, with the award-winning Denzel Washington in the title role. In 1994, "The American Experience", an award-winning PBS television series, created a documentary that was produced, directed, and co-written by Orlando Bagwell, called *Malcolm X: Make it Plain*—a phrase that Malcolm urged on those who preceded him to the podium at any Nation of Islam event. The documentary included interviews with colleagues and friends in and out of the Nation, journalists' commentaries, and original black and white footage of Malcolm's speeches and interviews. The Spike Lee film catapulted a re-issue of the 1965 book to the top of *The New York Times* best-seller list in 1993 and critical re-reviews of the Malcolm X / Alex Haley collaboration became a staple item in major metropolitan papers.

ROOTS OF TWO COLLABORATIVE COMPOSITION STRATEGIES

Black Elk & John Neihardt

When Neihardt met Nicholas Black Elk for the first time, he spent four and a half hours listening to the older man's stories. Neihardt returned the following summer, with Black Elk's permission and with his daughters Enid and Hilda, to receive the whole story. Black Elk's son, Ben, acted as interpreter, and over several days, with a gathering of tribal friends adding their memories, he told his life story. Neihardt felt obligated to preserve Black Elk's Great Vision. Back home in Branson, Missouri, using Enid's stenographic notes, he composed *Black Elk Speaks: As told to John G. Neihardt (Flaming Rainbow)*, and published it in 1932. It was reissued in paperback in 1961, and, based on an interview with the television talk show host, Dick Cavett, emerged again in the early 1970s. Raymond J. DeMallie published *The Sixth Grandfather: Black Elk's Teachings Given to John G. Neihardt*, in 1984, based on the unedited stenographic notes of Black Elk's words and those of his tribesmen.

Malcolm X and Alex Haley

Alex Haley composed a seventy-three page *Epilogue* after Malcolm died, but had received permission to do so, without editing, at the very beginning of their work together. In this reflective commentary, Haley, the journalist, reminisced about the special relationship between him and Malcolm, its many turning points, and documented the biographical events that took place while the narrative was being composed. He recalled how Malcolm stared him down after signing the initial book contract and told him he wanted a writer and not an interpreter. Haley tried to capture this life as a chronicle of events, but admitted that the power of Malcolm's electric personality made a dispassionate account almost impossible to achieve.

The project began in 1963; Haley proposed to Malcolm that they collaborate on an "as told to", full-length autobiographical work. Haley met with Mr. Elijah Muhammad, the head of the Nation of Islam, who responded that Allah approved the book. For the next two years, Malcolm and the journalist met in a Greenwich Village apartment, traveled together around New York City to his public speaking events as well as to family gatherings, and attended Nation of Islam mosques and meetings in other cities. They dialogued most of the autobiography during a period when Malcolm's life was unraveling, and saw each other face to face for the last time in January 1965. Malcolm read it and they revised it, together, many times just before he died. Malcolm phoned Haley on Tuesday, February 18; he was assassinated five days later when Haley was in the final editing stages of the manuscript.

In the last chapter, "1965", Malcolm ended his story by saying that his heart was invested in this book in the hope that its readers would learn from his life, and understand that the cancer of racism was still alive in America. If he had helped to destroy it, any success should be attributed to Allah, and the mistakes and failures to him. His sense of forthcoming death was loud and clear.

FRUITS OF COLLABORATIVE AUTHORSHIP

Nicholas Black Elk through John Neihardt

Sally McCluskey interviewed John Neihardt in April, 1971, the same month in which Dee Brown, author of *Bury My Heart at Wounded Knee*, appeared on the Dick Cavett show and called *Black Elk Speaks* the finest American Indian book ever written. She was investigating the language of the text, and was complimentary about their collaborative process: ". . .the book's power is in the persona of Black Elk and in the texture of the prose itself," "making him a complex human being who walked real roads, saw real clouds, smelled real winds, and tasted real meat."[25] She asserted that "it is ultimately the *way* the story is told that endows it with greatness, and Black Elk's language which creates the power of *Black Elk Speaks.*"[26]

Neihardt told McCluskey that he had decided to give her his "once and for all" statement. The following quote has inspired thirty years of scholars' commentaries about this work.

> *Black Elk Speaks* is a work of art with two collaborators, the chief one being Black Elk. My function was both creative and editorial. I think he knew the kind of person I was when I came to see him—I am referring to the mystical strain in me and all my work. He said, "You have been sent so that I may teach you and you receive what I know. It was given to me for men and it is true and it is beautiful and soon I will be under the grass." And I think he knew I was the tool—no, the medium—he needed for what he wanted to get said. And my attitude toward what he has said to me is one of religious obligation.
>
> But it is obsurd (sic) to suppose that the use of the first person singular is not a literary device, by which I mean that Black Elk did not sit and tell me his story in chronological order. At times considerable editing was necessary, but it was always worth the editing. *The beginning and the ending are mine; they are what he would have said if he had been able. At times I changed a word, a sentence, sometimes created a paragraph. And the translation—or rather the transformation—of what was given me was expressed so that it could be understood by the white world.*[27]

McCluskey proclaimed that neither Dee Brown nor Robert Sayre (a distinguished American literature scholar) discerned Neihardt's hand in the opening and closing chapters of the book. She reported that Black Elk adopted Neihardt as his spiritual son to legitimate the passing to him of such sacred mysteries. Neihardt told her that the old man felt that his own son did not care about such matters, having become more white than Indian.

G. Thomas Couser, in his book *Altered Egos*, was less positive about these dynamics. He acknowledged the unique mixture of Black Elk's status and initiation of the story telling project, John Neihardt's impressive poetic and spiritual gifts, and the historical and cultural ingredients that elevated the text as both Native American autobiography and a Lakota-based prophetic statement. Neihardt's understanding of the performative characteristics of a Native American story, his care in including the polyphonic qualities of other voices to remember tribal events, framing the bookend chapters that were primarily his own prose—all were essential and positive contributions. DeMallie also had noted how Neihardt struggled with the publisher to keep Black Elk's description of his vision within its chronological context versus being relegated to an appendix as a quaint spiritual footnote to an Indian's history of epic battles and reservation life.

Despite this confluence of positive elements, Couser opened his critique with this summary: "In it we see Black Elk not face to face, but through the gloss of a white man—a translation whose surface obscures Black Elk by reflecting the culture of his collaborator."[28] Neihardt said that he had transformed the narrative and that was Couser's criticism. He regarded the collaboration's product as a study of cultures in collision—Native American oral tradition versus Euramerican written culture, Native American spirituality's groundings in sacred geography and ritual performance versus Judeo-Christianity's emphasis on salvation history and chosen persons. Couser noted that even DeMallie's efforts to get back closer to the original Black Elk utterances cannot do so, because of the complex translation processes at the actual meetings in 1930 and 1931, and despite the complex intertextual annotations that he constructed. Couser concluded that Native American autobiographies, despite what their collaborative bicultural authors may assert, remain captivity narratives.[29] In his most pejorative statement, Couser labeled the book "an act of bicultural ventriloquism."[30]

Consider two of the most often quoted (and dramatic) passages attributed to the holy man in the text of *Black Elk Speaks*—ironically, both were composed by Neihardt, but only confessed to McCluskey forty years later. In the first chapter, Black Elk acknowledged the power of his sacred vision and his failure in being able to properly use it. What might have flourished had he been stronger, withered, and a people's dreams died in the bloodshed at Wounded Knee. In the last chapter, using apocalyptic language, he described himself as a pitiful old man, but more tragically, that the sacred hoop was broken and the sacred tree of his people was dead.

Did Black Elk sound like James's and Christianity's "sick soul"? Recall that Neihardt came to the West to examine the Ghost Dance and its inexorable progression to Wounded Knee. What purpose did such gloom serve for his intended white audiences? If Black Elk had in fact appropriated the Catholic faith and became its articulate teacher, then how do these passages reflect his experiences of conversion and redemption? Why was any inkling of a more hopeful view, grounded in Black Elk's Catholicism, deleted by Neihardt in his transformations of the interviews? Couser rightly concluded that it was Neihardt who needed apocalyptic tones in these passages to be consistent with his personal vision for the work. Neihardt's portrayal erased Black Elk's embrace of the anti-assimilation Ghost Dance religion and any referents to his conversion to Catholicism thirty years earlier and the power both faiths afforded him. Couser contested Neihardt's motivations as a product of his times, portraying Black Elk as powerless before inevitable white domination of the land and their people's souls. By muting Black Elk's conversion to Catholicism and his various reservation strategies to maintain his Lakota heritage, Neihardt perpetuated a tragic interpretation of Indian defeat, leaving no clues about his subject's wily capacity to keep his vision alive, until someone came to write it down and get the word out.

Teachers and scholars evolve their interpretations of texts just as authors revise their memory's episodes. In a 1996 essay on strategies for interpreting this multicultural text, Couser wrote that "the challenge of teaching *Black Elk Speaks* is, in a way, the challenge inherent in any process of cross-cultural translation: to make the 'other' comprehensible without erasing its difference."[31] He recommended that students receive heavy dosages of social history to appreciate the context and the message of the work.

Brian Swann and Arnold Krupat offered another literary theory perspective about the collaborative composition strategy.

> That form of writing generally known to the West as *autobiography*
> had no equivalent among the oral cultures of the indigenous
> inhabitants of the Americas. Although the tribes, like people the
> world over, kept material as well as mental records of collective
> and personal experience, the notion of telling the whole of any one
> individual's life or taking merely personal experience as of
> particular significance was, in the most literal way, foreign to
> them, if not also repugnant.[32]

The 1800s saw a spate of battle epics, solicited by well-meaning journalists or historians, with male Indian chiefs as their protagonists, attempting to document the West's "winning" from the "losing" Indians' point of view. In the early twentieth century, anthropologists like Franz Boas and his many doctoral students took up the cause of preserving Indian culture by finding, recording, and publishing Indian lives before they were lost. Like the Black Elk text, these stories continued the tradition of "as told to" collaborations because indigenous languages could not be used if a mainstream publisher were to be secured. Autobiographical works by Indians who knew English and were willing to conform to standard publishing requirements appeared in the 1930s and 1940s. During the 1970s, life narrative works by N. Scott Momaday and Leslie Marmon Silko appeared, recognized as both uniquely Native American and contributing to a widening canon of American literature and culture.

It took awhile for standard literary criticism to catch up with a rapidly expanding corpus of resurrected texts and contemporary variations by American Indians.

> . . .Western literary criticism had been and—so long as it remains
> Western literary criticism—will continue to be text-based (regardless

of the existence of audio and videotapes, etc.), while reminding the
reader that Native literatures are and continue to be oral and performative.
To produce the texts of an Indian literature requires the
work of transcribers (because Indian literary performances are
oral performances) and of translators (because it has always been, and,
unfortunately, remains the case—with to be sure, significant exceptions—
that a majority of the literary critics of Indian literatures, myself included,
have little or no competence in Indian languages).[33]

Krupat formulated ethnocriticism, an interdisciplinary strategy drawn from
ethnographic, historical, and literary theorists and his close readings of American Indian works. Indigenous texts can be understood from a variety of perspectives, like working one's way around a circle, striving for different, perhaps conflicted points of view, to arrive at holistic understandings.

Looking at a life narrative like *Black Elk Speaks* requires that we let indigenous epistemologies challenge our traditional genre-based thinking about
the self (*autos*), life history and its development over time (*bios*), and texts
that are written (*graphe*). Critical analyses of life narratives are replete with
Western assumptions about autonomy and civilization, that individuals make
independent choices by which they ideally progress towards a personal maturity that in turn produces culturally sophisticated authors and texts. This
was Gusdorf's prescription for what was necessary for autobiographical production. Western sciences, social sciences, and humanities scholarship are
thick with such constructs, even when the epistemological assumptions about
their origins are being challenged (e.g., modernist versus postmodernist definitions of the self). Moreover, notions about what is public versus private information are grounded in similar ways of seeing the world.

Krupat pointed out that cosmology, psychology, sociology, economics, and
nature are inseparably woven threads of these ethnic lives and their stories.
He distinguished between Indian autobiographies—those bicultural compositions about a Native American and written by a Euroamerican whose form
and style are evident—and autobiographies by Indians—although self-
composed, they still must be understood as part of the bicultural, civilizing
process because of their translation from oral story to written form. *Black Elk
Speaks* was an Indian autobiography because, for Krupat, its bicultural composition strategy demonstrated the cultures in collision phenomenon addressed by Couser. Krupat concluded that Neihardt turned the story into one
about "romantic transcendence", [34] replete with moral conflict, a death struggle, and the discovery and recognition of a hero who does not survive the conflict. Neihardt's Black Elk is a story with an ending, not a continuing process;
the tale reflects his nostalgic yearning for a better world with less material
power and more mystical beauty. Krupat criticized buying into the same

dream and urging the text as a new bible for Indians and Anglos alike who suffer from a too-technological world. Romantic longings for transcendence yield some of our best images in utopian and literary plots; whether it is solid ground for justice and social change is a continuing topic of lively debate.

The Autobiography of Malcolm X was a unique synthesis of religion and an unequivocal call for social justice and change, embedded within the character development of a charismatic, ethnic leader. As we shall see, it could make Augustine and the Puritans smile proudly of their inherited contributions to composing stories of the self.

Malcolm X as told to Alex Haley

After Haley retired from the U.S. Coast Guard and embarked on a journalism career, a friend told him about her family's conversion to a remarkable religion called The Nation of Islam. Mike Wallace of CBS narrated a New York telecast in 1959 called "The Hate that Hate Produced", introducing America to its tenets and its two most important leaders—The Honorable Elijah Muhammad and his Harlem, New York Minister, Malcolm X. Haley developed background material and *Reader's Digest* approved a feature story. He met with a skeptical Malcolm who sent him for approval to Elijah Muhammad. "Mr. Muhammad Speaks" was published in 1960; it was the first featured magazine article on the movement and its leaders. Haley followed in 1961 and 1963 with a feature in the *Saturday Evening Post* and an extensive *Playboy* interview. Malcolm's skepticism about Haley diminished somewhat when the journalist and his publisher kept their promises to print verbatim what he had said.

For these early articles, Malcolm was circumspect, shining the bright light on Mr. Elijah Muhammad and his message to Black people. When Haley approached him about a full-length autobiographical, *as told to* text, he was taken aback, sending the journalist once again to seek approval. All the parties agreed and Malcolm immediately produced a hand-written dedication to the spiritual leader who cleaned him up made him the man he had become. Haley agreed to Malcolm's terms that everything in the book would be exactly what he had said and nothing would be left out without his approval. Malcolm, in turn, pledged to spend the time, despite his chaotic schedule, to work together on the projected one hundred thousand word manuscript. And so they began their intense series of two to five-hour sessions, beginning usually at 10:00 pm after Malcolm's full day of speeches, meetings and recruitment activities.

For the first month, Malcolm gave Haley sermon after sermon about Mr. Muhammad's message and harangued him about white devils. The journalist took notes and Malcolm constantly scribbled on paper napkins that Haley placed on the table and then left them behind for Haley to gather when gone. Based on these napkin notes, Haley one time probed Malcolm about his feelings towards women and trust in relationships. It was a turning point because he began to talk more personally about his wife and memories. Several sessions later, Malcolm arrived exhausted after a day of constant criticism by non-Muslim Negro leaders. Intuitively and with trepidation, Haley asked him to talk about his mother. That night's monologue produced the autobiographical substance for the first two chapters, "Nightmare" and "Mascot". Talking about his mother was the stimulus for subsequent revelations about his most private experiences. Some time after, Malcolm left the city without telling Haley why, but when he returned, he announced that he and his sister and brothers had secured the release of their mother from the Michigan state institution where she was confined for a quarter century.

Malcolm became more energized, sometimes lively and other times grimly somber when he remembered from childhood to hustler days to prison experiences. His mood at night and how he captured life events mirrored whether the day had been marked by affiliation or anger in his dealings with others. The reader can sense a growing relationship developing between the two men. Haley described his contacts with Malcolm's wife, Betty, and the daily appearances at his side with an immediacy of experience that is woven into the final chapters of the narrative as well as into the Epilogue. Malcolm grew more trusting of selected whites, like M.S. Handler of *The New York Times*, and other black men, like the photographer, Gordon Parks, actor Ossie Davis, and scholars C. Eric Lincoln and Kenneth Clark. His increased trust emerged at the same time while he had to grow more vigilant about those around him because death threats began and his ostracism from the Nation of Islam was becoming a relentlessly tragic script.

In retrospect, Haley saw that Malcolm's split with Elijah Muhammad and his inner circle was growing wider but he never knew, nor appreciated, the deeply personal consequences of the rift. After Malcolm's caustic remarks about John Kennedy's assassination, he was suspended. Silenced, he wrote Haley that it was a good time to devote their full attention to completing the book. Haley produced a draft of "Nightmare" and the editing and revision process on the early chapters began. Malcolm became a careful line editor with a very active red pen. Several weeks later, he asked Haley to change their original contract so that the proceeds from the book would go now, in the case of his death, directly to his wife, Mrs. Betty X Little. In the same note, he mused about the perils of composing a coherent story about one's life when everything was changing so fast and while life was in imminent peril.

In March, 1964, Malcolm made a trip to the Muslim holy cities, signing his correspondence as "El-Hajj Malik El-Shabazz", and writing Haley that he expected good progress on the book because his time was short. The awakening to traditional Islam after Mecca caused a crisis in the life of this text. Malcolm returned chapters with substantial red-penned revisions about his father-son relationship with Elijah Muhammad. Haley worried because a similar conversation had taken place before the trip, about robbing the narrative of its drama by telegraphing the rift early in the book. After several testy exchanges, Malcolm backed off and agreed to maintain the linear progression of the already composed story without foreshadowing. In subsequent editing sessions with the two men in the room together, Malcolm was often chagrinned at his earlier, uncritical commitments, shaking his head in disbelief at what he read, but he let the text remain the way he originally told the story to his scribe.

Malcolm journeyed again to Africa in 1964, as his newfound religious and political affiliations were more public than ever. The feud between him and Elijah Muhammad intensified. He was now keeping a diary and shared these notes with Haley to be included in the autobiography—for as long as he could stay alive. He called Haley one time during this period and told him that he trusted him seventy percent now, only somewhat less than his wife, Betty. On Tuesday, February 16, 1965, Malcolm canceled a planned trip to upstate New York to finish off the book editing; he told another associate that day that he had been marked for death in the next five days. He predicted accurately. The last twenty pages of the Epilogue described the immediate events leading to his assassination at the Audubon Ballroom, the local and national reactions to his death, Elijah Muhammad's speech about Malcolm at the Black Muslim National Convention taking place in Chicago at the very same time, and the funeral in Harlem.

The literary criticism on *The Autobiography of Malcolm X* demonstrates a similar evolution of ideas as the commentaries on *Black Elk Speaks*, with increasingly complex analyses. Malcolm's text was compared to the American master narrative by Ben Franklin. Both men rose from humble beginnings to world prominence and in doing so, they represented the exemplary possibilities of American achievement. The virtues espoused by the Nation of Islam and lived by Malcolm matched those qualities that Franklin touted. I believe that Malcolm's post-Mecca self had to incorporate the heart's affect with his mind's strategic decision making about religion and politics. Moving from radical separatism to a brotherhood of man was a psychological maturing of a previously one-dimensional self.[35]

Integrating literary theory with psychological concepts, Paul John Eakin[36] began with the premise that unlike the conversion narrative or spiritual autobiography themes that other scholars used to situate this work, Malcolm's was an unfinished self, working through provisional identities in his stormy life. Haley's remarks in the Epilogue confirm this viewpoint. The first dedication that Malcolm wrote to Elijah Muhammad signaled his intent to describe an exemplary life and was the motivation for his meetings with Haley and the recollection of memory's episodes. His was the classic before-and-after fruits of conversion story that I described for Saint Augustine in Chapter One and for Thomas Merton in Chapter Two. Eakin deftly integrated his analysis of the evangelical certainty of a convert's religious change with the narrative tone that characterizes the highly-scripted life story. However, in Malcolm's life, the story line was interrupted when he was "Out" (16). His consciousness changed so dramatically with this loss; a new identity took shape with a second conversion at "Mecca" (17).

Eakin saw two identity stories in the text. The first came in two parts—Sinner and Saved—with two turning points—the Ostrowski comment about being a "nigger", made to him in elementary school, and then his epiphany and kneeling in prayer in prison.[37] Mecca produced a second identity, but the fruits of conversion, even the rich joys that James described, were conflicted by Malcolm's awareness of his impending death. Eakin interpreted the immediacy of Malcolm's words as critically important to the voice that emerged after Mecca and in the last months/pages of this story.

Eakin appreciated Haley's intuitive understanding that Malcolm's world was in jeopardy; that awareness was essential to the shape of the final text.

> Despite his tactful protest that he was only a "writer," Haley himself
> had been instrumental in playing out the autobiographical drama
> between one Malcolm X, whose faith in Elijah Muhammad had
> supplied him with his initial rationale for an autobiography, and another,
> whose repudiation of Elijah Muhammad made the *Autobiography* the
> extraordinary human document it eventually became.[38]

It was Haley who early on dutifully recorded Malcolm as he harangued him about white devils and Elijah Muhammad, and Haley who later brought to the surface another Malcolm who scribbled onto napkins the subtexts of his day's experiences and its significance. Malcolm's dictations to his scribe exploded the conventional wisdoms about autobiographical forms. Malcolm had to compose a self on the run, with the end of his available tape, imminent. Merton had the luxury of looking back and declaring that he did not know his character in *The Seven Storey Mountain*. Malcolm never had such distance and the illusion of objectivity that Gusdorf described as a hallmark of life narrative. With insightful and appreciative language, Eakin concluded the following about the literary status of this work and its psychological lessons, comparing it to another autobiographical classic, *The Education of Henry Adams*:

Paradoxically, nowhere does the book succeed, persuade, more
than in its confession of failure as autobiography, . . .Malcolm X,
like Adams, leaves behind him the husks of played-out autobiographical
paradigms. . . .Malcolm X's work, and Adams's as well, generate a sense
that the uncompromising commitment to the truth of one's own
nature, which requires the elimination of false identities and careers
one by one, will yield at last the pure ore of a final and irreducible
selfhood. This is the ultimate autobiographical dream.[39]

A collaborative effort can be examined from a therapeutic perspective as
well. Eugene Wolfenstein [40] characterized Malcolm as the psychoanalytic
analysand, reclaiming stored-away events from his emotional past, and Haley
as the analyst who was the oblique screen onto which to project these
episodes. The original premise of their relationship was instrumental. Haley
would be the scribe for Malcolm as he held up a mirror to white racism in a
monologue of self-criticism, then affirmation, and above all else as a testi-
monial to Elijah Muhammad. Beginning with the night when Malcolm's de-
fenses were down and Haley skillfully probed his memories about his mother,
however, the agenda shifted. The past was painful, but the only way to gain
control over it was not through his affiliation with a substitute father-figure
and espousing the Nation of Islam, but through gathering memory's episodes
in response to Haley's prompts. Wolfenstein described this collaborative relationship as fostering the psychoanalytical working-through sequence, sur-
facing the roots of Malcolm's conflicted feelings and behaviors, and even
making him psychologically ready for the spiritual epiphany at Mecca.
Speaking the autobiography was his vehicle to reconsider the journey of transitional selves from Malcolm Little to Detroit Red to Satan to Minister Malcolm X, finally becoming El-Hajj Malik El-Shabbazz.

As a Marxist, Wolfenstein conceptualized this journey as not only one of
inner reflection, but of external political activism with the important agenda
of contesting class differences. Self-examination opened Malcolm's eyes to
the complex causes and consequences of American racism; Malcolm's history
became Black American history. Malcolm's assassination aborted his discovery of the economic roots of American *apartheid*. In therapy, one's conversa-
tional partner stimulates insight via helping the other to make new connections, and in its most elegant moments, two individuals disrupt power
differences and move beyond the expertise and epiphanies that either could
have discovered alone. This was the power of change that justified Erikson's
comparison of his psychoanalytic methods with Gandhi's (and Martin Luther
King's) militant nonviolence.

Albert Stone, a literary scholar, characterized the fruits of the Malcolm X and
Alex Haley collaboration as an "oral social history and spiritual confession"[41]

having moral leverage in both Black and white communities, especially in urban America of the twentieth century. Like Wolfenstein's therapeutic ethic, the
text's power was in its synergy of Malcolm as autobiographical voice and Haley as facilitator. Neihardt, the poet, transformed Black Elk's oral text, attempting to be true to what he would have said. Haley, the journalist, was scrupu-
lously faithful to Malcolm's rhetorical prowess and brilliant turns of a phrase,
recording anecdotes and aphorisms used from his bully pulpits and in private
on the napkin notes in Haley's Greenwich Village apartment. This only could
have happened because Malcolm told his scribe-therapist that he trusted Haley
about seventy percent (just like his wife) as their relationship matured.

 After his death, Malcolm X's legacy ebbed and flowed in the Black community and in American history. Malcolm has been portrayed as hero and
saint, often woven together with Martin Luther King, Jr. as two shining examples of Black advocacy. Each inspired other leaders and other methodologies in behalf of Black Power and pride, racial self-determination, cultural autonomy, and black capitalism. The separatist political agenda of Black
nationalism stood against dominant white values and economic forces. Recall
that some of Malcolm's earliest memories were of his parents' devotion to
Marcus Garvey's Universal Negro Improvement Association (UNIA). Malcolm has been cast by others as a public moralist, consistent with the vibrant
tradition of advocacy for social reform in Black Christian churches. Malcolm's legacy offered hope to the urban north's ghetto poor and disenfran-
chised, with a message of pride for individuals. He elevated their collective
pride as being a chosen people.

 James Baldwin once reminded the White community of a biblical warning:
God gave Noah the rainbow sign, no more water, the fire next time! Almost
forty years after publishing *The Fire Next Time*, he collaborated with Arnold
Perl and Spike Lee to recast the *Autobiography* into a film. The filmmaker,
Spike Lee, told a reporter that one of his messages in *Malcolm X* was for au-
diences to leave theaters believing that he was alive today. Thus, the final im-
ages in his 1992 film are of Nelson Mandela and school children in Soweto,
South Africa, who stand and proclaim: "I am Malcolm."[42]

MEMORY'S EPISODES

Identity

In Erikson's first psychosocial stages— Basic trust versus mistrust, Autonomy
versus shame and doubt, Initiative versus guilt, and Industry versus inferiority—extended family members and friends enable the young person to navi-

gate the conflicts. Resolutions yield in succession the virtues of hope, will, sense of purpose, and competence. In his last statement on the life cycle, Erikson fleshed out the dimensions of his ages and stages model.[43] Antipathies were contrasted with basic virtues and strengths in a similar manner to the alternatives of the eight stage conflicts: hope versus withdrawal, will versus compulsion, purpose versus inhibition, and competence versus inertia. The accomplishment of the stages' virtues sets the table for a youth's adolescence when identity and fidelity were the fruits of internal reflection and external expectations. In both Saint Augustine's and Thomas Merton's life narratives, I examined textual passages that illuminated these epigenetic dynamics.

Ten of the first twelve chapters of *Black Elk Speaks* charted his developing identity as an epic warrior in keeping with tribal patterns and his recognition of Crazy Horse as an ideal model. These chapters sketched his earliest memory from age three at the Battle of the 100 Slain in 1866 when his father was permanently injured, boyhood initiations into his tribe (2) and into the bison hunt (4), first encounters at age ten with the *Wasichus* (5), vicariously experiencing a friend's courting trials and triumphs (6), and participating in actual battles with the U.S. Calvary, Custer's killing at Little Big Horn, and taking his first scalp (8, 9). When he reached adolescence, Black Elk was "walking the black road" (10) of imminent destruction, that led to the death of Crazy Horse (11), his tribal chief and role model, and the forced march of his band to Canada (12) when he was sixteen years old. The episodes composed from Black Elk's reminiscences suggest a young man who consolidated one identity as a competent warrior and member of his tribe. A case can be made from these chapters' episodes for the Eriksonian movement from conflict to conflict, acquiring successive virtues by their resolutions—autonomy and will, initiative and sense of purpose, and industry and competence.

The pessimistic narrative tone woven into the recollections, however, ought not be traced back, in Eriksonian fashion, to the earliest stages of Black Elk's life. Rather, it reflects a foreshadowing of "The End of the Dream" that seems to have been Neihardt's interpretive message. Using the traditional chronological order of events for a memoir, Neihardt recounted Black Elk's first vision received at age five in "Early Boyhood" (2) and the "Great Vision" (3) which he received at age nine. There are episodes bundled together as "The Compelling Fear" (13) that can be interpreted as intentionally splitting Black Elk's identity between warrior and religious figure. At seventeen, he called on the Six Grandfathers directly and they responded by sending the thunder beings to protect the tribe when it fled danger.

On the reservation and under the *Wasichus* control, this power felt like a curse to him because he was unable to tell anyone. His mother and father brought him to a medicine man, Black Road, to whom he confided his visions and his sense of a calling. The older man counseled him to perform his vision as an obligation to his people; not to do so publicly would mean harm to both him and them. "The Horse Dance" (14), "The Dog Vision" (15), "Heyoka Ceremony" (16), "First Cure" (17), and "The Powers of the Bison and the Elk (18) chronicle how the vision was proclaimed, received by the tribe, and bore its fruit with external respect from his people and Black Elk's internal confidence in its power. The virtues required for a warrior's identity and growing into the role of healer and seer effectively integrated all prior virtues: hope, will, sense of purpose, competence, and now most importantly, fidelity. In Lakota spiritual life, the warrior and the religious dimensions are not antagonistic. Neither were the consequences of redemption for the individual and the community. This identity laid the groundwork for the adulthood virtues of love, care, and ego integrity that biographical information suggests would follow after John Neihardt's "dream" in this text had ended, and Black Elk's adult life began.

When Black Elk was twenty-three years old, he recalled that his vocation as a healer was recognized and with great benefit to his people. Yet, Neihardt described him as despairing over the continuing demise of his people. Erikson's psychological moratorium from identity work began when Black Elk joined Buffalo Bill's Wild West show and toured Europe (19 & 20). He returned to find that the relations between his people and the *Wasichus* had become dreadful and thus begins Chapter 21, "The Messiah". He explored the Ghost Dance rituals and rekindled his commitments to his own vision, despite feeling a kindred spirit with what he saw there (22).

Black Elk Speaks ends at Wounded Knee in 1890. When John Neihardt arrived in 1930, Black Elk was in his sixties, having theoretically navigated Erikson's stages of identity, intimacy, and generativity. The identity as healer and seer remained intact despite all of the historical circumstances of reservation life and its interplay with the federal government's suppression of Indian religion. His reflections on life's meanings were thus communicated to Neihardt during the psychosocial stage of Ego integrity versus despair, a time when reminiscence bestows on memory's episodes either fruitful meaning or a sense of tragedy.

Malcolm X composed his narrative in his thirties. Having broken with the Nation of Islam, his mentor Elijah Muhammad, and as a husband and father, Malcolm was squarely in the midst of generativity issues. In 1964, he founded the Muslim Mosque as part of the religious dimensions of his life and the Organization of African American Unity for the political dimensions. *The Autobiography of Malcolm X* became the vehicle whereby he articulated the pathway to his final identity as a religious activist. His memories of earlier life follow the Eriksonian progression very well.

"Nightmare" (1) established the theme of racial oppression and violence that was at the heart of the experience of being a Black man in America. The chapter covered his *bios* from birth through early childhood to school age; psychologically, his *autos* was being formed in the crucible of relationships between his dark-skinned father and light-skinned mother, among his siblings, and from racist America's actions against the Little family. After the fire that was his earliest memory at age four, Malcolm discovered a basic survival skill—protesting with a loud voice got heard. After Earl Little died when Malcolm was six years old, however, not even making noise could help. At age nine, his family circle's sense of pride deteriorated. They were placed on relief and the finger was pointed at the children at school so that both race and class were a constant stigma. Malcolm stole from local stores and the state welfare system focused on him during home visits, until it shifted to his mother and a lack of control over the large family. The state dispersed the children to foster homes and he sensed the worst was about to happen, being sent to live with another family. When he was twelve, his mother was institutionalized and remained there until 1963 when the family got her released. Malcolm visited her occasionally, seeing her in 1952, at age twenty-seven, after being released from prison.

After Haley got him to talk about his mother, it changed the nature of their collaboration and the emotional quality of the episodes from that point on. In Erikson's early stages, we establish a platform of trust that the world is a relatively safe place and then develop a sense of autonomy built on predictable boundaries being enforced to keep us safe as we venture forth. Without being overly interpretive, I believe that Malcolm may have been still working through these very basic issues when he was dictating his story. Gathering memory's episodes and making them public via a composition strategy is an act of generativity that continues to refine one's sense of identity, and draws deeply on basic trust, especially in a collaborative effort.

With the pejorative chapter title, "Mascot" (2), Malcolm continued his description of these early stages. He was expelled from school and sent to a detention home at age thirteen. The couple he lived with was physically benign but thoroughly racist. He felt treated like a pet, first realizing that being Black meant he would never receive comparable credit for any sensitivity, talents, or intelligence. He began to understand how fitting in among white people did not mean that they would ever regard him as an equal. Mrs. Swerlin advocated against Malcolm's being sent to reform school. He enrolled in junior high school in the seventh grade at the age of thirteen. Popular by virtue of his social skills and athletic talents, he was still a mascot and navigated the daily experiences of some teachers' encouraging comments and others' stereotypic portrayal of blacks in American history and contemporary life. At age fourteen, he was elected president of his school class, trying every way he could to be as white as his peers. DuBois's double consciousness dynamic is rife through this whole chapter and its contribution to Malcolm's diffuse identity became clearer in subsequent episodes.

At age fourteen, in the eighth grade, two encounters framed his ethnic identity. They formed a Manichean dualism for the rest of his life and it is obvious that he understood that while he dictated the passages to Haley. A step-sister from his father's first marriage, Ella from Boston, came to visit the family in Lansing, and in her, Malcolm met his first truly proud Black woman. She filled Malcolm with stories of family members who were doing well with their families and in their work, and how each of them never forgot to help the rest because that was what the Littles were supposed to do for each other. She praised Malcolm's intellectual accomplishments and then organized the whole family to visit their mother in the Kalamazoo hospital. Malcolm spent the summer in Boston and was introduced to Ella's Black society, a world never known to him in Michigan. When he returned home, everyone in his family and school noticed the difference—Malcolm identified as a young Black man.

The second critical event in this chapter cemented the negative pole of that identity. Talking to an English teacher, Mr. Ostrowksi, who he respected and felt respected him, Malcolm said he was thinking about becoming a lawyer. The teacher's response was a critical turning point and Malcolm labeled it as such in dictating the narrative to Haley. The teacher told him that people of his race ("niggers") do not become lawyers; he should be a carpenter because he was good with his hands and people liked him doing that kind of work. At its best, this passage captured the historical debate between Booker T. Washington's advocacy for vocational trade training versus W.E.B. DuBois's value in the liberal arts and what type of education was best suited for a young Black man in America at that time. At its worst, and this was Malcolm's memory, it was his psychosocial ticket out of formal schooling as a reservoir of racism in 1941 America. He never got over it and among teachers and classmates whose casually used hateful descriptors once rolled off his back, he now stared down anyone who used them. Students and teachers alike didn't know what had changed in the once affable "boy". He graduated and took a bus to Boston. Twenty years later, he praised Allah for separating him from that heritage.

Chronicling the period from 1941 to 1946, Malcolm described how he honed his skills as a hustler. Ella introduced him to Roxbury, Massachusetts, populated by Black families that considered themselves a cut above their brothers and sisters in the Boston ghetto. Malcolm scorned them and began to identify more with the inner-city poor. A new pal, Shorty, introduced him to city life and he became a successful apprentice in the world of hustling.

Malcolm shifted to New York City and Harlem and built his reputation as "Detroit Red" (6) with a full repertoire of skills in narcotics and prostitution. He received a 4-F from the military by intimidating a psychiatrist at his interview and telling of his plan to go south, organize other colored soldiers, and kill White boys. In February, 1946, he was sentenced to serve ten years on burglary charges, a conviction that typically brought two years for a first offender. His accomplices had been White girls and for that crime, he was made to pay dearly.

Conversion

In Erikson's model, Malcolm's psychosocial development seemed more on the role diffusion end of the continuum than on identity. His first conversion experience would resolve that conflict. In "Satan" (10), he described incarceration and how he earned the newest name on his identity journey for all his vitriolic anti-religion statements. Malcolm met Bimbi, a prison philosopher and the library's best customer, and discovered an individual for whom words were power. Malcolm began taking correspondence courses and taught himself how to read and to write more effectively. At the behest of his brothers, Philbert and Reginald, Malcolm stopped eating pork and the news spread throughout the prison. Ella got Malcolm transferred from Charlestown to the Norfolk Prison Colony which was an experimental rehabilitation jail. The inmate culture affirmed intellectual discussions; teachers from Harvard and Boston University offered courses; the prison library was its most outstanding feature.

During a visit with Reginald, Malcolm was first told the reason why he had been asked to give up pork and smoking. His brother told him about Allah, that God had come to America and revealed himself to Elijah Muhammad, a humble Black man, and that the time was up for the White man who was the devil. Letters and visits from Little family members followed and the seeds were sown as Malcolm turned these ideas over and over in his head, fusing them with the history of religion and Black-White relationships he learned from his self-designed reading program. He wrote daily to Elijah Muhammad and to family members who beckoned him to submit to Allah. Finally, one night, Malcolm had an apparition in his cell, that he believed was of Master W.D. Fard, the Messiah, who had appointed Elijah Muhammad to be the messenger to Black people. Malcolm grew more militant in his preaching among the inmates and was sent back to Charlestown Prison from where he was finally released in 1952.

Malcolm's second conversion experience took place in Mecca in April, 1964. Ella paid his way. He was out of the Nation of Islam, and she had also been thrown out of the Nation's Boston Mosque # 11. When he left America traveling first to Europe, then to Cairo, and on to Jedda, he was met with one after another kind and hospitable person. For Malcolm, the term, *White American*, was a constellation of negative values and attitudes, but he was confronted with the opposite in light-complexioned peoples in the Muslim world. When he finished the Hajj, Malcolm embraced a brotherhood of all peoples under the power of Allah. He urged his followers to turn to a spiritual path of truth, parting ways with the suicidal path of racism. This second spiritual conversion guided his actions until his death less than one year later, and inspired El-Hajj Malik El-Shabbazz' continuing prophetic voice.

Using James's paradigm described earlier in this chapter, the dramatic episodes in the cell and on the pilgrimage to Mecca suggest a sudden conversion experience. My interpretation favors an evolving new consciousness leading to a capstone experience, rather than something all-at-once—whether the life narrative text comes from Saint Augustine, Thomas Merton, Malcolm X, or Black Elk. Reading DeMallie's transcription of the original oral history notes, one appreciates the progressive conversion more in James's terms, and with less of a Neihardt-edited perspective. I believe that there is ample evidence to suggest that James's lectures on mysticism could be used to examine the phenomenology of Black Elk's visions, as well.

At age five, while hunting with his father in the woods, Black Elk saw two men coming out of the clouds, singing. This episode lasted twenty minutes. At age nine, he became very sick, and while lying in his tipi, the same two men came to him. Thus began the account of the vision of twelve horses from four directions, the six grandfathers (north, south, east, west, sky, and earth), sacred roads (black and red), four ascents, and receiving the gifts of the north's healing herb and cleansing sacred wind, the south's sacred hoop and tree to bloom, the east's daybreak star and pipe, and the west's cup of living water with the sacred bow and the powers to make life and to destroy. At age seventeen, returning from Canada, his prayers to the grandfathers were answered and re-awakened his consciousness of his powers. With a renewed confidence, he began his public witness to his vision.

DeMallie's transcriptions of Black Elk's Ghost Dance Visions suggest active participation versus just the role of an observer. He contrasted his understanding of personal vocation and identity with what others were identifying as a means of radical social change. Neihardt's account minimizes this recognition of the Ghost Dance and the poet made it seem like Wovoka was just another false prophet on the road to the brutal ending at Wounded Knee. The DeMallie account lends support, to my mind, that this immersion was a continuing chapter in the conversion process. Black Elk, using Erikson's terms, was grappling with the virtue of fidelity versus the repudiation of what he had received and incorporated into his adult vocation.

In the final section of the DeMallie record, "Teaching Flaming Rainbow", the "Ceremony on Harney Peak", which became Neihardt's *Author's Postscript*, Black Elk spoke in a more optimistic tone. Recall that Black Elk was sixty eight years old—a time of ego integrity versus despair—when he told his story to Neihardt. His Roman Catholic catechetical accomplishments and continued healing practices formed the heart of his generativity period. Recognizing this set of later adulthood dynamics, at a psychosocial stage with wisdom as its virtue and the disdain that grows out of dogmatism as its antipathy, I read the following passages from DeMallie differently.

> In sorrow I am sending a voice, O six powers of the earth, hear
> me in sorrow. With tears I am sending a voice. May you behold
> me and hear me that my people may live again. [The transcript
> noted here that "it did rain out of a perfectly bright sky and then
> it cleared up immediately afterward".] Grandfathers, behold this pipe.
> In behalf of my children and also my nephew's children, I offer this
> pipe, that we may see many happy days.[44]

In the final chapter in the Neihardt version, Black Elk's saga ends with tears running down his cheeks, and the sounds of his feeble voice that would never speak again. He wept in the drizzling rain, and then the sky cleared, and the sun returned. An Eriksonian interpretation of the DeMallie record suggests that the life cycle virtues of hope, fidelity, and wisdom are operative, not the antipathies of withdrawal, repudiation, and disdain. This is a redemptive episode, from a spiritual and a psychological perspective, that I interpreted differently than Neihardt intended.

Conversion experiences require giving up something and gaining something. Neihardt turned Black Elk's last words into a mystical and romantic scene of the tragic hero with an apocalyptically powerful message for all peoples. Rice offered a different interpretation about the Black Elk final message. Common to all Sioux narrators were several themes: after creation, the world was and always will be fraught with conflict and the potential for both generativity and destructiveness; human beings are charged with responsibly completing what spirits have initiated; loss is a constant reality and must never diminish living; a healthy sense of the world is one that accepts its contradictory and absurd nature; tolerance of diverse spiritualities is not based on a reverence for any one divinity. And there are four "personality 'types', necessary to tribal strength—active, contemplative, inspired, directive."[45]

James always took an agnostic stance on the "roots" of profound religious insights, one of them being the conversion experience. Scientifically, the "fruits" can be the objects of careful scrutiny. In this section, I tried to integrate identity formation and conversion events by examining their fruits as revealed in the authors' memory's episodes. I now turn, finally, to the transformation of author and text into being "prophetic", one fruit that stands the test of time. In psychological terms, becoming prophetic may be a natural progression and the development of complex identity. In sacred terms, becoming prophetic may be understood either as demanded by the transcendent, or as coming full circle to what was always intended to be.

PROPHETIC VOICES

Tom Merton's mentor, Mark Van Doren, told him that the mark of a good book was if it stayed in print for fifty years. Buddhist, Christian, Hebrew, Hindu, Islamic, and Taoist sacred scriptures certainly have trumped this secular literary standard. Why do some life narratives stand the test of time? The story must transcend its historical boundaries by tapping into a more existential or spiritual set of questions and meanings.

Black Elk Speaks was rediscovered in the 1970s while the American Indian Movement (AIM) and the environmental rights agenda became national issues. Vine Deloria Jr. described it as a Bible for a new generation of Native Americans, offering a message that we all should not ignore. Becoming prophetic involves a message that emerges from one time and communicates inspired meanings to subsequent generations, weaves them into their consciousness, and becomes a call to action. *Black Elk Speaks* is considered by some as such a work.

The American Indian Religious Freedom Act was passed in 1978 and acknowledged a long history of suppressed First Amendment rights for Native American spiritual practices. How Native Americans resisted this suppression continues to be resurrected by historians.

> . . .the origins of this resistance came from a variety of Native religious
> leaders who emphatically called for an assertion of Native beliefs
> and practices as an affirmation of intrinsic, inherited spiritual values
> and as a rallying cry for the preservation of the many diverse paths
> found in Native religious life. . .This affirmation was strengthened by
> the emergence of a significant number of prophetic spiritual leaders
> whose visionary experiences confirmed and celebrated Native religious
> orientation as a primary source of empowerment for resisting colonial
> advancement.[46]

Irwin chronicled the repetitive pattern of racist legislation in the twentieth century that kept indigenous spirituality in hiding. In 1969, George Mitchell and Dennis Banks (Chippewas) founded the AIM and were joined by Clyde and Vernon Bellecourt (Chippewa) and Russell Means (Oglala). "The 'spiritual rebirth' of Indian rights was affirmed as a union between traditional religious and political leaders espousing a revival of Native identity and a rebirth of religious practices as a means for political empowerment."[47]

In 1995, Irwin spoke at a Sun Dance with a Lakota tribal leader about the history of religious oppression on the Pine Ridge Reservation.

> You know, Black Elk was part of a conspiracy, a cover up among the Lakota. What he says there about the Indian religion being dead, over, was part of a plan to stop the oppression here at Pine Ridge. It worked too. After that book came out, things got better; we just said it was over, dead, a thing of the past. We still had to do it secretly, but things have gotten better. Now we can do it more openly and bring other people in . . . .I don't believe our religion is something that should be hidden or kept from other people who are not Lakota or Indian. But for a long time, we had to keep everything hidden, even from other Lakota.[48]

Black Elk Speaks has lasting value because it teaches continuing generations. It is a portal into American history because students must struggle to make sense of its narrative in the context of Indian cultural traditions and their responses to government policies. It is a portal into articulating their social philosophy as they contrast their Euro-American and Christian beliefs in developmental progress with Native American cosmologies that celebrate place more than time. It is a portal into having empathy for multicultural differences, neither grounded in a need for universalism nor in romantically manufactured similarities. Like Augustine and Merton, Black Elk's life reflects the quest to incorporate ideas and new experiences while affirming a value system and memories with a rich continuity.

Malcolm X witnessed how an individual can overcome debilitating experiences and vicious social circumstances, to continually re-create himself. Violence and a life at the margins of American society have been daily and withering experiences for many people of color. Malcolm's psyche continually beat back Mr. Ostrowski's message. He absorbed the betrayal and then the public humiliation by his second father, Elijah Muhammad. His memory's episodes were bracketed by the fire at age four and then the fire that destroyed his family's home again over thirty years later. Yet, he prospered and led his people to consider themselves beautiful and chosen. Cornel West wrote that "Malcolm X's notion of psychic conversion depends on the idea that black spaces, in which black community, humanity, love, care, concern, and support flourish, will emerge from a black boiling rage."[49]

The Autobiography of Malcolm X is a classic of the American prophetic tradition, a didactic narrative about an exemplary life expressing Puritan values in contemporary times. It is a spiritual autobiography about conversion—an individual standing out because of and in behalf of a community of values. In contrast to evoking Jeremiah's vision about future redemption for a chosen people after they turned away from sinful ways, Malcolm's message evoked Ezekiel's vision of resurrection. One vision yearned for a future, better place; the other heralded its power in the here and now.

John Edgar Wideman captured prophetic legacy in a poetic way:

Malcolm Martin, Martin Malcolm, the *m*s are some ancient sister
in the amen corner *mmmmmm*, they are great mountains, cloud
crowned, silhouetted against red dawn, as close to sky as solid
as earth ever reaches. They are men, mortals, mothers' sons;
they were murdered, martyred, mirror our suffering, our history—
betrayed, torn apart, dispersed. They wear the masks of men, of
life or death, but it is not those accidental features we mourn. We
are seeking always the body of our wholeness, what we once were
and could be again, the promise of redemption Malcolm Martin
Mandela seem to carry in their persons, a new day close enough
to touch, to bestow a name upon—Malcolm, Martin, Mandela.
What is snatched always just as it appears close enough to grasp.[50]

The Autobiography of Malcolm X and *Black Elk Speaks* challenge American readers to understand racism as part of their history, and to be more humble in relations with people of color in global contexts. Both authors epitomized the relentless struggle and burden of DuBois's double consciousness. Both challenged assimilation strategies and faced the real possibilities of death, then composed a unique resistance to the status quo. Black Elk and Malcolm X gave witness to conversion and redemption in life's stories. Their prophetic texts became the fruits for subsequent readers.

In the next chapter, I turn to women's stories that diversified even more the colorful palette used to paint twentieth century life narrative texts.

NOTES

1. Martin Marty, "Introduction", in William James, *The Varieties of Religious Experience* (New York: Penguin Classics, 1982), *xi, xvi* (Original work published in 1902).

2. Richard R. Niebuhr, "William James on Religious Experience," in *The Cambridge Companion to William James,* ed. Ruth Anna Putnam (Cambridge, UK: Cambridge University Press, 1997), 215.

3. William James, *The Varieties of Religious Experience* (New York: Penguin Classics, 1982), 31.

4. Charles Taylor described the "sick souls" and "twice born" concepts as central, reminding us that James even inserted an autobiographical passage about one of his own depressive episodes, but that he attributed to another person. Taylor wrote: "This is at the heart of religion for James, because this experience meets our most dire spiritual needs, which are defined by the three great negative experiences of melancholy, evil, and the sense of personal sin. Some of the perennial interest of James's book comes from his identifying these three zones of spiritual anguish, which continue to haunt our world today". Charles Taylor, *Varieties of Religion Today: William James Revisited* (Cambridge, MA: Harvard University Press, 2002), 37.

5. James, *Varieties,* 189.

6. James, *Varieties,* 377.

7. James, *Varieties,* 487. Rorty goes so far as to say, that for James, ". . .talk about our responsibility to truth, or to reason, must be replaced by talk about our responsibility to our fellow human beings. James's account of truth and knowledge is a utilitarian ethics of belief. . ." Richard Rorty, "Religious Faith, Intellectual Responsibility, and Romance" in *The Cambridge Companion to William James*, ed. Ruth Anna Putnam (Cambridge, UK: Cambridge University Press, 1997), 84.

8. John Barbour, *The Conscience of the Autobiographer: Ethical and Religious Dimensions of Autobiography* (Hampshire, UK: MacMillan, 1992), 14. He described "truthfulness in autobiography not as a strange hybrid of history and fiction, but in terms of a continual dialogue between a writer's conscience and his imagination", 28.

9. Peter Dorsey, *Sacred Estrangement: The Rhetoric of Conversion in Modern American Autobiography* (University Park, PA: The Pennsylvania State University Press, 1993), 2. He recognized that "A number of feminist critics—among them Mary Mason, Carolyn Heilbrun, Felicity Nussbaum, and Sidonie Smith—support [the] claim that the hermaneutics of conversion has marginalized certain writers—particularly women", 6.

10. *Shorter Oxford English Dictionary* (Oxford, UK: Oxford University Press, 2002), 2499.

11. Dan P. McAdams and Regina L. Logan, "What is Generativity," in *The Generative Society: Caring for Future Generations*, eds. Ed de St. Aubin, Dan P. McAdams, & Tae-Chang Kim (Washington DC: American Psychological Association, 2004), 16.

12. McAdams & Logan, "Generativity", 22. Respondents ". . .highlight scenes in their life stories in which extremely bad events (e.g., death, loss, failure, frustration) are followed by good outcomes (e.g., revitalization, improvement, growth, enlightenment). This way of telling a story about one's life is what we call a *redemption sequence*. A bad scene is redeemed, salvaged, made better by that which follows. The opposite sort of sequence in narrative is what we call a *contamination sequence*, where an extremely good scene is ruined, spoiled, or sullied by a bad scene that follows it. Highly generative adults rarely construct contamination sequences in accounting for their own lives, whereas less generative adults are more likely to speak of good scenes turning bad", 25–26. McAdams's most recent book, *The Redemptive Self: Stories Americans Lives By* extends this psychological argument with an historical and socio-cultural analysis; that book's ideas will be discussed in more detail in Chapter Six.

13. Dan P. McAdams, *The Stories We Live By* (New York: Guilford, 1996). Mental health researchers, especially in the tradition of George Vaillant's *Adaptation to Life* (Boston: Little, Brown, 1977) 25-year longitudinal study, have discovered that it is not the amount or severity of stressful life experiences, but a maturing set of coping strategies that predict overall physical and psychological well-being. The cognitive-behavioral therapeutic approaches to maladies such as depression now reflect this belief, based on continuing empirical evidence.

14. *Shorter Oxford English Dictionary*, 2369–2370.

15. G. Thomas Couser, *American Autobiography: The Prophetic Mode* (Amherst: University of Massachusetts Press, 1979), 3–4. The author concluded that: "Often a way of measuring individual achievements against cultural standards, autobiography becomes, in the prophet's hands, a medium for measuring communal achievement against individually intuited standards. . . .Confronted with the contradiction between what America is and what it could be, our autobiographers have yielded again and again to the prophetic impulse; they have sought analogies between their own experience and that of the community; they have tested cultural myths in the crucible of their own experience; and they have distilled from that experience new visions and values to urge on their audiences", 5.

16. *Shorter Oxford English Dictionary*, 3255.

17. Arnold Krupat, "The Indian Autobiography: Origins, Type, and Function," in *Smoothing the Ground: Essays on Native American Oral Literature*, ed. Brian Swann (Berkeley: University of California Press, 1983), 28–53.

18. DeMallie described how the actual bestowal of these names was proclaimed, using Neihardt's daughter Enid's hand-written notes: "Whenever the rain is over there is always the rainbow with a beautiful sight. Your thoughts are beautiful and from your thoughts the rainbow goes out and they get knowledge out of it. Gives acclaim to his work. His world is like the garden and his words are like the drizzly pour of rain falling on the thirsty garden. Afterward the rainbow stands overhead. The rainbow is like his thoughts and whenever the rain passes over there will be a rainbow." Raymond DeMallie, *The Sixth Grandfather: Black Elk's Teachings Given to John G. Neihardt* (Lincoln: University of Nebraska Press, 1984), 36.

19. Nicholas Black Elk, *Black Elk Speaks. As Told through John Neihardt (Flaming Rainbow)* (Lincoln: University of Nebraska Press, 2000), *xxix*. This 2000 edition contains all of the prior editions' Prefaces and will be used for this chapter.

20. Hilda Neihardt and Lori Utecht, *Black Elk Lives: Conversations with the Black Elk Family* (Lincoln: University of Nebraska Press 2000), *ix*.

21. Black Elk was born in December, 1863, a member of the Lakota tribe, on the Little Powder River. When he was three, his father's leg was broken in the Battle of the Hundred Slain, and he limped until he died, at about the time when others died at Wounded Knee in 1890. He was born during times when everything seemed troubled in their world.

22. DeMallie, *Sixth Grandfather*, 31.

23. DeMallie, *Sixth Grandfather*, 71.

24. Malcolm X, *The Autobiography of Malcolm X, As told to Alex Haley,* (New York: Ballantine, 1992), 150.

25. Sally McCluskey, "Black Elk Speaks: And So Does John Neihardt," *Western American Literature* 6, (1972), 232.

26. McCluskey, "So Does John Neihardt," 234. She concluded her support of Neihardt's approach in this way: ". . .the peculiar collaboration that is *Black Elk Speaks* reads not only as the voice of a holy man, but of a poet as well. Neihardt listened to Black Elk's story with a poet's ear, and he retold it with a poet's gifts. Black Elk speaks, and Neihardt, under "religious obligation," gave that speech to the white world; but his own voice, giving form and beauty to that utterance, is softly audible behind every word.", 241.

27. McCluskey, "So Does John Neihardt," 238–239, emphasis added.

28. G. T. Couser, *Altered Egos: Authority in American Autobiography* (New York: Oxford University Press, 1989), 190.

29. Couser, *Altered Egos*, 196. In Black Elk's story, the captivity dynamic operates at several levels. "The vision, therefore, if not the entire narrative, is twice mediated: first from his ancestors through Black Elk, and then from Black Elk through Neihardt. (Unlike the poet, the holy man admits that the vision is ineffable and that he is an imperfect vehicle.) In spite of Black Elk's efforts to locate the narrative's authority in a communal and transcendent source, the basis for that authority has slowly but inexorably shifted: from the supernatural to the secular, the tribal to the individual, the Lakota to the written, and the visionary and oral to the written and printed," 198.

30. Couser, *Altered Egos*, 203.

31. G. Thomas Couser, "Indian Preservation: Teaching *Black Elk Speaks*," in *Teaching American Ethnic Literatures*, eds. John R. Maitino & David R. Peck (Albuquerque: University of New Mexico Press, 1996), 23.

32. Brian Swann and Arnold Krupat, *I Tell You Now: Autobiographical Essays by Native American Writers* (Lincoln: University of Nebraska Press, 1987), *ix.*

33. Arnold Krupat, *Ethnocriticism: Ethnography, History, Literature* (Berkeley: University of California Press, 1992), 175–176.

34. Arnold Krupat, *For Those Who Came After: A Study of Native American Autobiography* (Berkeley: University of California Press, 1985), 131.

35. Couser understood the text in the Puritan autobiographical tradition where private spiritual conversion and public communal affiliation are co-mingled because history is teleological and Americans belong to a new chosen people. Malcolm staked his claim for Black people's chosen-ness in keeping with an American tradition of Franklin, Frederick Douglass, Walt Whitman, and Henry Adams. Being "Saved" (Chapter 11) was at the center of this story. Leaving prison in 1952, he purchased new glasses for his new vision, a suitcase for his new career, and a new watch because time was ever so important in his achievement ethic. Life in the Nation of Islam became one pathway after that conversion (Chapters 12 to 16); a second conversion at Mecca (Chapter 17) became the soul of a new story that was abbreviated at age thirty-nine with his assassination in 1965 (Chapters 18 to the Epilogue). G. Thomas Couser, *American Autobiography: The Prophetic Mode* (Amherst: University of Massachusetts Press, 1979).

36. Paul John Eakin, "Malcolm X and the Limits of Autobiography," in *Autobiography: Essays Theoretical and Critical*, ed. James Olney (Princeton, NJ: Princeton University Press, 1980), 181–193.

37. "It seems probable that when Malcolm X began his dictations to Haley in 1963 he anticipated that his narrative would end with an account of his transformation into the national spokesman of Elijah Muhammad's Nation of Islam. . . .This was not to be the end of the story, however, because the pace of Malcolm X's history, always lively, became tumultuous in 1963 and steadily accelerated until his assassination in 1965." Eakin, "Malcolm X Limits", 187.

38. Eakin, "Malcolm X Limits, 190.

39. Eakin, "Malcolm X Limits", 193.

40. Eugene V. Wolfenstein, *The Victims of Democracy: Malcolm X and the Black Revolution* (Berkeley: University of California Press, 1981).

41. Albert E. Stone, *Autobiographical Occasions and Original Acts* (Philadelphia: University of Pennyslvania Press, 1982), 250.

42. When he was doing a high school report on Malcolm X, I urged my son to read Cornel West's essay on Malcolm X and Black rage. When he finished his school project, he told me that his generation knew more about Malcolm and JFK and the historical figures from my generation via Spike Lee's and Oliver Stone's interpretations than from any other source. Cornel West, *Race Matters* (New York: Vintage Books, 1994).

43. Erik H. Erikson, and Joan M. Erikson, *The Life Cycle Completed: Extended Version with New Chapters on the Ninth Stage of Development*, (New York: Norton, 1997).

44. DeMallie, *Sixth Grandfather*, 296.

45. J. Rice, *Before the Great Spirit: The Many Faces of Sioux Spirituality* (Albuquerque: University of New Mexico Press, 1998), 13.

46. Lee Irwin, "Freedom, Law, and Prophecy: A Brief History of Native American Religious Resistance," in *Native American Spirituality: A Critical Reader,* ed. Lee Irwin (Lincoln: University of Nebraska Press, 2000), 298. Irwin's chapter is a cogent review of this history. The Indian Religious Crimes Code, promulgated by the Secretary of the Interior in 1883, and the subsequent directives to all Bureau of Indian Affairs agents, suppressed dances and feasts and especially the medicine men. These practices reflected dangerous tendencies not aligned with the mainstream Christian missionaries working to elevate primitive Indians to Euro-American civilized values and behaviors. Accommodation strategies practiced by many tribes only revealed that there would be no reciprocity by the *Wasichus*. The alternative was resistance, from coast to coast. The most suppressive measures were exemplified in 1889 with Secretary Morgan's statement in the annual report of the Bureau of Indian Affairs: "The Indians must conform to "the White man's ways," peaceably if they will, forcibly if they must. . . .The tribal relations should be broken up, socialism destroyed, and the family and the autonomy of the individual substituted." (Quoted in Irwin, p. 300). Wounded Knee in December, 1890, was one result of the Lakota Sioux people's participation in religious activity. After that event, Native American religious practice went underground, into secret gatherings, remote sites on the reservations far away from detection and the possibility of a similar response by the *Wasichus*.

47. Irwin, "Freedom, Law and Prophecy", 303. In 1971, Sun Dancers were arrested on Pine Ridge reservation. AIM and federal authorities engaged in another con-

frontation at Wounded Knee in 1973, with the result of changing federal response in favor of Native American rights. Over the next twenty years the following acts were passed, all having direct bearing on religious issues: Indian Self-Determination and Education Assistance Act (1974), Indian Child Welfare Act (1978), American Indian Religious Freedom Act (1978), Archeological Resources Protection Act (1979), National Park Service policy statement on Native American sites and practices (1987), National Museum of the American Indian Act (1989), Native American Grave Protection and Repatriation Act (1990), Religious Freedom Restoration Act (1993), and the Native American Free Exercise of Religion Act (1994).

48. Irwin, "Freedom, Law and Prophecy", 308.

49. West, *Race Matters*, 141.

50. John Edgar Wideman, "Malcolm X: The Art of Autobiography," in *Malcolm X: In Our Own Image*, ed. Joe Wood (New York: St. Martin's Press, 1992), 102.

Chapter Four

Coloring Women's Stories

PRECIS

*In the first three chapters, we focused on four men's stories and the perspectives used by scholars in literature, psychology, and multicultural and religious studies to understand their maps, metaphors, composition strategies, and memory's episodes. Women's life narratives in the English language, "written by herself", date to the fourteenth century. Yet, autobiographical studies scholars ignored these texts by and about women. Two of the products of the Women's Movement during the 1970s were first the resurrection of their works and then the scholarly commentaries that examined their contributions to this genre. These commentaries shifted the proportional emphases on au*tos, bios, *and* graphe. *Beginning in the 1980s, feminist scholarship and critical works by people of color interrupted prevailing assumptions about autonomy, authorship, and subjectivity.*

This challenge to business as usual was not limited to gender, but to studies of ethnicity, class, and sexual orientation. From 1980 to 2000, any illusion that life narratives could be understood using a monochromatic lens was left behind. We had inklings of these changes from examining The Autobiography of Malcolm X *and especially the ethnocriticism debates over* Black Elk Speaks. *By the end of this chapter, you will appreciate that expecting differences and respecting differences became a compelling force in literary studies and across the scholarly fields and teaching curricula in the academy.*

I will highlight the scholarly work of feminist literary theorists, and focus especially on Sidonie Smith and her analyses of life narratives. Using her theoretical perspective and selected other scholars in literary studies and psychology, we will then examine one of the most critically acclaimed life nar-

rative texts—Maxine Hong Kingston's The Woman Warrior: Memoirs of a Girlhood among Ghosts.

After the mid-1970s, the genre of autobiography and critical essays analyzing its complexities multiplied. Smith and Watson[1] identified fifty-two different labels to describe life narratives and three waves of scholarly commentary. The first was represented by Misch's touchstone work in the early part of the century. Gusdorf's essay was at the heart of the second wave. This chapter will focus on Smith and Watson's third wave—a spider's web-like set of perspectives from Euro-American women and women of color who wrote about the social constructions of the self. They changed the rubrics by which we judge texts.

Smith and Watson noted several transitional works between their second to third waves. Sayre[2] judged an autobiography to be significant when its authors articulated a compelling American idea or virtue. In a country of equals, persons stand out due to some common denominator that an audience recognizes easily; the author must declare having accomplished it bigger or better or at least differently than others. Sayre recognized that standing apart was also a necessity for subsets of the American people not allowed to participate in assumed equality. He used a geographical analogy to describe the array of American selves illustrated in four prototypical texts. Benjamin Franklin's story symbolized the East, a European literary and intellectual heritage that valued economic prosperity. Frederick Douglass represented the South, using his life and multiple autobiographical texts to bear witness to freedom and its conflicts. Walt Whitman was the West—mythical, adventurous, tapping into very different motivations than Franklin to realize the possibilities of a boundless physical and psychological territory. Henry Adams was the North with its inherited opportunity and privilege. These four men were the past's "leading architects of American character", and he predicted that ". . .to tell the rest of the story—of what went on in the house—will be a challenge for the years ahead."[3]

Smith and Watson's history of autobiographical criticism situated Gusdorf's essay at the heart of their second wave, with Olney's [4] works as important transitions. Their third wave was characterized by diverse authors and composition strategies that shifted the historical emphases, first on *bios*, and then on *autos*, to *graphe* and how varied constructions communicated complex and heterogeneous selves. Autobiography became a "performative act" [5] or a "pact" [6] between the author/narrator and the reader. Relationships became paramount as authors continually re-constructed themselves via composing new stories.[7] Interdisciplinary examinations of memory and multicultural experiences enhanced notions about autobiography as a performance to be appreciated by diverse audiences.

Feminist scholars, with the advent of the Women's Movement and the resurrection of many women's life narratives, fostered an empathic understanding of constructed selves and the composing of stories. Women of color deepened this understanding as they integrated experiences of silenced anger and
discontinuity, and of relationships and identities forged by oral traditions.
Sidonie Smith described the new agenda for a poetics of women's autobiography as the study of how gender affects the qualities of the composed text,
the silencing constraints of patriarchal societies and an androcentric literary
genre, and the role that sexuality plays in its presence or absence in stories.[8]

In the next two sections, I sketch an overview to feminist commentaries on
life narratives, and then turn to an in-depth focus on the works of Sidonie
Smith.

SCHOLARSHIP BY AND ABOUT WOMEN AUTHORS

Mary Mason examined early autobiographical works in English: Dame Julian
of Norwich (*Revelations*, ca. 14th century), Margery Kempe (*The Book of
Margery Kempe,* ca. 1432), Margaret Cavendish (*True Relation of My Birth,
Breeding and Life*, 1656), and Anne Bradstreet (*To my Children*, ca. 17th century). She placed these resurrected texts in the spiritual autobiography tradition begun by Augustine, but saw the authors' plot structures and constructions of identity as different from male models.

> The dramatic structure of conversion that we find in Augustine's
> *Confessions,* where the self is presented as the stage for a battle of
> opposing forces and where a climactic victory stage for one force—
> spirit defeating flesh—completes the drama of the self, simply does
> not accord with the deepest realities of women's experience and so is
> inappropriate as a model for women's life writing. . . .On the contrary,
> judging by our four models, the self-discovery of female identity
> seems to acknowledge the real presence and recognition of another
> consciousness, and the disclosure of female self is linked to the
> identification with some "other". [9]

Mason felt that identifying with an "other" freed these four women to be self-
disclosing in times and places where such statements were not at all accept-
able. The women's rhetoric demonstrated that their partnerships were freely
chosen, and not with the deference demanded of their public selves. Julian of
Norwich's and Margery Kempe's "other" was a divine being and Anne Bradstreet's was her spiritual community. Margaret Cavendish's secular story was
composed as a matched pair with that of her husband, the Duke of Newcastle.

The selves revealed in these four works expressed clear identities as authors, responding to Julian's pointed query: "Why hath this lady writ her own life?"

Estelle Jelinek compared women's autobiographies with those from the male tradition. Starting with the emergence in the early 20ᵗʰ century of literary criticism on the genre, she described the omission of all but a few women authors in the commentaries, lasting deep into the century. When attention was paid to women's work, it was less than complimentary. The critic, Louise Montague Athearn, wrote about Kate Millett's iconoclastic *Flying,* published in 1974:

> ... a book? No. It is the personal outpouring of a disturbed lady—albeit genius—whose eclectic life is of more interest to her than to the reader. There is no story line, no plot, no continuity. Her writing is a frantic stringing together of words, without any thought for the ordinary arrangement of noun and verb. It is hard reading. . . .It is utter confusion. [10]

Jelinek evaluated women's autobiographies against canonical benchmarks. First, autobiographies were judged by the substantive content of public stories and the significance of those events. (Recall Misch's representative lives and Sayre's notion of linking personal experiences to great virtues.) The turning points of political his-story were the sources for men's reflections. In contrast, women's texts were produced at times when her-story was critical. For example, there was a spate of publications during the Progressive Era and its social changes that influenced other women's public service, as well as in that period's echo during the late 1960s and 1970s. Second, the life scripts of public personalities were primary in men's texts; accounts of private lives received more emphasis in women's texts, even when composed by distinguished public figures. Third, Jelinek evaluated critics' expectations for personal disclosures and judged that both women and men had established boundaries for such revelations. Fourth, the rhetorical styles in women's autobiographies were honest and understated. Instead of proclaiming one's self in aggrandized terms as a male hero figure, women's stories reflected less certainty yet portrayed a resolute working-through of problems. Fifth, and finally, she addressed Gusdorf's standard of articulating unity in one's life. Women's lives were rich in discontinuities and adaptations, disconnections and wholeness, diversities and common denominators; their narratives reflected as much. In the last two decades of the 20ᵗʰ century, both women's and men's postmodern narratives would discard the expectation for unity in daily life and record its variations in journals, memoirs, and nonfiction essays. In a 1998 essay, Smith and Watson summarized, appreciatively, the contributions and the limitations of Jelinek's early work. Questions of textuality, gender and identity, race, class, and location motivated subsequent work, broadened the field, and rendered it more lively.[11]

The 1988 essays in Benstock's *The Private Self: Theory and Practice of Women's Autobiographical Writings* were responses to Olney's 1980 volume of critical work and especially to Gusdorf's assertion that autobiography is a mirror of the self. Self and reflected self may not be necessarily the same. Stanford Friedman's chapter applied this challenge broadly.

> That mirror does not reflect back a unique, individual identity to
> each living woman; it projects the image of WOMAN, a category
> that is supposed to define the living woman's identity. . . .Isolate
> individualism is an illusion. It is also a privilege of power. A white
> man has the luxury of forgetting his skin color and sex. He can think
> of himself as an "individual." Women and minorities, reminded at every
> turn in the great cultural hall of mirrors of their sex or color, have no
> such luxury.[12]

In *Subjectivity, Identity, and the Body,* Smith also challenged the reliance on a "universal self", an idealized characteristic by which men's narratives connected to their audiences, but to which women's experiences had little to no resemblance.

Another scholar, Leigh Gilmore, proposed that although women's autobiographies were ignored in literary criticism, feminists had developed tools in other disciplines to understand these texts. Gilmore affirmed the multiplicity in and of women's lives.

> Insofar as feminist criticism of autobiography has accepted a
> psychologizing paradigm, it reproduces the following ideological
> tenets of individualism: men are autonomous individuals with
> inflexible ego boundaries who write autobiographies that turn on
> moments of conflict and place the self at the center of the drama.
> Women, by contrast, have flexible ego boundaries, develop a view
> of the world characterized by relationships (with priority given
> to the mother-daughter bond), and therefore represent the self
> in relation to "others".[13]

Gender politics is inextricably linked to a critique of the individualism doctrine—from Augustine to Rousseau to Franklin and their critical commentators. Neither men nor women had universal selves and few authors used uniform composition strategies. Gilmore evaluated life narrative strategies in refreshingly new ways. She advocated an approach to reading that listens to an author's voice for its uniqueness, not for common denominators, for specific declarations of self, not for universals. This stance requires that readers engage a text with strong and resilient empathy. We must do the hard work to see a life through an author's eyes, not requiring their assimilation into some larger group identity to elevate their text's status as representative.

Gender, class, ethnicity, sexual orientation—all categories of difference—were the focus of many scholars' commentaries in the last two decades of the twentieth century. Smith and Watson summarized this new perspective as a challenge to a one-dimensional self examined in many disciplinary fields, and with it, to the celebration of master narrative composition strategies that placed certain texts in a canon of exemplary autobiographical works.[14] Our understandings of texts benefited significantly from an outpouring of critical work in the 1990s about women authors who were African American, Asian American, Latina, and American Indian. The emphasis was on the interaction of multiple identifying characteristics whereas in earlier studies, scholars' conceptual focus was often dichotomous (e.g., women vs. men; gay vs. straight, etc.).

As part of the Wisconsin Studies in American Autobiography, Smith & Watson assembled a reader with forty critical essays composed from 1980 to 1996 on women and autobiography, several of which have been mentioned already.[15] In their introductory chapter, they examined theories of women's autobiographies; analyzed different perspectives on subjectivity; proposed twelve scholarly tasks (e.g., ethics, memory, interdisciplinary studies, therapeutics) as promising areas for continuing study; and predicted future directions for the field. "In summary, we suggest that the real legacy of the last twenty years in women's autobiographical theorizing has been the emergence of a heterogeneous welter of conflicting positions about subjectivity and the autobiographical." [16]

COMMENTARIES BY SIDONIE SMITH AND COLLEAGUES

Smith's first book explored the styles used by Black American authors in their search for identity, and the themes of masking, naming, mastery, and expatriation in Black American autobiographies, with slave narratives as touchstone for subsequent texts.[17] In her first chapter, "Flight", she examined the Southern Black's acts of rebellion demonstrated first in fleeing their bondage of slavery and second in writing about that experience. Literary issues included writing to northern White audiences, declarations of authorship, and their focus on public versus private experiences. In her final chapter, "Transcendence", she highlighted a traditional arc of a life narrative—the movement from death to life, from slavery to freedom. All of the chapters in between catalog the difficult trade-offs required to survive in an Apartheid America. The last chapter began with the existential question that Claude Brown used to begin his own autobiography: "Run! Where?"

Smith captured the corrosive and life/spirit threatening choices in her portrayal of the styles used by different authors to do more than just survive. Evaluating the assimilation strategies of Booker T. Washington, she described "the acrobatics of the mask of Christian invisibility."[18] Writing an autobiography bestows a "rite of coherence upon the chaos of their lives."[19] For Richard Wright, "the meaning of living came only when one was struggling to wring a meaning out of meaningless suffering." [20] For Malcolm X, it was a journey from anger (the "nigger" in Malcolm Little) to love (the freedom in El Hajj Malik El-Shabazz). For Maya Angelou, writing became her way to recapture past memories too painful to examine and to fly from the cages of one's life. Smith's attribution of transcendence to these stories derived from an interpretation that writing one's story was bearing witness about the struggle, affirming the emancipating power of anger and love to whomever would listen.

A Poetics of Women's Autobiography

In the opening chapter of this 1987 work, Smith sketched the historical changes in genre criticism.[21] When the emphasis on *bios* shifted to *autos*, Smith the critic became "a psychoanalyst of sorts, interpreting the truth of an autobiography in its psychological dimensions rather than in its factual or moral ones."[22] She decried the practice of scholars' reviews in which only one or two were written by or about women. It was time for a change in the gender of examined authors and for the placing of more emphasis on feminist *graphe*: "plural, continuous, interdependent, nonsensical, roundabout, a narrative of ruptures, gaps, wordplay, and *jouissance*. . ." [23]

Critics neither explored this terrain nor deemed it worthy of scholars' mappings. The dimension of continuity versus discontinuity became an issue, as did the quest to define women's nature. Smith's objective was to create a poetics of women's texts; autobiography was a story about stories. Their compositions were interpretations of a life, bestowing meanings on memory's episodes that may or may not have been evident earlier. She captured the ironies and nuances of human behavior dynamics revealed in literary works, characterizing the strategies used by women as:

> An effort of recovery and creation, an exploration into the
> possibility of recapturing and restating a past, autobiography
> simultaneously involves a realization that the adventure is informed
> continually by shifting considerations of the present moment.

. . .she renders in words the confrontation between the dramatic present
and the narrative past, between the psychological pressures of discourse
and the narrative pressures of story.[24]

Women have many stories to tell. Recall Arnold Krupat's interpretations
for Native American writers and the difficulties of their transcriptions of an
oral tradition into written Euro-American forms. Women know, when they
write, that audiences will read them as women authors. People of color bear
the same burden and opportunity. They compose their narratives with readers' responses in mind. Their strategies, historically, required addressing
many unstated questions:

Did this (woman) author actually compose this story?

*By what authority does this (woman) author write about private, non-public
(read unimportant) experiences and thus what contribution to man's (read
universally important) narratives can this text make?*

*How do I communicate who I am in ways that others' gender, race, class, and
sexuality constructions of my story will be interrupted or even dismantled?*

"Written by herself" became a signatory declaration. Smith defined the
choice for women autobiographers as perpetuating "cultural ventriloquism"
versus "embracing the polyphonic possibilities of selfhood." [25]

With an autobiographical disclosure, she previewed what would become
the themes for twenty years of her scholarly work after *Poetics*:

. . .woman speaks to her culture from the margins. While margins
have their limitations, they also have their advantages of vision.
They are polyvocal, more distant from the centers of power and
conventions of selfhood. They are heretical. Perhaps that is why
I have found women's autobiographies to be both eccentric and
alive, whatever their limitations. There is a theatricality about
them, but of the regional stage. Characterized by dysphoria, by
the restlessness and anxieties of self-authorship, women's stories
frustrate expectations and thoroughly enchant the reader
because they are vital, unconventional. From them erupt,
however suppressed they might be, rebellion, confusion,
ambivalence, the uncertainties of desire. But always there
is that voice, close to the surface of the story, telling about
woman's life, negotiating the stories of man and woman.[26]

Like Gergen's review of Erik Erikson, Smith's critical judgments, communicated with such clarity and verve, invite a warm and admiring 'yes'.

Subjectivity, Identity, and the Body

Psychological research about gender differences came to an empirical conclusion in the 1980s that literary scholars had arrived at as well—there are as
many, if not more, differences among women as there are between women
and men. Smith's 1993 book asked the question whether women's life narratives were unique? Women at the turn of the 21st century were creating new
metaphors and maps, new composition strategies, and new ways of gathering
memory's episodes. They blurred boundaries and crossed borders of literary,
psychological, and political significance.

Women's autobiographical practices are occasions to 'talk back'.[27] Talking
back involved for Smith an examination of how women confronted a universal selfhood as the model for subjectivity and the "I" of autobiographical
writing, and how the body and its many images were either a source of outlaw practice or of continuing repression and a veiled narrative.[28] She tracked
the expanding consciousness in women's life narratives across the nineteenth
and twentieth centuries. The acrobatics challenge she interpreted for Black
authors was apt for women writers, as well. Her analysis of Harriet Jacobs'
slave narrative was a compelling illumination of how women of color confronted so many universal expectations; it was "consigned to obscurity for
over one hundred years. . . .it went unread, perhaps because it was, precisely,
unreadable".[29] Her chapters in this book on Hurston, Dillard, Moraga, and
Spence are especially helpful for a reader to better understand the gender, sexuality, ethnicity, and identity themes in Hong Kingston to be reviewed later in
this chapter.

Smith addressed similar issues in her 1995 chapter, "Performativity, Autobiographical Practice, Resistance", examining again the concepts of self and
performance. "Autobiographical storytelling becomes one means through
which people in the West believe themselves to be 'selves'. In this way, autobiographical storytelling is always a perfomative occasion. . ." [30] She critiqued the notions we hold about an Enlightenment self, asserting that "there
are many stories to be told and many different and divergent storytelling occasions that call for and forth contextually-marked and sometimes radically
divergent narratives of identity". [31] ". . .the cultural injunction to be a deep,
unified, coherent, autonomous 'self' produces necessary failure, for the autobiographical subject is amnesiac, incoherent, heterogeneous, interactive."[32]
As we will explore in the next chapter, using Dan McAdams's perspectives,
the paradigm of scientific psychology splintered trying to predict such variations for human behavior; cognitive research on autobiographical memory
points to similar findings as those stated in her chapter.

For Smith and other literary scholars, audience is a critical factor in life
narrative stories, just as it is for any performance.

An audience implies a community of people for whom certain discourses of identity and truth make sense. The audience comes to expect a certain kind of performativity that conforms relatively comfortably to criteria of intelligibility. Thus, a specific recitation of identity involves the inclusion of certain identity contents and the exclusion of others; the incorporation of certain narrative itineraries and intentionalities, the silencing of others; the adoption of certain autobiographical voices, the muting of others. But audiences are never simple homogeneous communities. They are themselves heterogeneous collectives that can solicit conflicted effects in the autobiographical subject.[33]

In the next section, we explore the work by Smith and her colleagues that contributed to shining the floodlights on women and their experiences around the diaspora.

The Global Importance of Stories

Four of Smith's edited volumes after the *Poetics* and *Subjectivity* texts brought to critical attention highly diverse authors and their narratives about empowerment. *Moving Lives: 20ᵗʰ Century Women's Travel Writing* was a sole-authored reflection that synthesized her continuing construction of a woman's poetics of autobiography with the ever-widening forms for which this agenda was very important.

De/Colonizing the Subject: The Politics of Gender in Women's Autobiography was Smith's first collaborative text with Julia Watson and grew out of the scholarly work by feminist scholars who met, wrote, and exchanged texts at scholarly meetings, enabling each other's genre commentaries during the 1980s. The volume's thesis was that "the axes of the subject's identifications and experiences are multiple, because locations in gender, class, race, ethnicity, and sexuality complicate one another, and not merely additively. . ."[34]

Similar themes and writing strategies were evaluated, and with global diversity, in: *Writing New Identities: Gender, Nation, and Immigration in Contemporary Europe*; *Indigenous Australian Voices: A Reader*; *Human Rights and Narrated Lives: The Ethics of Recognition*.[35] The anthology about voices from the New Europe—from Ireland to Russia and Sweden to Italy—explored self-representations in autobiography, film, magazines, and novels as cultural forms of gendered nationalism. "The writing of/toward new identities is a writing driven by memory and amnesia. . .the relationship of memories to amnesia is ever adjustable, fluid, and productive of new meanings and new narratives."[36]

"I give you this story" was the editors' choice to begin the volume of Australian narratives; it opens with the prefatory remarks:

> It is a common assumption that all indigenous people of Australia
> constitute one group, the Aborigines. However, we do not think of
> ourselves as "Aboriginal" but rather identify ourselves within our own communities. The first thing you are asked when meeting a member
> of another indigenous community is, "Where do you come from?"[37]

This comment echoes the first-week question I hear in my college teaching about Native American literature, or for that matter, any ethnic narrative. "Professor, what is the Indian perspective on. . .?" Over the years, expecting students' attempts to understand groups who are different from their own, I will respond: "Would we ever ask how all Europeans see this issue, demanding some homogeneous statement about Poles, Italians, and Bosnians?" However, in post-911 classrooms, I have been struck by how many students assert that there is, and should be, one, clear "American perspective" on any number of complex questions.

The 1990s brought to center stage the study of diverse life narratives in literary scholarship as well as human rights testimony in socio-political and journalistic venues. *Human Rights and Narrated Lives: The Ethics of Recognition*, was a text crossing many boundaries of cognitive and affective experience. It

> understands "the political" as inclusive of moral, aesthetic,
> and ethical aspects of culture. It treats life narratives and human
> rights campaigns as multidimensional domains that merge and
> intersect at critical points, unfolding within and enfolding one
> another in an ethical relationship that is simultaneously productive
> of claims for social justice and problematic for the furtherance
> of this goal.[38]

Life narratives and human rights testimonies intersect. Two themes can be found in such texts. First, they give voice to those who were formerly silent and become an imperative to those willing to listen. Second, hope is the very real product of storytelling, if and when people are willing to be empathic and then are motivated to join others in action.

Smith's *Moving Lives: Twentieth-Century Women's Travel Writing* had a simple premise: "Journeys by foot across the hard and soft earth, journeys by air high above the huddling masses below, journeys along the rigid rails, haphazard journeys along the highways and backstreets— women on the move have taken them all."[39] Smith took simple concepts—travel by foot, plane, train, and automobile—and illuminated their unexamined assumptions. From women's stories, she unpackaged the acts of leaving and returning home, by what mode of transportation and for what reason, to where do women intend to go (or not go), why this journey, and how does its very initiation and going someplace-else challenge assumptions about boundaries and appropriateness. Specific geographies and differing modes of identification were important—a woman's Tibetan journey across the Himalayas by foot, going by camel into the Australian outback, traveling by train from Beijing to Berlin, taking anonymous Greyhound buses or being driven in highly stylized American automobiles—and they are not the same on any dimension. However, unlike the stories in her collaborative anthologies, the women who pursued these travel "quests" that Smith examined were all White and with the economic wherewithal to do so. Smith focused solely on the relationships between gender and mobility and the modernist linking of technology to progress; she recognized the constraints that women of color encounter when they must get to the other side of inhospitable places.

I conclude with Smith's and Julia Watson's three important theoretical projects on life narratives for a new century.

Getting a Life: Everyday Uses of Autobiography

In this volume, Smith and Watson added the following examples to Sayre's list of autobiographical forms: political candidates' "personal" ads, daytime television's confessional obsessions, self-help groups' formulaic self-disclosures, dressing for success in ways that are "me", family albums, elongated medical histories for social services or financial services applications, and personal ads in all media. The distribution lists that we create or to which we belong, our selections of journal subscriptions, organizational memberships, charitable donations, and products consumption, our personally tailored "home pages"—all present to the public what used to be a private self. All are consumed and re-distributed to others by selected and unselected publics so that they all can better "serve the special me that I am".

> *In postmodern America we are culturally obsessed with*
> *getting a life—and not just getting it, but sharing it with*
> *and advertising it to others. We are as well, obsessed*
> *with consuming the lives that other people have gotten.*
> The lives we consume are translated through our own
> lives into story. Getting a life is a necessary negotiation
> in the every day practice of American culture/s.[40]

Smith and Watson portrayed America as an imagined community of auto-biographical storytellers. This was their brilliant synthesis of the differing emphases of *autos*, *bios*, and *graphe* in studying texts. Early in the twentieth century, autobiography was construed as *bios*; the canon standards expected that the author's life spotlight a distinctive American virtue. By adhering to literal veracity, the record of building America would not be spotted with untrue or partially accurate documents. With more emphasis on *autos*, or the psychology of troubling questions that yielded highly individualistic responses, expectations for universal meanings of the subjective self declined. Now, the canon was constituted by what represented the most individualistic in creative imaginings. Previously erased lives and texts by women and people of color could be included, but only with the grudgingly slow changes in defining what was the "best" of and for America. With the uniform, agreed-upon standards cat-out-of-the-bag, *graphe* became primary. "Autobiographical discourse continues, to a considerable extent, to be a palpable means through which Americans know themselves to be American and not-American in all those complexities and contradictions of that identity."[41]

Smith and Watson raised questions about privacy, individualistic culture, commodification, identity and identity politic(s), ethos of disposability of just about everything and everyone. They suggested that we repetitively assemble, reproduce, and consume autobiographical stories. Are we becoming hollowed "profiles", "sound-bites" (a curious two-worded term), or just "bytes" with technological sophistication? Hope springs from "talking back"—a theme that has remained consistent throughout the corpus of Smith's works:

> "*On a daily basis, then, personal narrators assume the role of*
> bricoleur *who takes up bits and pieces of the identities and narrative*
> *forms available and, by disjoining and joining them in excessive ways,*
> *creates a history of the subject at a precise point in time and space.*"[42]

McAdams arrived at a similar position with his description of constantly revising one's stories, creating an anthology of the self in his life story model of identity. Watson and Smith articulated from whence we derive those stories for our anthologies. Moreover, they understood that "*the everyday uses of autobiography can produce changes in the subject, for narratives are generatively excessive as well as reconstitutive.*"[43]

Women, Autobiography, Theory: A Reader

The legacy of women's autobiographical theorizing from 1980 to 2000 was the emergence of multiple conflicting positions about subjectivity and autobiographical composition strategies. This Smith and Watson anthology of scholarly pieces was ". . . like paintings at a museum exhibit or patches on a quilt, putting together diverse perspectives on the same topic puts all of them into sharper focus."[44]

In their Introduction, the authors told a story about building the archive of women's writing and simultaneously encountering the masculine autobiographical standards of the twentieth century. The narrative of feminist theoretical development had its early voices in women like Mary Mason and Estelle Jelinek, a second stage during the decade of the eighties, and then the platform was established with single-authored works by Sidonie Smith, Francoise Lionnet, Carolyn Heilbrun, and with the anthologies edited by Bela Brodzki and Celeste Schenck, and by Shari Benstock. Smith and Watson evaluated these contributions, were critical of their limitations, yet appreciative of their ground-breaking perspectives. Post-colonialist and postmodernist perspectives extended this platform constructed in the 1980s.

In Part Two of the Introductory chapter, Smith and Watson compared feminist theorists of autobiography (many of whose abridged original essays were included in their anthology) with more general theorizing about subjectivity. This section enables the student, the more advanced reader, and the scholar to make connections between the array of perspectives in the humanities and cultural studies with specific authors and their examinations of life narratives. After mapping the terrain of twentieth-century scholarship, the authors ventured into compass-making in Part Three's "prospects for theorizing women's autobiography". Interdisciplinary studies of autobiography will nuance future criticism and composition of life narrative works.

Reading Autobiography: A Guide for Interpreting Life Narratives

I first discovered this book buried amidst a stack of bibliographic references that my undergraduate assistant gathered to update a reading list for my next year's course. Now, I return often to individual chapters when preparing specific presentations. I read it with even more appreciation and envy when I was three-quarters finished composing the text you are now reading. Smith and Watson's intended audiences were advanced undergraduate and master's level graduate students and for the general reader, and as a teaching resource for faculty in literature, American studies, women's studies, African-American and ethnic studies, history, and other courses. It is without equal as both a starting point, and as a scholarly companion to primary source autobiographical material.

As you have read, beginning in Chapter One, my schema to evaluate reading and writing of autobiographical works includes: Maps and Metaphors; Composition Strategies; and Gathering Memory's Episodes. This organizational approach reflects the interdisciplinary commentary about life narratives, especially via research advanced during the 1990s. Two terms—psychology and cognitive neuroscience—will not be found in Smith and Watson's index. Identity and memory, however, are two terms that cross-over the work by scholars in literature and psychology and have ample references in their index. Their schema for analyzing texts had three elements, as well, inspired by the psychologist, Jerome Bruner, "getting a life means getting a narrative, and vice versa": Life Narrative Definitions and Distinctions; Autobiographical Subjects (memory, experience, identity, embodiment, agency); and Autobiographical Acts (poetics: a matrix of story narrators, motivators, and consumers).

They provided an historical analysis of life narratives and chapters on the three waves of autobiographical criticism to which I have referred often in previous pages. "A tool kit: Twenty strategies for reading life narratives" is a fine guide; their twenty strategies are truly interdisciplinary. Yet, specific scholarship from psychology is never explicitly mentioned.

During the 1970s, more and more texts by women and ethnic authors were written and made their way into public view; others were resurrected as the study of non-canonical texts gathered momentum. As part of an overall consciousness raising taking place in scholarly communities, the critical commentaries on these texts began to take form in the early 1980s and into the 1990s. Two overlapping phenomena took place during this era. First, scholars now had diverse texts with which to work. Second, scholars themselves became more diverse in their gender, ethnic heritages, and points of view. For literary critics like Smith, this was a time of polyphonic possibilities via a carnivalesque forum for differences. Psychologists were less appreciative of such heterogeneity in assumptions and analytical methods.

In my exploration of Maxine Hong Kingston in the following pages, her literary predecessors, and the paradigm-shifting consequences of her composition strategies, I will use the feminist theoretical perspectives advanced by Sidonie Smith and her colleagues. I also will compare and contrast these perspectives with the commentaries by multicultural literary scholars whose intellectual and experiential subjectivities wove in and out of the texts they evaluated.

MAXINE HONG KINGSTON'S TALKING STORIES

Maps and Metaphors

The Woman Warrior: Memoirs of a Girlhood among Ghosts [45] is among the most often assigned texts in American higher education, used in literature, history, anthropology, sociology, cultural studies, ethnic studies, and feminist studies courses. Each word of the title spotlights its complex metaphors.

Woman advances this story as a feminist analysis of patriarchy, mother-daughter relationships, and the social constructions of gender in China and America. *Warrior* signifies its appeal to the mythic stories of historical Chinese figures like Fa Mu Lan and Ts'ai Yen. Their tales transcend time and place as road maps for women's encounters with sexism. *Memoirs*, in the plural form, demonstrate the text's polyphonic character, with similar tracings to an oral tradition like Black Elk's or Leslie Marmon Silko. Her five chapters are auto/biographical accounts of Maxine's stormy relationships with her mother, of a no name aunt from China whose life and name the family erased from their history, and about another aunt whose story lost its definition when she became an American mental health tragedy. *Girlhood* tells the reader that these are episodes from Maxine's adolescence, and her developmental changes always took place *among Ghosts*. The preposition, *among*, denotes walking in the midst of, neither of them or with them, and *Ghosts* are the dizzying array of cultural "others" and the historical memories with whom an ethnic Chinese person constructed her hyphenated identity in America.

Smith first wrote about *The Woman Warrior* in her *Poetics* book, in the concluding chapter entitled "Filiality and Woman's Autobiographical Storytelling". Hong Kingston's book epitomized the themes that Smith examined in all women's lives and their texts: interdependent characters connected but also silenced by others' words, narratives replete with ruptures and gaps, polyphonic voices discovering their power at the margins of American society. "No single work captures so powerfully the relationship of gender to genre in twentieth-century autobiography." [46] Smith's subsequent analyses of colonizing subjects, Australian voices, and human rights narratives can be linked directly back to her examination of *The Woman Warrior*–narratives are women's and peoples of color's means for talking back when its authors discover the hope of stories instead of being beaten down and silenced.

Life's metaphors grow out of stories that often come from our mothers, but are revised through memory's episodes into those we now call our own.

> In dialogic engagement with her mother's word, she struggles to
> constitute the voice of her own subjectivity, to emerge from
> a past dominated by stories told to her, ones that inscribe the
> fictional possibilities of female selfhood, into a present
> articulated by her own storytelling. [47]

As I described in Chapter Two, disciplinary scholars study the driving forces of nature's inheritances and the wide variability of nurturing factors in fashioning an identity during the second decade of life. Hong Kingston's magical realism prose enlivens these processes so that we can learn from them and weave them into our own stories. Smith noted the exhilarating possibilities and the problems

from episodes passed from one generation on to the next: "...they generate confusions and ambiguities, since as a child Kingston inflected the narratives with
her own subjectivity...tales of bravery and exoticism are underwritten by an alternative text of female vulnerability and victimization."[48]

Suzanne Juhasz summarized the book in this way: *"The Woman Warrior* is
about trying to be an American, when you are the child of Chinese emigrants;
trying to be a woman, when you have been taught that men are all that matter;
trying to be a writer, when you have been afraid to speak out loud at all".[49] Hong
Kingston, thirty-six years old when she published her book, captured the perspective, confusions, and still weak voice of a young Maxine, as did Maya Angelou in the first of her serial autobiographies, *I Know Why the Caged Bird
Sings*. The character Maxine dons and doffs storied roles like so many garments.

The opening chapter is a cautionary tale about her father's sister and the social constraints imposed by cultures and history on women. Maxine turned
the story over and over to eke out her meanings from it, all the while deci-
phering what was fact and fiction in her mother's account. Hong Kingston
created herself, the writer, as a woman warrior after the Fa Mu Lan tale told
her by her mother, just as Leslie Marmon Silko appropriated the Yellow
Woman traditions into her *Storyteller* narrative.[50] This life narrative is about
being a Chinese American woman who grew up in Stockton, California, in a
household filled with stories from her mother's and father's past as well as
their contemporary glosses on American life.

Smith situated *The Woman Warrior* in the history of life narratives in this way:

> ...an autobiography about women's autobiographical storytelling.
> A postmodern work, it exemplifies the potential for works from
> the marginalized to challenge the ideology of individualism and
> with it the ideology of gender... to consider the complex imbroglios
> of cultural fictions that surround the autobiographer who is engaging
> two sets of stories: those of the dominant culture and those of an
> ethnic subculture with its own traditions, its own unique stories.[51]

To appreciate the intricate maps and metaphors created by Hong Kingston in
The Woman Warrior, we must absorb the author's lesson that we must grow our
minds larger, like the universe, so that we can manage its paradoxes more ably.

Composition Strategies

Hong Kingston

> ...creates a careful, highly polished stylistic surface in order to
> give form to a world that is invisible, the imagination, wherein

dwell the reality that shapes existence. Kingston's approach makes
creating, rather than recording, the significant autobiographical act.[52]

Members of the Asian American creative community gave this text a less appreciative reception. Frank Chin scathingly criticized the author for perpetuating popular stereotypes of Chinese Americans held by many Americans and
literary critics by the use of exotic tales and caricatures, rather than accurate
history and strong characters. In her important casebook of critical essays on
the book, Cynthia Sau-Ling Wong identified three critical assumptions of
Chin and others that seemed to be behind all the vitriol hurled at the book and
its author: (a) the changing paradigm of the genre of autobiography, (b) critical responses to life narratives written by American ethnic writers, and (c) issues specific to the Chinese American audience and its authors.[53]

By the 1970s, texts by women and people of color were brought to the foreground by popular audiences; commentaries by literary scholars followed in
the 1980s. Women had always been telling their stories in memoirs and in fiction. The *bios* tradition emphasized descriptive histories of public lives, with a
sprinkling of private, behind the scenes episodes to add context and emotional
qualities to the story. The *autos* tradition elevated the importance of self-
scrutiny about the meanings of gathered episodes. Scholarly interpretations
tried to discern authors' motivations and intentions, often using available *bios*
evidence to compare and contrast that which was revealed by the *autos*. However, oral traditions of different ethnic cultures and the writing styles of fiction
authors did not translate easily into the truth-telling, journalistic prose that
characterized many works in the ever-changing life narrative canon.

Hong Kingston told Wong, in response to all the questions about whether
The Woman Warrior should have been classified as "fact" or "fiction", that it
was her publisher who decided on the non-fiction category.[54] Wong understood how an ethnic author is particularly vulnerable to criticism because
readers' responses are so variable to stories of families, cultures, and histories
about which Anglo-Americans may know little and may stereotype very
much. Wong did acknowledge all the reservations about how Hong Kingston
stretched the boundaries of the original stories from which she drew inspiration for the characters in this book.

Recall Couser's admonition that teachers of *Black Elk Speaks* should provide students with historical background as part of their close readings of a
text. In contrast, the ethnic woman author is expected to educate the reader
about socio-cultural and historical dynamics as part of the actual text. Perhaps
in response to these expectations, Hong Kingston inserted a chapter on Chinese immigration history right in the middle of her second memoir about her
father, *China Men*, published several years later.

Some of the criticisms by ethnic scholars echoed the earlier standards, that a life narrative should reflect the virtues and ethos of a larger community, affording its readers educational and inspirational value as "representative". The individual story must generalize to some idealized collective history to advance aesthetic qualities and civilizing characteristics in the population at large. As I will describe in the next chapter, Richard Rodriguez also received stinging criticisms for positions he took in his first memoir, *Hunger of Memory*, when he violated Chicano norms.

Hong Kingston's feminist perspective vexed some Chinese men, as well, because they perceived her tales to portray all Chinese men as patriarchal sexists. She suffered the double burden of gendered and ethnic identities in presenting her story to a general audience that included those looking for exotic images and those hoping to find an autographical "I" constructed and composed in comparable ways to their own strategies. King-kok Cheung, in contrast, described Hong Kingston's composition strategies as consistent with women's continuing efforts to "talk-back":

> Her ploys are reminiscent of the tactics that feminist critics
> have associated with women's writing generally: the
> appropriation and subversion of dominant discourse. . . .The
> first ploy is to declare open warfare: explicit protests, mythic
> re-visioning, blatant defiance of traditional precepts. The
> second is to engage in guerilla tactics—irony, indirection,
> and understatement—to vitiate the assertions in the text.[55]

Hong Kingston declared, when recalling an episode about being silenced as a young girl, that if she did not talk, she would not have any personality.

In addition to violating the conventions about truth telling in memoirs, *The Woman Warrior* did not conform to the linear, narrative structure that characterized older texts like those by Augustine, Merton, Black Elk, and Malcolm X. A chronological progression from early life to contemporary experience reflects a belief in a unified developmental history and a continuous self and identity. Hong Kingston composed her life narrative as five intersecting chapters, each with a different female protagonist, but all constructed to illuminate Maxine thinking out-loud about her mother's fantastic stories and how she must respond in order to create her own story.

Whereas the adolescent Maxine was trying out all of the stories that her mother gave her, the thirty-year old Hong Kingston was testing out the stories in written form. She transformed her oral story telling culture into the Euro-American written traditions. She created a composition strategy that fostered ambiguities, making our task as readers to listen carefully, to respond with empathy, and to form our own judgments. Maxine became Hong Kingston in the text. Her composition strategy asks us as readers to become more sophisticated in our acceptance of ambiguity in human life, in our knowledgeable appreciation of gendered and ethnic identities, and perhaps in our capacities to weave her experiences into our own life narratives—as did she.

In the next section, I will evaluate these five chapters as episodes, told in a postmodern literary fashion, consistent with the layers of memory that form life narratives at any one point and at every point in our continuing story.

Gathering Talk-Story Episodes from Memory

There are five chapters in *The Woman Warrior* portraying five central characters from whose tales Hong Kingston patterned her identity:

> "No Name Woman": her father's sister in China
> "White Tigers": historic figure of Fa Mu Lan
> "Shaman": Maxine's mother, Brave Orchid
> "At the Western Palace": Maxine's maternal aunt, Moon Orchid
> "A Song for a Barbarian Reed Pipe": historic figure of Ts'ai Yen.

She sequenced these five characters' episodes so that her text begins with her mother's cautionary tale about becoming a woman and being silenced, told to her in adolescence, and she finishes the final chapter with the discovery of her own voice. She wove autobiographical details all through the chapters as memories of the personal responses she made to these epic characters and what they demanded of her. Smith interpreted her merged composition and identity strategies as trying to compose a self via inherited cultural stories about women.[56] Paul John Eakin described the same dynamic: "the art of self-invention is governed by a dialectical interplay between the individual and his or her culture."[57] These are American stories, mythic and ethnic Chinese stories, women's stories, and working class stories. Maxine listens obediently, tries to makes sense of them, and responds as a young person in the process of constructing a self; then, she remembers them as an adult writer in order to create her own vivid and meaningful text. Stories are the pre-texts for *The Woman Warrior*.

No Name Woman

The book's narrative opens with Maxine's mother's dramatic prohibition. She must never repeat the story told about her father's sister who killed herself, because they erased her from all memory as if she had never been born. Brave Orchid described how her sister-in-law became pregnant after her husband left their village, and the villagers raided their house and wreaked havoc. The aunt gave birth in the pigsty, and then drowned her child and herself in the well. Maxine's mother told her that with the onset of her menstrual cycle, the same could happen to her and she would bring the same humiliation and shame to the family. She must be vigilant lest her memory be forgotten as well. In the rest of the first chapter, Maxine thinks out loud about her no name aunt, placing herself in her shoes, imagining what motivated her to make the choices she did. Was this a rape? Was it an act of pleasure, seeking to break out of the imposed boundaries? She concludes with a feminist critique of patriarchy. Her aunt was punished because she acted as if she were entitled to a private life, apart from what men provided and allowed.

Hong Kingston placed Brave Orchid's no name woman story at the very beginning of her narrative, signaling the book's social, economic, political, biological, and symbolic meanings. Maxine must weave Brave Orchid's story about China and its rules into her Chinese American strivings at both the psychological and cultural levels because this terrible, ancestral tale will have no benefit unless she can weave it into her own story. Maxine must evaluate why the aunt never revealed the man's name, why she took her child's life as well as her own, and why she chose the well to poison the drinking water of those who would not protect her life. Is there a different social contract for boys versus girls, and how does it manifest itself in all countries? Eakin construed the suicide as an act of ultimate autonomy, sealing her story from the villagers who violated her privacy. The terrible consequences of this defiance, however, were her death and erasure from memory and family history. Brave Orchid, mindful of Maxine's predilections, double binds her daughter with a "tell no one" admonition, that became the seeds for the provocative silences of *The Woman Warrior*. The chapter ended with Hong Kingston's sober acknowledgement that her aunt haunts her and so she writes about her. What always haunts her are her mother's talk stories, never to be forgotten, always a leaven in her consciousness.

White Tigers

Hong Kingston established characters who framed the two ends of her identity continuum. No name woman was erased from the family tradition. Girls could grow up to be wives and slaves. Fa Mu Lan was the standard against which to measure a young girl's aspirations and a young woman's accomplishments. She could also grow up to be a heroine, a warrior woman, like her own powerful mother, talking story. In this chapter, we are introduced to a house filled with Brave Orchid's stories and their lingering power. Hong Kingston shifted to the pronoun "I" to create her own magical realism version of the mythic tale where a seven-year old girl went into training with an elderly couple in the mountains, the land of white tigers. She learned how to live in harmony with nature, how her woman's body was part of the natural order and all the seamless connections that were possible. Most importantly, she had to grow her mind as large as the universe in order to be more at home with its paradoxes.

After fifteen years, the young trainee came down from the mountain and re-entered a world filled with violence and oppression. Her parents welcomed her home, and with her consent, carved words on her back. She put on men's clothes and armor, recruited the villagers' sons, and led them off to battle. She fell in love, had a child, but never revealed her woman's identity until she returned once more to her parents' home, married, and committed to the traditional chores of farm work, housework, and breeding sons. The domesticated warrior mused that her new legend would be about being a perfect daughter and Maxine fretted that her American life could only be judged as very disappointing.

Hong Kingston ruminated about her heroine's accomplishments versus the realities of her actual life in Stockton, California, listening to countless slurs about girls oft repeated in her Chinese American community. Raising geese was better than raising girls; the former were useful but the latter left their families to live with strangers. While at Berkeley, she wanted to come home as her parents' son, so they would be proud of her. She also stopped pursuing academic achievements because the American standard for women was not to be intelligent if you wanted to have dates. Nevertheless, Fa Mu Lan became the standard by which Maxine filtered her remembered episodes.

How confusing it was to grow up as a young woman receiving abundant contradictory messages from multiple cultural sources—American society, Chinese history, the Chinese American community, and the working class environment of her California family. Hong Kingston's concluding statement in this chapter captured her emerging consciousness that author's words are more powerful than the strength of swords. Hong Kingston had recycled a Chinese myth and changed the genders in the original story. Yueh Fei was a male general whose mother had carved slogans about being loyal to China on his back. Whereas both the No Name Woman and Fa Mu Lan capitulated to the ethos of their Chinese villages and had their identities thereby foreclosed, Maxine's fate was more ambiguous after Chapter Two. She still could not figure out her true village.

Shaman

This chapter is at the apex of the book; it is auto/biography at its best. Brave Orchid re-enacted the Fa Mu Lan story, but as an adult in China. She left home to be educated as a physician, and returned to battle villagers' ills. After her husband had been gone for years in Gold Mountain/America, she took the money he sent her to go to medical school. After graduation, she was heralded as a new woman scientist who transformed China's medical rituals.

Brave Orchid came to America in 1940, and Maxine was born several years later during World War II. Brave Orchid's American life must have been a disappointment for her, too. She and her husband owned a laundry with life among the "ghosts"—white ghosts, black ghosts, police ghosts, taxi ghosts. In China, Brave Orchid achieved recognition from her medical school peers for her intelligence and as a slayer of ghosts. In America, she was forced to assimilate, neither to slay nor to heal. Maternal heroic tales came from China, but Maxine had to make sense out of their meaning and adaptability to her life in California.

Hong Kingston concluded this chapter with a fond memory of the last time she visited her parents. She recalled the long conversation she had with her mother, now reconciled to never return to China. Mother and daughter try to make sense of each other's world, from its complexly layered symbols to the daily medications taken to ease their headaches and colds, the foods they eat and the ones they avoid. Brave Orchid called Maxine "little dog", and she warmly ended this chapter of her life feeling that a great weight had been lifted from her. Her mother called her little dog, affectionately, but recognized that she and her daughter were both dragons in actual life. The passage signals Maxine's increasing consciousness of her interdependence with her mother as well as the possibilities of her independence that will blossom. Like Fa Mu Lan, legends can be made also from perfect filiality.

At the Western Palace

Brave Orchid's sister, Moon Orchid, came to America after her husband left her behind in China for more than thirty years. At Brave Orchid's nagging insistence, she timidly confronted her husband, a wealthy physician, who had taken another, younger wife. He rebuffed her in a scene witnessed by Maxine's brother, then told to her sister, and finally passed along to Hong Kingston. The entire fourth chapter was written in the third person and the author informs the reader in the fifth chapter that she was passing on a multiply told version. This composition strategy is similar to the oral tradition captured by Leslie Marmon Silko in *Storyteller.* She composed variations of the Yellow Woman tale several different ways, some spare, some grandly described, some humorous, and some laced with irony. All keep circling around the moral lesson that the author hopes to convey, first by her own experience, and then in dialogue with her listeners/readers.

Moon Orchid was fragile, refined, and understood her life as revolving in a lesser orbit around others. When her husband scorned her "at the western palace" and sent her away, she vanished herself from his life and into madness. Despite Brave Orchid's persistent challenges, Moon Orchid misplaced herself; her spirit just drifted into the universe. Hong Kingston took this anecdote from her brother's memory and created her own cautionary tale about ethnic women in America, echoing her mother's earlier talk-story strategy. Instead of Brave Orchid warning Maxine about the dangers of female sexuality, Hong Kingston tells the reader how women may lose their psyche, and wove this text using quote-threads of her mother's voice. Brave Orchid's "diagnosis" was that people who are sane talk story in a variety of ways; mad people only have one story and they tell it over and over again.

Moon Orchid, like no name woman, informs Maxine's life narrative deeply. Her mother's sister's rejection and ensuing madness was woven into her own identity. At the end of this chapter, Brave Orchid harangues her husband about taking another wife and admonishes her daughters to never let men be unfaithful to them. Challenging the realities of American women's undergraduate enrollment patterns at the University of California at that time, Hong Kingston declares that Brave Orchid's daughters will all major in science or mathematics. She was writing a new script for the women of her family, and beyond, that had to be different from no name woman, Fa Mu Lan, and Brave Orchid who lost their power when they returned to their villages and their assumptions. It had to be different from Moon Orchid who was set adrift with no village and with no role to play without a spousal identity. In the fifth and final chapter, Hong Kingston gave readers that new script out of history, memory, her mother's talk-story, and her growing feminist consciousness.

A Song for a Barbarian Reed Pipe

In the fifth chapter, Hong Kingston declares a new identity—as a Chinese outlaw knot-maker. The narrative comes full circle with another mythic talk-story told to her by her mother on a recent visit. Most importantly, for this last chapter and for the entire life narrative text, Hong Kingston proudly announces that the beginning of this whole story belonged to her mother, but the ending now belonged to her.

This chapter has the most traditional autobiographical details about the young Maxine's development. Hong Kingston, the accomplished adult writer, understood deeply what we have learned about memory in recent cognitive neuroscience research. She must sift through memory's episodes and sort what was an actual childhood event, what came from her multi-layered family stories, and what even invaded her psyche from popular culture, like the American movies. In *Storyteller,* Leslie Marmon Silko declared a similar preoccupation with trying to distinguish between what was in fact a true memory and what was vivid imagination.

Discovering a voice was at the heart of the two most vivid episodes in this chapter. The first scene took place in elementary school between Maxine and a girl who could not speak. Maxine verbally bludgeoned the voiceless peer. Hong Kingston may have composed the girl as her mirror image for an actual illness that kept her home from American school where she felt persecuted, ridiculed, and characterized as stupid. She hammered the voiceless girl with visions of a future that were dreary and subservient. After the incident, Maxine was muted and mysteriously ill for eighteen months, but at least she did not have to go back to where her test scores indicated that her IQ was zero!

The second episode was a classic adolescent tirade. Maxine had grown a list of over two hundred things to tell her mother why she felt oppressed in the family. Fearing that her parents had identified a potential mate, she unleashed her grievances one night during supper at the laundry. She continues to use the academic achievement standards that concluded the previous chapter and announced how smart others thought she was. She not only can get A's, but she can win scholarships, and her intellectual acumen was high enough to be a scientist or a mathematician. On and on she went. About China. About her mother's stories. About making sense about everything in their ethnic household. Then, Brave Orchid decided this must be a debate, not a monologue. She told the verbally spent Maxine that if she were so smart, why hadn't she ever gotten the point that Chinese always say the opposite to stretch the mind. Besides, Brave Orchid was a doctor, so the family already had one scientist in its story!

Erikson understood that identity is about reconciling opposites for our entire lives. Families, peers, and cultures bombard adolescents with possible identifications. The younger persons try on roles in whole and in part, struggling to be separate and unique, but longing to be merged and part of something larger, while they eke out a fledgling consciousness of their limitations. Hong Kingston wrote a brilliant declaration of independence episode. How to resolve all her conflicted polarities was the conclusion of the book. She knew the stakes were high and needed a mythic character like Ts'ai Yen to do so.

She ended the fifth and last chapter with a blended talk story begun by her mother and concluded by her. It was about Ts'ai Yen, a Chinese poetess who was taken involuntarily from her homeland. Those who listened heard about forever wandering, and her children learned to sing their mother's song. Hong Kingston created a story within a story as her vision for her life narrative. Ts'ai Yen and Brave Orchid had to discover ways to live among barbarians. Their struggles were fraught with loneliness, sadness, and displacement. To finish *The Woman Warrior*, Hong Kingston has Ts'ai Yen compose a song of anger and of sadness, in response to the foreign peoples among whom she must live, and even weaving their notes into hers. Finally freed, Ts'ai Yen returns home, bringing her captive songs with her, then passing them down from generation to generation. Thus, Hong Kingston celebrates differences and similarities; hers is an ethic not of assimilation, but of intercultural dialogue and harmony. Moreover, her writing enabled her to achieve an inner harmony among all the different chords of her ethnic and gendered life.

REMEMBERING CONTINUED

Saint Augustine reviewed all of his published work near the end of his life, asserting that *The Confessions* needed no revisions because it continued to inspire others. Thomas Merton wrote in his journals not too long after publishing *The Seven Storey Mountain* that he did not recognize the younger monk who penned the original narrative. He had moved on, psychologically and spiritually. Nicholas Black Elk continued talking to John Neihardt over the years, and then shared more time with Joseph Epes Brown, not to revise his memory's episodes, but to amplify the complex spirituality that he created after the Battle of Wounded Knee in 1890. Malcolm X's assassination while Alex Haley finished the final revisions of the dictated narrative foreclosed any new meanings from his dramatic life work.

Maxine Hong Kingston had the opportunity on many occasions after publishing *The Woman Warrior* to revise her understandings of her life narrative text. She published a second memoir, *China Men*, then a novel, *Tripmaster Monkey: His Fake Book*, in 1989, and a blended work of fiction and nonfiction, *The Fifth Book of Peace*, in 2003. All these works received positive national reviews, awards, and critical commentaries by scholars and journalists, and prompted re-evaluations of *The Woman Warrior* in academic and popular press publications. Paul Skenazy and Tera Martin edited an anthology of *Conversations with Maxine Hong Kingston* that had been published between 1977 and 1996. In these interviews, she answered the myriad criticisms about the original work, its metaphors, composition strategies, and how her memory's episodes first took shape and evolved during and after writing the original work. Compared to Augustine, Black Elk, Merton, and Malcolm X, this opportunity for continued remembering via twenty years of published interviews offers insights into the literary and psychological processes of life narrative construction. The story about the story was able to continue.

Writing Identity

Hong Kingston composed poetry when she was eight years old and first published at fifteen with her essay, "I am an American", in *American Girl* magazine. She did not publish again until *The Woman Warrior* when she was in her thirties. In the fifth and sixth grades, she discovered her first Chinese character in a book and a Chinese woman author after reading Jade Wong Snow's autobiography, *Fifth Chinese Daughter*. It was a healing experience, having just read Louisa May Alcott's caricature of a Chinaman. Reading Jade Wong Snow enabled Hong Kingston to continue writing during her adolescent, identity years.

When asked about becoming and being a writer, she told Gary Kubota in 1977 that she didn't do research before she wrote on a topic, believing that she could tap into creative muses and discover images and stories about which she never really knew anything.[58] It was a powerful vision, composting since adolescence, that launched her successful first work. Ten years after publishing it, she summarized its developmental and gender identity themes to Kay Bonetti in 1986. Hong Kingston judged that *The Woman Warrior* was a young person's story, someone in the process of creating herself in words. In *China Men*, she extended her narrative voice to discover men's development. The process of completing both enabled her to compose an adult woman's identity, capable of telling the stories of both women and men.[59] With Judy Hoy in 1986, she mused that a narrator's struggle was to follow along the path of powerful and eccentric women without losing one's own way.[60]

Recall how Augustine saw memory processes as critically important in the development of identity. After a decade of explaining herself and the how and why of *The Woman Warrior*, Hong Kingston articulated similar understandings about memory. She told Paula Rabinowitz, also in 1986, that a writer's memory "winnows", and then the narrator must decide what is absolutely essential to get down on paper or else she will be haunted by what remains unspoken and unwritten.[61] A common denominator in Alice Walker, Toni Morrison, Leslie Marmon Silko, Judith Ortiz Cofer, and Maxine Hong Kingston is the way they weave their ethnic oral traditions into their fiction and nonfiction works. Their works' touchstone is always the collective memories of their communities. Again, to Paula Rabinowitz, she described how her memory inspired her to blend the rugged individualism themes of strength and standing alone, so prevalent in American writing with the collective strains of an ethnic family and circle of intimates.[62]

In 1996, in an interview with Eric Shroeder, she compared her composition strategy of telling a community secret with how Alice Walker began *The Color Purple* and Toni Morrison's opening of *The Bluest Eye*. She chose "No Name Woman" as her way into *The Woman Warrior* in order to overcome the most elementary obstacle we encounter—our mother's prohibitions. Doing so in the very first lines allowed her to declare her lifetime of disobedience right away.[63] "Tell no one" is all about being an "outlaw Chinese knot-maker", or as I tell my students to be playful with responding to her words—what does it mean to be build their identities as "in-law not-makers"? She is always "talking back", so that she and her people will not forget their families, communities, history, and the stories on which they rest. Yet, in a 2004 interview with Andrea Lewis, she was adamant that she wanted to be remembered not as a feminist writer or a Chinese American writer, but as a writer.[64]

Transforming the Genre

The complexity of Hong Kingston's composition strategies is how she blurs the boundaries between fiction and non-fiction, especially in *The Woman Warrior*. In a 1980 interview with Arturo Islas and Marilyn Yalom, she reflected on oral tradition's influences on the static prose of written forms. Oral tradition is immediate, commanding, directly influencing how one responds by its dialogic nature. The story changes from telling to telling based on who is the storyteller, not just on who is the listening audience, and on the circumstances surrounding the telling. The written form must remain fixed on the page. To overcome this static quality of written text, she tried to weave as much ambiguity into her writing at every turn.[65]

As I detailed earlier in the chapter, she was criticized for her publisher Knopf's label of autobiography for this work. Ten years after it appeared, in 1986, she told Kay Bonetti that calling her books novels would have been o.k. with her. She had arrived, however, at an entirely new perspective on the traditional separations and dichotomies. While working on her novel, *Tripmaster Monkey*, she came to the realization that she was always writing a new kind of biography. When one's subjects are "imaginative people", the lives and dreams and memory's episodes necessarily lean towards fiction. Stories of storytellers cannot be narrated in documentary journalism ways. Families do not create their histories and her-stories with that type of prose.[66] To Paula Rabinowitz that same year, she described such work as a biography of the imagination.[67]

Hong Kingston not only made up the stories of lives, but she transformed the mythic stories from her oral tradition in ways that enraged some critics and Asian writer/scholars. She transposed genders, adapted story lines and re-visioned the outcomes. In 1989, she spent a week as a Regents Lecturer at the University of California at Santa Cruz, meeting with students and faculty. She revealed to her audiences that in the no name woman chapter, her imagination constructed so many possible ways that this life may have been led. The tale was rife with ambiguity on the page, because her memory's reconstructions of her mother's initial telling of it were just as ambiguous. The entire tale could have been an exaggerated homily by her mother.

The "outlaw knot maker" delighted in composing intricate new forms to capture "talk-story". Like Jade Wong Snow had done for her, Hong Kingston gave life narrative writers permission to discover distinctive voices, and to color their own metaphors, composition strategies, and memory's episodes.

In her anthology of American women's autobiographical writings, *Written by Herself*, Ker Conway captured the effects from listening to all these stories. After reading women's autobiographies, we savor the memories of a splendid cast of characters, having learned powerful lessons from new friends. The memories that we now have from meeting them challenges us to be more reflective about working on our own story scripts, composing the meanings of our own lives.[68]

In the next chapter, I turn to the serial autobiographies published by Richard Rodriguez in 1982, 1992, and 2002. More than just a snapshot of a storytelling moment, Rodriguez's works enable us to more fully appreciate the life story model of identity and its applications to our own self-awareness and writing efforts.

NOTES

1. Sidonie Smith and Julia Watson, *Reading Autobiography: A Guide for Interpreting Life Narratives* (Minneapolis: University of Minnesota Press, 2001).

2. Sayre wrote about the ubiquity of life narrative texts in the American culture and listed: Puritan diaries, travel narratives, captivity narratives, "biographies" and "autobiographies" of Indian chiefs, success and immigrant stories, protest stories, apologies from public figure scoundrels and rogues, "True Confessions" in magazines, cryptic entries in high-school yearbooks, photograph albums, and academics' *vitas*. Robert F. Sayre, "Autobiography and the Making of America", in *Autobiography: Essays Theoretical and Critical*, ed. James Olney (Princeton, NJ: Princeton University Press, 1980).

3. Sayre, "Making of America", 168.

4. James Olney, ed., *Autobiography: Essays Theoretical and Critical* (Princeton, NJ: Princeton University Press, 1980).

5. Elizabeth Bruss, *Autobiographical Acts: The Changing Situation of a Literary Genre* (Baltimore: Johns Hopkins University Press, 1976).

6. Philippe Lejeune, "The Autobiographical Pact", in *On Autobiography*, ed. Paul John Eakin, trans. Katherine Leary (Minneapolis: University of Minnesota Press, 1989).

7. Paul J. Eakin, *How Our Lives Became Stories: Making Selves* (Ithaca, NY: Cornell University Press, 1999).

8. Sidonie Smith, *A Poetics of Women's Autobiography: Marginality and the Fictions of Self-Representation* (Bloomington: Indiana University Press, 1987).

9. Mary G. Mason, "The Other Voice: Autobiographies of Women Writers", in *Autobiography: Essays Theoretical and Critical*, ed. James Olney (Princeton, NJ: Princeton University Press, 1980), 210.

10. Quoted in *Women's Autobiography: Essays in Criticism*, ed. Estelle C. Jelinek, (Bloomington, IN: Indiana University Press, 1980), 4. Jelinek suggested that if works composed by women would have been published with a man's name, the response would have been very different. "As men, these women's experiences would be de-

scribed in heroic or exceptional terms: alienation, initiation, manhood, apotheosis, transformation, guilt, identity crises, and symbolic journeys. As women, their experiences are viewed in more conventional terms: heartbreak, anger, loneliness, motherhood, humility, confusion, and self-abnegation", 5.

11. Sidonie Smith and Julia Watson, eds., *Women, Autobiography, Theory: A Reader* (Madison, WI: University of Wisconsin Press, 1998).

12. Susan Stanford Friedman, "Women's Autobiographical Selves: Theory and Practice", in *The Private Self: Theory and Practice of Women's Autobiographical Writings*, ed. Shari Benstock (Chapel Hill, NC: University of North Carolina Press, 1988), 38–39.

13. Leigh Gilmore, *Autobiographics: A Feminist Theory of Women's Self-Representation* (Ithaca, NY: Cornell University Press, 1994), xiii. Gilmore urges the reader to meet others who are different and who are the same by not confusing one for the other: ". . .the history of autobiography reveals that the self is not a transcendent construct that is recorded in its essential continuity by generation after generation of autobiographers. Indeed, one might well look to autobiography as a place to begin interrogating the value-laden assumption of the immutability and deep-down sameness of selves, for one finds in autobiography a virtuoso display of the complexities and differences within gender, place, time, religious practice, the aesthetic, the family, work, as well as the experiences of class, race, and ethnicity which self-reflexive narratives must manage", 82.

14. Sidonie Smith and Julia Watson, *Reading Autobiography: A Guide for Interpreting Life Narratives* (Minneapolis: University of Minnesota Press, 2001), 135.

15. Smith and Watson described *Women, Autobiography, Theory: A Reader* in this way. "Think of it as a set of tools—or building blocks, guides, recipes—for enabling your own entry into the activity (and the self-reflexivity) of theorizing women's autobiography", 4. Recall how O'Donnell described his authoritative study of Saint Augustine as a "set of grappling hooks".

16. Smith and Watson, *Women, Autobiography, Theory,* 37.

17. Sidonie Smith, *Where I'm Bound: Patterns of Slavery and Freedom in Black American Autobiography* (Westport, CT: Greenwood Press, 1974). She analyzed: William W. Brown's *Narrative of the Life of William W. Brown, A Fugitive Slave: Written by Himself*; Frederick Douglass', *My Bondage and my Freedom, Part I—Life as a Slave, Part II—Life as a Freeman*; Booker T. Washington's *Up from Slavery*; Richard Wright's *Black Boy*; Langston Hughes's *The Big Sea*; Malcolm X's *The Autobiography of Malcolm X*; Eldridge Cleaver's *Soul on Ice*; Maya Angelou's *I Know Why the Caged Bird Sings;* Horace Cayton *Long Old Road*; and Claude Brown's *Manchild in the Promised Land.*

18. Smith, *Where I'm Bound,* 47.

19. Smith, *Where I'm Bound,* 46.

20. Smith, *Where I'm Bound,* 112.

21. After Misch's work early in the century, she saw Gusdorf's 1956 essay as critical, as was Francis R. Hart, "Notes for an Anatomy of Modern Autobiography", *New Literary History* 1 (Spring 1970) and James Olney *Metaphors of Self: The Meaning of Autobiography* (Princeton: Princeton University Press, 1970).

22. Smith, *Poetics*, 5.

23. Smith, *Poetics*, 13.

24. Smith, *Poetics*, 46.

25. Smith, *Poetics*, 57–58.

26. Smith, *Poetics*, 176.

27. Sidonie Smith, "Who's Talking/Who's Talking Back: The Subject of Personal Narrative", *Signs* 18 (Winter 1993).

28. In Maxine Hong Kingston's narratives, women were "outlaws"—in fact, she actually assigns herself that possibility, but with the impish trickster approach that characterizes many such experimental works—only if she had lived in China. For another author of this era, Leslie Marmon Silko's Yellow Woman character and her identity as a Laguna Pueblo storyteller brim with challenges to the Euro-American and masculine scripts held sacred until the 1980s.

29. Sidonie Smith, *Subjectivity, Idenitity, and the Body.* (Bloomington, IN: Indiana University Press, 1993), 61. The "master narratives" of the first wave and continuing into the second wave of autobiographical commentary provided no standards by which to judge such texts as those by three modernist writers—Gertrude Stein's *The Autobiography of Alice B. Toklas*, Virginia Woolf's "A sketch of the past", and Zora Neale Hurston's *Dust Tracks on a Road*—as well as more recent works—Annie Dillard's *An American Childhood*, Cherrie Moraga's *Loving in the War Years*, Jo Spence's *Putting Myself in the Picture*, Helene Cixous's essay "The Laugh of the Medusa", Gloria Anzaldua's *Borderlands/La Frontera: The New Mestiza*, and Donna Harraway's essay "A Manifesto for Cyborgs: Science, Technology, and Socialist Feminism in the 1980s".

30. Sidonie Smith, "Performativity, Autobiographical Practice, Resistance", *Auto/biography Studies* 10 (1995), 18.

31. Smith, "Performativity", 18.

32. Smith, "Performativity", 20.

33. Smith, "Performativity", 19–20.

34. Sidonie Smith and Julia Watson, eds., *De/Colonizing the Subject: The Politics of Gender in Women's Autobiography* (Minneapolis: University of Minnesota Press, 1992), *xiv.* The two editors gathered essays from authors in colonial, transitional, and postcolonial geopolitical environments, neither purporting any representative sampling nor intention to discover some universal paradigm. Consistent with Smith's stance in *Poetics*, it was inappropriate to read global texts against Western or Euro-American literary conventions and canons. The texts of these stories become scenes where authors from Kuwait, Australia, France, United States, India, and the Caribbean encountered, maintained, or disrupted a particular place's conventions about gender and identity.

35. Gisela Brinker-Gabler and Sidonie Smith, eds., *Writing New Identities: Gender, Nation, and Immigration in Contemporary Europe* (Minneapolis: University of Minnesota Press, 1996); Jennifer Sabbioni, Kay Schaeffer, and Sidonie Smith, eds., *Indigenous Australian Voices: A Reader* (New Brunswick, NJ: Rutgers University Press, 1998); and Kay Schaeffer and Sidonie Smith, eds., *Human Rights and Narrated Lives: The Ethics of Recognition* (New York: Palgrave Macmillan, 2004).

36. Brinker-Gabler and Smith, *Writing New Identities,* 17.

37. Sabbioni, Schaeffer, and Smith, *Australian Voices, xix.*

38. Schaeffer and Smith, *Human Rights, 2.*

39. Sidonie Smith, *Moving Lives: Twentieth-Century Women's Travel Writing* (Minneapolis: University of Minnesota Press, 2001), *xvii.*

40. Sidonie Smith and Julia Watson, eds., *Getting a Life: Everyday Uses of Auto-biography* (Minneapolis: University of Minnesota Press, 1996), 14, *italics* in original.

41. Smith and Watson, *Getting a Life,* 6–7.

42. Smith and Watson, *Getting a Life,* 14, *italics* in original.

43. Smith and Watson, *Getting a Life,* 15, *italics* in original.

44. Smith and Watson, *Women, Autobiography, Theory,* 42.

45. Maxine Hong Kingston, *The Woman Warrior: Memoirs of a Girlhood Among Ghosts* (New York: Vintage International, 1989).

46. Smith, *Poetics,* 150.

47. Smith, *Poetics,* 152.

48. Smith, *Poetics,* 162. Hong Kingston's story and text reveal developmental outcomes about identity: through "the syncopated rhythm of statement and rebuttal, she answers her mother's vision of things with her own, challenging unremittingly the power of her mother to control interpretations", 163.

49. Suzanne Juhasz, "Towards a Theory of Form in Feminist Autobiography: Kate Millet's *Flying* and *Sita*; Maxine Hong Kingston's *The Woman Warrior,* in *Women's Autobiography: Essays in Criticism,* ed. Estelle C. Jelinek (Bloomington, IN: Indiana University Press, 1980), 231.

50. Cheung wrote how important Hong Kingston's and Alice Walker's identities were as writers (as I interpreted Thomas Merton's dual vocation in Chapter Two). "Their needs for self-expression are obvious; they hang on to sanity by writing; they defend themselves with words; they discover their potential—sound themselves out—through articulation. . . .They work their way from speechlessness to eloquence not only by covering the historical stages women writers have traveled—from suffering patriarchy, to rebelling against its conventions, to creating their own ethos—but also by developing a style that emerges from their respective cultures. King-kok Cheung, "Don't Tell": Imposed Silences in *The Color Purple* and *The Woman Warrior. In Reading Literatures of Asian America,* ed. Shirley Geok-lin Lim (Philadelphia: Temple University Press, 1992), 163.

51. Sidonie Smith, *Poetics,* 150–151.

52. Suzanne Juhasz, "Towards a Theory of Form", 237.

53. Cynthia Sau-Ling Wong, ed., *The Woman Warrior: A Casebook* (New York: Oxford Press, 1999). Cheung put it this way: ". . . the braiding of gender and ethnicity in these texts [i.e., *Woman Warrior* and *China Men*] produces an unusually resonant double-voiced discourse, one that upsets the opposition between women and men, East and West, fable and fact, orality and chirography, talking and listening, (re)vision and history". King-kok Cheung, "Provocative Silence: *The Woman Warrior* and *China Men*", in *Articulate Silences,* ed. King-kok Cheung (Ithaca, NY: Cornell University Press, 1993), 74.

54. Cynthia Sau-Ling Wong, *Casebook,* 30. Critics persisted in attacking Hong Kingston and her publisher for cashing in on the public's interest in ethnic autobiographies, recognizing that first-works of fiction written by female authors were

significantly less marketable. Many of the criticisms continued to come from Chinese authors and reviewers. Wong cited a letter written by Katheryn Fong (1977) in the *Bulletin for Concerned Asian Scholars*. "I read your references to mythical and feudal China as fiction. . . .Your fantasy stories are embellished versions of your mother's embellished versions of stories. As fiction. these stories are creatively written with graphic imagery and emotion. The problem is that non-Chinese are reading your fiction as true accounts of Chinese and Chinese-American history. "(Quoted in Wong, 30–31).

55. Cheung, "Provocative Silence", 80.

56. Smith, *Poetics*, 150–151.

57. Paul John Eakin, *Fictions in Autobiography: Studies in the Art of Self-invention*, (Princeton, NJ: Princeton University Press, 1985), 256.

58. Gary Kubota, "Maxine Hong Kingston: Something Comes from Outside onto the Paper" In *Conversations with Maxine Hong Kingston,* eds. Paul Skenazy and Tera Martin (Jackson, MS: University of Mississippi Press, 1998).

59. Kay Bonetti, "An Interview with Maxine Hong Kingston" in *Conversations with Maxine Hong Kingston*, eds. Paul Skenazy and Tera Martin (Jackson, MS: University of Mississippi Press, 1998).

60. Judy Hoy, "To Be Able To See the Tao" in *Conversations with Maxine Hong Kingston*, eds. Paul Skenazy and Tera Martin (Jackson, MS: University of Mississippi Press, 1998).

61. Paula Rabinowitz, "Eccentric Memories: A Conversation with Maxine Hong Kingston" in *Conversations with Maxine Hong Kingston*, eds. Paul Skenazy and Tera Martin (Jackson, MS: University of Mississippi Press, 1998).

62. Rabinowitz, "Eccentric Memories".

63. Eric Shroeder, "As Truthful as Possible: An Interview with Maxine Hong Kingston" in *Conversations with Maxine Hong Kingston*, eds. Paul Skenazy and Tera Martin (Jackson, MS: University of Mississippi Press, 1998).

64. Andrea Lewis, "Maxine Hong Kingston", *The Progressive* 68 (February 2004).

65. Arturo Islas and Marilyn Yalom, "Interview with Maxine Hong Kingston" in *Conversations with Maxine Hong Kingston*, eds. Paul Skenazy and Tera Martin (Jackson, MS: University of Mississippi Press, 1998), *italics in original*.

66. Bonetti, "Interview with MHK".

67. Rabinowitz, "Eccentric Memories".

68. Jill Ker Conway, ed., *Written by Herself. Autobiographies of American Women: An Anthology* (New York: Vintage, 1992).

Chapter Five

Continuing Anthologies of the Self

PRECIS

In Chapter Two, I described psychobiography as an early application of psychological theory to the analysis of individual lives. Erik Erikson's concept of identity in our psychosocial development was a critically important example of interdisciplinary thought. Building on Erikson's early work in the 1950s, the subfield of personality psychology became a lens to examine diverse life narratives. In this chapter, we will explore the narrative of Dan McAdams's theory and research. He developed a life story model of identity. As individuals continue to mature, we accumulate experiences and express them in stories. Beginning with the early stories we compose as adolescents, our task is to continually remember and edit this ever-expanding and diversifying anthology. His work fused psychological and literary perspectives to understand the construction of self in contemporary American culture.

In this chapter we will discover identity themes in three texts that Smith and Watson categorized as "serial autobiographies". Richard Rodriguez is an essayist and public intellectual who revised his anthology of the self with three autobiographical texts published when he was thirty-eight, forty-eight, and fifty-eight years old. As his memory's episodes accumulated in the public and private spheres of his life, his maps and metaphors shifted and his composition strategies grew in interesting ways that affected the life narrative genre. He composed his three texts as a set of interdependent essays. Collectively, they offer us an opportunity to consider how gender, class, ethnicity, culture, religion, sexual orientation, and geographical place became the complex ingredients for composing twenty-first century stories and constructing the selves that they reveal.

Psychology is not only with us, but swamping us. Its
popularity is so great as to arouse suspicions of superficiality,
or even quackery. It has become almost a fashion, so that
publishers claim that the word psychology on the title page
of a book is sufficient guarantee for a substantial sale.[1]

This observation was made in 1926.

Eighty years later, psychology competes with religion as a source of individuals' values. It became an academic discipline and a powerful explanation
for everyday questions about human behavior in the twentieth century, but its
emphasis on methodology moved researchers away from questions that were
important to the humanities. Psychology still may be "swamping us", but
with one hundred years of scientific pursuits and reflective professional practice, the discipline offers much to our understanding of life narratives and
those who compose them. This is especially true as interdisciplinary scholars
re-discover the qualitative importance of stories in all of our lives.

We first encounter academic subject matter and its problem solving methods in university classrooms. This material becomes popularized with its lifelong consumption by students as relevant to their lives and by the capacity of
professors and practitioners to speak to public audiences. Charles Brewer and
I [2] reviewed the history of academic psychology from the founding of the
American Psychological Association in 1892 to the end of the twentieth century. The 1900–1901 Columbia University catalog showed the introductory
course was taught by an interdisciplinary faculty in a department called "Philosophy, Psychology, Anthropology, and Education". Laboratory courses in
the undergraduate curriculum at the turn of the 20th century included experimental, physiological, abnormal and pathological, and comparative psychology. Specialized seminars were forums for faculty research interests (e.g.,
mental measurement, race psychology, or pedagogical psychology). William
James offered a course called "Psychological Basis of Religious Faith" at
Harvard at the time when he published the *Varieties of Religious Experience*
that we discussed in Chapter Three.

The field continued its centrifugal trajectory with more and more research
topics turned into the teaching curriculum. In the 1950s, colleges and universities taught introductory, social, abnormal, experimental, child, and educational psychology courses most often. Beginning in the 1970s, psychology
experienced tremendous growth in its enrollments. Today, more than one mil-
lion undergraduates take Introductory Psychology as part of their general education requirements every year. Psychology has become the most popular
disciplinary degree in the humanities, social sciences, and sciences, graduating 80,000 plus baccalaureates every year.

Baron Perlman and Lee McCann captured a comprehensive snapshot of the field at the end of the century, sampling catalogs, nationally, from 2-year and baccalaureate colleges, comprehensive universities, and doctoral universities. "Cognitive, biological, human growth/development, adult development/ gerontology, and psychology of women moved into the Top 30." [3] A three-decade pattern of the most frequently offered undergraduate courses continued: introductory, abnormal, social, and personality psychology. Course titles reflected twentieth century psychology's subfields; closer scrutiny of course content reveals the comings and goings of topics deemed important and the methods used to build the knowledge base of this very popular discipline.

This evolution of ideas within American psychology is characterized in introductory textbooks as an array of perspectives or ways of seeing human behavior through lenses that integrate theory, research methods, and applications. In the first half of the twentieth century, Freud's psychoanalytic perspective was predominant in psychotherapy practice and in scholarly and popular interpretations of society and culture. Alfred Adler, Anna Freud, Erich Fromm, Karen Horney, Carl Jung, and Harry Stack Sullivan offered psychodynamic understandings of the self and its problems. Beginning in the 1950s, the humanistic perspective, exemplified in the writings of Abraham Maslow and the clinical theory and applications of Carl Rogers, offered an optimistic, alternative view of human nature and its potential. Popular jargon adopted from psychology shifted from "excavating a person's past" and their "defense mechanisms" to the benefits of becoming "self-actualized" and offering one's children "unconditional positive regard". The psychoanalytical perspective inspired archaeological metaphors to capture human dilemmas; the humanistic perspective used astronomical, even astrological ones. Self-help and parenting guides flew off bookstore shelves.

Beginning in the 1960s, behavioral and cognitive psychology perspectives were transplanted from their research laboratory origins and applied to clinical diagnoses and treatments. Phobias were treated using scientifically established behavioral methods, and the results verified via single subject case studies. In a similar way, cognitive perspectives were applied to understanding depression; the work of psychotherapy required individuals to re-think their attributions about adversity, not to invest in lengthy examinations of early childhood traumas or to fret about their low self-esteem.

The neuropsychology perspective emerged in the 1970s and grounded abnormal psychology in brain and behavior research. The consequences were beneficial advances in health psychology and behavioral medicine, but becoming a Prozac Nation was judged in the discipline and by the general public less positively. In the 1970s also, feminist and sociocultural perspectives focused our attentions on different identity composites derived from the gender, ethnicity, class, religion, and sexual orientation characteristics of individuals living in a more tolerant and pluralistic society.

The cumulative result of all these perspectives and their direct applications to human experience moved psychology away from its dichotomous conceptualizations of human behavior: male versus female, white versus "other", abnormal versus normal, nature versus nurture. Individual differences were expected and then respected by the discipline's scientists and practitioners. The educated reading public who had taken introductory psychology courses as undergraduates grew more facile with the terms and explanations of complex human behavior provided by this discipline. From *Time* magazine to movie thrillers to television talk shows, psychology became a sub-text for every script about human interactions. Today, psychological ideas and methods derive from multiple interdisciplinary connections within the sciences, and across the social sciences, humanities, and the arts. As the twenty-first century began, it became increasingly apparent that to fully understand individuals and their differences, complex interdisciplinary models were needed.

PERSONALITY PSYCHOLOGY

McAdams [4] characterized his subfield as a dissident in the scientific aspirations of psychology. By studying the whole person, addressing the problem of motivation and its often unobservable derivatives, and investigating what makes for differences versus common denominators among people, personality psychology tackled topics that required innovative methods for gathering data. Depending on one's epistemological stance about what is scientific knowledge and how we acquire it, personality could be characterized as the most comprehensive or the most superficial of subfields. A blue ribbon panel of experts in the 1950s recommended either Personality Psychology or History of Psychology as the best capstone course for undergraduate students because of their integrative value for study in the major field. Gordon Allport's humanistic alternative to psychoanalysis and behaviorism in studying individuals and Henry Murray's efforts to plumb the complexities of individuals' subjective lives recognized the drama in most people's stories.

After 1950, priorities in this sub-field shifted; specialization prevailed and personality research turned to the rigorous definition of constructs and their measurement. In his conceptual history, McAdams linked the popularity of particular constructs to the social historical context in which they emerged. The study of "authoritarianism", for example, was an antidote to the horrific experiences of World War II. "Need for achievement" was manifested by men in grey flannel suits employed in the expanding corporate ethos of the post-war period. This was an age of ubiquitous "anxiety", concomitant with the Cold War nuclear peril. Measuring such personality constructs required reductionistic strategies; the goal was to predict behavior more than to understand its complexities and conflicted nature. As a result, the major debates in personality psychology centered on two positions: measurable dispositional traits that could be generalized versus explaining human behavior as dictated by the variability of situational determinants. In 1971, Rae Carlson wrote: "Where is the person in personality research?" mourning the loss of the Allport and Murray tradition of inquiry.

> Personality psychology would seem to be paying an exorbitant price
> in potential knowledge for the security afforded by preserving norms
> of convenience and methodological orthodoxy. Must these important,
> unanswered questions be left to literature and psychiatry? [5]

Advances in cognitive psychology prompted the inclusion of its dimensions in statements about individuals and their remembered histories, their present responses, and their future goals, aspirations, and intentions.

The 1980s and 1990s brought new life and new methods to personality psychology. Individual differences, across the lifespan and in multicultural and international settings, were mapped with a taxonomy of five, empirically validated traits: emotional stability, extraversion, openness, agreeableness, and conscientiousness. Studies of motivation incorporated cognitive and biological factors. Finally, the study of the whole person was revived by intersecting cognitive developmental psychology and personality psychology to understand how the "self" emerges, grows, changes, and maintains consistency.

DAN MCADAMS AND THE LIFE STORY MODEL OF IDENTITY

In *Power, Intimacy, and the Life Story*, McAdams introduced his unique point of view as

> . . .an *exploration* in personality. It ventures into the unmapped
> continent of human identity with a topographical hunch. The hunch is
> that the landscape takes the form of story. More accurately (and this is
> where the metaphor of geography breaks down), the hunch is that we—
> as scientists, therapists, and human beings—can come to comprehend
> the region of human identity *as if* it were laid out as a story. The "as if"
> reminds us that scientific models and theories are, by necessity, *fictions*,
> we impose upon experience in order to render it more sensible; in order to

transform the buzzing, blooming confusion of our confrontation with the cosmos into a relatively simple picture, a laconic statement, and an elegant framework.[6]

Scientists ask "big questions—questions about love, power, identity, adaptation—and can design reasonable methodologies and measurement techniques for examining these questions in disciplined empirical ways."[7] In the early 1980s, McAdams and his students at Loyola University and Northwestern University integrated two ways of understanding the world as the paradigmatic mode and the narrative mode. Paradigms are the bread and butter of psychological science; they are parsimonious, reasoned, empirical observations that lead to new questions and greater predictability in human behavior. Narratives mean more than the words actually say, prompting listeners' reflections and responses and new, often unpredictable stories. McAdams situated his explorations as a postmodern project. His writings are replete with literary, historical, and spiritual references. The overarching goal of his lifework was stated in his very first book:

> . . .elaborate and illustrate a life-story model of identity by integrating
> a number of diverse theories and concepts in the social sciences and
> humanities and by describing and analyzing personological data
> collected from college students and men and women at midlife.[8]

There are three distinct threads in this earliest work that appear again and again. First, McAdams was grounded in the empirical and theoretical tradition of personality research taught by Harvard faculty like Henry Murray, Gordon Allport, David McClelland, and Robert White. McClelland asserted two agendas for a scientific discipline of personality psychology: to understand lives and to predict behavior. McAdams's focus on power and intimacy motives in his first book was in this tradition. Second, he drew deeply from Erik Erikson's groundbreaking theory of psychosocial development, with its understandings of identity and generativity. Third, McAdams was inspired by existential writers like Samuel Beckett, T.S. Eliot, Robert Langenbaum, Robert Jay Lifton, and Jean Paul Sartre. Identity for them was not only a psychological but a spiritual problem and literature its best medium for expression. McAdams used Northrop Frye's mythic archetypes as labels for his identity stories and their characters or imagoes.[9] The weaving together of these three threads inspired his model, with identity development as central, but constructed via a continuing narrative of a life-story that has unity and purpose. Twenty years later, in his most recent work, he still described its thematic focus as a: "psycho-cultural-literary portrait of the redemptive self."[10]

In the following four sections, organized chronologically, we will evaluate how McAdams's model evolved with continuing empirical research and led to his integration of the values and methods of multiple disciplinary perspectives.

Making Stories

Fusing Murray's proposition that the history of the organism *is* the organism with Erikson's epigenetic understanding of identity, McAdams proposed:

> . . .the main thesis of my life story model of identity is that
> a person defines him- or herself by constructing an autobiographical
> *story* of the self, complete with setting, scene, character, plot, and
> theme (McAdams, 1985, 1987). The story is the person's *identity*
> (Erikson, 1959). The story provides the person with a sense of unity
> and purpose in life—a sense that one is a whole being moving
> forward in a particular direction. From the standpoint of personal
> identity, therefore, the person is both historian and history—a storyteller
> who creates the self in the telling. . .[11]

He asserted that identity has markers available for study across the entire lifespan, before and after one's adolescence. One task of infancy is to form attachment bonds with responsible adults. Successful attachment experiences can be read in the narrative tone of someone's story: optimistic stories with romance and comedy themes reflect positive attachments whereas pessimistic stories of tragedy and irony reflect negative experiences. During early childhood, youngsters listen to stories and develop images to use in their later constructions. These compositions become more complex during elementary school years as they learn that stories also have intentions, motives, and themes. In adolescence, the person establishes an ideology or ethic of care or justice, translated into the settings of a story, replete with nuclear episodes or scenes. With the increased cognitive maturity that prompts their reflections about ideology, adolescents now turn childhood tales into myths, also recognizing that there are sacred stories to draw on and that heroes and heroines suffer.

McAdams synthesized psychologist Jerome Bruner's notion that our "mythologically instructed community provides its members with a library of scripts"[12] with which to compare and contrast one's emerging story, and Jean-Paul Sartre's philosophical perspective that the "person's past is reconstructed within the current demand of the myth."[13] The young adult discovers that personality contains many characters or imagoes, sometimes in harmony with one another but more often in conflict. Exploring who I want to be(come) and developing a narrative is the task of adulthood—to resolve differences until a

generativity script emerges and the individual orients to endings and the meanings of the story for others, not just the primary agenda of self-definition.

> . . .the life story of a middle-aged man or woman is likely
> to be more philosophical, ironic, and sculpted than the hot-from-
> the-fire narrative produced in early adulthood. The story is likely
> to place greater emphasis on themes of loss and separation and to
> incorporate a greater variety of self-relevant material suggestive of
> contrasexual and other previously suppressed or unarticulated aspects
> of the self. . . . If identity is an integrative life narrative providing the
> person with a sense of unity and purpose in life, then it is probably in
> mid-life that the adult becomes especially concerned about how the
> story is going to end. One's sense of wholeness and direction in life
> is teleologically anchored.[14]

Drawing on gerontology research from the 1970s and 1980s, McAdams understood middle and later adulthood as the time for review of one's story, reflection on the processes of its construction, and resolving what Erikson out-
lined as the final two conflicts of generativity versus stagnation and ego
integrity versus despair.

In his 1991 "Self and Story" article, he intersected psychological science
with a literary understanding of the nature of story. Stories have grammars;
rules for their construction and for their evaluation by others begin in adolescence. Stories have settings. Characters are described in place and time.
Episodes combine to create a plot structure. Events have sequences of initiating action, internal and external responses by the main character, consequences from the responses leading to more reactions and then a new cycle
of initiating actions by the key players in the story. Children and adults learn
these rules and find stories easier to remember if they have a predictable
canonical form. The composition of one's autobiography and the storytelling
that is required of the individual in the psychotherapy relationship or in personality research are examples of the construction of self through stories.
McAdams grounded the function of stories in constructing a self, thus:

> We *choose* in the *present* to remember the past in a certain way. In the
> making of the self, there is no objective bedrock of the past from which
> to fashion the myth. The past is malleable, changing, ever synthesized
> and re-synthesized by present life choices. . .History and the self are not
> total fabrications of the imagination; nor are they pure discoveries of
> fact. The self as story is *both* "made" and "found out". . .[15]

Advances from 1980 to 2000 in cognitive psychology research in memory,
specifically on the topic of autobiographical memory, would add considerable

scientific support to these well-turned phrases. Recall the very early understandings of this recapturing of memory phenomenon that I described in Chapter One from Book X of Saint Augustine's *The Confessions*, composed a mere 1500 years earlier, and interpreted so insightfully by James Olney in 1998.

McAdams articulated the goals of his life-story model of identity using Erikson's optimistic statement from *Young Man Luther*.

> To be adult means among other things to see one's life in continuing perspective, both in retrospect, and prospect. By accepting some definition as to who he is, usually on the basis of a function of an economy, a place in the sequence of generations, and a status in the structure of society, the adult is able to selectively reconstruct his past in such a way that, step for step, it seems to have planned him, or better, he seems to have planned it. In this sense, psychologically, we *do* choose our parents, our family history, and the history of our kings, heroes, and gods. By making them our own, we maneuver ourselves into the inner position of proprietors, of creators.[16]

The texts for his 1990s research program were elicited either from a structured interview or as a written response to a protocol asking about: life chapters, eight defining ("nuclear") episodes (peak experience, nadir experience, turning point, earliest memory, childhood memory, adolescent memory, adult memory, and any other important memory), four significant people, imagined future script, identification of predicted stresses and problems, definition of a personal ideology, and an overall life theme as currently understood. McAdams and his students examined the stories of undergraduates and adults in the community on these dimensions.

Paradigms versus Narratives for the Storied Self

Psychologists in the 1990s returned to the theory of traits espoused decades earlier by Gordon Allport. The contemporary version of this theory was that across many cultures, people described themselves and others in ways that were statistically summarized as "The Big Five" personality factors, discussed earlier in this chapter. By asking precise questions organized around these five factors, the personality researcher discovered stable, heritable, multicultural, and related characteristics about a person. Trait theorists emphasized biologically influenced dispositions (e.g., extraversion versus introversion) to behave in certain ways in the present, not the underlying antecedents or the variable situations that elicit these responses. As the most active research agenda in personality in the 1990s, other scholars necessarily compared and contrasted their perspectives with "The Big Five's" assumptions and impressive findings.

In a cluster of articles and chapters published from 1992 to 1996, McAdams addressed trait research. Traits offered lists of specific characteristics, but they were not sufficient for understanding complex persons. His journal article titles during this period shrewdly captured such comparisons: "A psychology of the stranger" or "What do we know when we know a person?" In the latter, he opened with an anecdote about a typical conversation that might take place between individuals at a neighborhood house party and then the debriefing about what they observed and interpreted. He summarized his evolving perspective on personality research thus:

> Personality traits, like those included within the Big Five taxonomy,
> reside at Level I of personality description and provide a general,
> comparative, and nonconditional dispositional signature for the person.
> Level II subsumes tasks, goals, projects, tactics, defenses, values and
> other developmental, motivational, and/or strategic concerns that
> contextualize a person's life in time, place, and role. Speaking directly
> to the modern problem of reflexively creating a unified and purposeful
> configuration of the Me, life stories reside at the third level of personality,
> as internalized integrative narrations of the personal past, present, and
> future. It is mainly through the psychosocial construction of life stories
> that modern adults create identity. . .[17]

Returning to William James's writings, he advocated a phenomenological understanding of individual lives and stories. The "I" is the verb of human experience; the "me" is its product developed over time, circumstances, and diverse experiences. Before late adolescence and adulthood, the "me" is a bundle of characteristics of Level I and Level II quality. After adolescence,

> The challenge of identity demands that the modern adult construct a
> "telling" of the self. . . . *A life story is an internalized and evolving*
> *narrative of the self that incorporates the reconstructed past, perceived*
> *present, and anticipated future*. . .within the modern world, the adult
> selfing process seems to seek out opportunities for integrating different autobiographical accounts into a narrated whole, aiming to construct a
> Me that exhibits a modicum of unity, coherence, and purpose.[18]

We can evaluate texts by asking five questions:

What is the structure and content of a life story?
What function does a life story have?
How does a life story develop over time?
What kinds of individually different life stories are there?
In mental health terms, what is a good life story?

A life story is a psychosocial construction that integrates the self. It educates and socializes others, manifests diversity, and demonstrates individuals' continuing pursuit of coherence, openness, reconciliation, and generativity. Having articulated for personality research audiences "what this framework can and cannot do"[19] and about "narrating the self into adulthood,"[20] McAdams situated his model within the new scholarship on narrative theory. He had to address postmodern understandings of the self that divided psychologists and cut across disciplinary boundaries.

Postmodern perspectives challenged Romantic and modernist assumptions. The search for unity and purpose amid constant change revealed the plight of Kenneth Gergen's "multiphrenic" individuals.[21] Edward Sampson[22] wrote about how persons in technologically complex and global environments became sites for unpredictable forces, disparate voices, and constantly changing social constructions. McAdams adroitly summarized these challenges to the modern self and the prevailing psychological paradigm thus: "The postmodern person seems to reside amid the stories that surround and define him or her on a moment by moment basis."[23]

Psychologists hold conflicted positions about the study of individual human lives, narrative theory, and qualitative forms of inquiry. Incorporating postmodern definitions remains difficult for mainstream scientific researchers. As I described in Chapter Four, humanities scholars, especially in literature and the arts, feel more kinship with these perspectives. McAdams attempted a preliminary integration in "The case for unity in the (post)modern self: A modest proposal". He began with Gergen's analysis in *The Saturated Self.*

> The postmodern condition generally is marked by a plurality of voices
> vying for the right to reality — to be accepted as legitimate expressions
> of the true and the good. . . .Under postmodern conditions, persons exist
> in a state of conscious construction and reconstruction; it is a world where any-
> thing goes that can be negotiated. Each reality of self gives way to
> reflexive questioning, irony, and ultimately the playful probing of yet
> another reality. The center fails to hold.[24]

In the final analysis, however, McAdams characterized a postmodern perspective as one that produces ambivalence and uncertainty, invoking James's statement in behalf of unity: "I am often confronted by the necessity of standing by one of my empirical selves and relinquishing the rest" and requires what James labeled the "selective industry of the mind".[25] He reiterated his life-story model of identity and the empirical support generated for the structure, content, and function of life stories as well as their significant relationships with aspects of the adult self.

A "narrative psychology of personality" for the 21st century can be characterized by seven critically important principles: selfhood is storied; life stories organize disparate experience into integrated wholes; life stories are cultural texts; people tailor their life stories for particular audiences; a person tells many stories, and those stories change over time; some stories are better than others; and the sharing of stories builds intimacy and community. He targeted three areas of primary research concern: personality coherence; personality change; and identifying different types of stories. McAdams remained true to his "topographical hunch" first articulated in his 1985 text, but now, narrative had truly become his "root metaphor" and his agenda remained—to widen that belief among his colleagues.[26]

I will review his work from 2000 to 2005 in the next section.

Post-Millennial Research

Traits and Stories

Within the personality psychology research community, the scientific construct of traits remains of paramount importance. McAdams and his colleagues at Northwestern University continued their efforts to bridge the findings from quantitative paradigms and those from empirical, but qualitative narratives. In "Traits and stories,"[27] they reported the results of a complex, two-study project with community adults and college students. Participants responded to a measure of the Big 5 personality traits and then composed brief narratives of ten life story scenes. The scenes came from McAdams's earlier research protocol in *Stories We Live By*. The trait of "Openness to Experience" was associated with life narrative complexity. The epiphanies and transformations that come with psychological or spiritual turning points were vivid in these individuals' stories. The trait of "Agreeableness", especially in the adult group, was linked to recalling episodes of love, friendship, caring and helping others. Contrary to the researchers' expectations, the "Extraversion" trait was not associated with a positive narrative tone. As he proposed ten years earlier, McAdams and his associates concluded that personality remains a complex, multi-level phenomenon, but empirical support was demonstrated for relationships between a broad description of a personality captured by traits and a more personal storied level.

In "A New Big Five: Fundamental Principles for an Integrative Science of Personality", McAdams and Jennifer Pals[28] proposed an organizing schema, synthesizing his paradigmatic and narrative projects over a twenty-year period. First, lives are individual variations on a more general evolutionary design pattern. Second, dispositional traits (e.g., "Openness to Experience", "Extraversion") are meaningful descriptors at this level, offering relatively stable and multiculturally effective ways to capture an individual's observable psychological features. Third, characteristic adaptations (e.g., goals, values, coping strategies) spotlight how individuals confront the challenges of everyday life, for better and for worse. Fourth, integrative life stories or personal narratives are psychosocial constructions that evolve as we continually remember our pasts and imagine our futures. Narrative identity is a measure of how we keep the story going. Fifth, culture delimits how we express our traits. It influences the timing and the content of our adaptation strategies. Moreover, culture provides an array of story forms for us to use, as well as cueing us on how to tell those stories, and to live them authentically.

How does this conceptual model of personality psychology help us to interpret life narratives as literary texts? The schema can be translated into the language of literary criticism in the following ways that are consistent with the anthology of stories we examined in the four previous chapters. We can make comparisons between texts by different authors because the dispositional traits used to describe an individual are akin to the broad American virtues touted by early literary scholars as the common denominators of exemplary lives. The schema's characteristic adaptations are compatible with the categorical labels that Smith and Watson used to inventory life narratives—ethnic or immigrant responses to the American experience, coping strategies recounted by slaves or abuse survivors, for example. The idiosyncratic qualities of the adaptations illuminate the narrative; the common denominators of the problem for a large population of readers generate the audience. When authors first consider how to capture their lives in a text, they can sample from "a menu of stories for the life course,"[29] and our cultures offer us "canonical narrative forms out of which people make meaning of their lives."[30] The intersections between psychology and literature were captured in McAdams's definition of integrative life narrative: "Internalized and evolving life stories that reconstruct the past and imagine the future to provide the person's life with identity (unity, purpose, meaning). Individual differences in life stories can be seen with respect to characteristic images, tones, themes, plots, and endings".[31]

Narratives and the Good Life

McAdams remained committed to Erikson's vision (i.e., hope) for identity and its integrative capacity across the lifespan. He synthesized cognitive, emotional, and behavioral aspects of development into the construction of an identity narrative, hypothesizing that different types of people worked on different aspects of their story at different times of their lives. The mid-life period of adulthood and generativity remained a fertile area for empirical study. McAdams and his colleagues studied individuals rated high in generativity concerns for the types and qualities of their constructed stories, and the relationship of story to other personality characteristics and overall mental health and life satisfaction.

After the millennium, a new set of voices emerged in the discipline to examine what they called "positive psychology". Since World War II, scientifically-based clinical practice devoted its efforts to precise definitions of abnormal behavior and the evaluation of psychotherapy treatment effectiveness. One of its most respected standard bearers, Martin Seligman, had an epiphany, and used his American Psychological Association presidential term to initiate basic research and applied projects on definitions of health, virtue, optimism, and the causes and effects of happiness in American life. His influence and ingenuity infiltrated many of the subfields of psychology, as he welcomed the traditions and wisdom of the humanities back to scientific endeavors. McAdams's scholarly work contributed to this new effort as well.

With Jack Bauer, he published the results of four projects on the elements of personal growth and the good life, with narrative theory as a distinguishing methodological feature.[32] The authors linked gratitude, one of the hallmark virtues in Seligman's approach to the well-adapted life, to its religious roots and explicated its importance in human development, successful midlife transitions, and as a characteristic of remembered episodes in the lives of generative adults. Using qualitative analytical methods of people's stories revealed more of the subtle, intentional features of personality development and growth, particularly in moments of career and religious transition. Finally, the authors summarized a good life and both the achievement of happiness and the capacity to extract rich meanings of how it was accomplished. Vibrant goals for the future and the non-defensive interpretation of past memories were critical features in adults' report of present-day happiness. A critical finding for our understanding of authors' composition strategies was that narratives may explain mature and happy people's lives, but they require constant editing to keep them genuine and enriching. The American Psychological Association enhanced the understanding and acceptance of narrative research with its publication of a series for which McAdams was one of the three editors.[33]

Post-Modern Self

The connections to literature and the humanities can be most clearly illuminated when McAdams addresses the challenges of post-modernism. Recall how perilous this effort could be, that its tenets had been labeled as "anthrax of the intellect" by one author in an *American Psychologist* comment on a Kenneth Gergen article.

Life stories are based on biographical facts, but they go considerably beyond the facts as people selectively appropriate aspects of their experience and imaginatively construe both past and future to construct stories that make sense to them and to their audiences, that vivify and integrate life and make it more or less meaningful. Life stories are psychosocial constructions, coauthored by the person himself or herself and the cultural context within which that person's life is embedded and given meaning. As such, individual life stories reflect cultural values and norms, including assumptions about gender, race, and class. Life stories are intelligible within a particular cultural frame, and yet they also differentiate one person from the next.[34]

McAdams's life-story model of identity was continually refined by other scholars' findings about how self-understanding emerged and became more complex, whether and how one's personality structures changed and how neurological and cognitive structures affected autobiographical memory. Early on, he recognized, however, that the paradigmatic mode of knowing the world and its peoples was not enough to understand complex lives. Thus, he embraced the narrative mode and fashioned a life-story model of identity to counter-balance the limits of his scientific community's analyses and interpretations. When Gergen and others challenged this worldview with their postmodern critique, the reader can almost feel McAdams's foundations being shaken.

The wild mix of cultural narratives and discourses determines a person's identity from one moment to the next. Each moment of discourse brings with it a new expression of the self. Over time, expressions are collected and patched together into a montage-like text whose development from one moment to the next can never be predicted.[35]

To work in a world where human behavior "can never be predicted" is a daunting prospect for any scientific psychologist.

When Gergen wrote "the center fails to hold," what he meant (among other things) was that (a) the subjective "I" (human agency) is no longer central to human life and can no longer hold together and appropriate subjective experience as its own, and (b) the objective "me" (the self-concept) can no longer be held together because, as an indeterminate text, it is changing from one moment to the next. . . .With respect to life stories, then, postmodern approaches suggest that there is not one integrative narrative to be found in any given life but, rather, a multiplicity of narratives.[36]

McAdams accommodated the postmodern critique by recognizing that multiplicity may be consistent with emerging research in many subfields of psychology. With a brilliant metaphor, he continued to affirm his belief in the person's pursuit of integration through identity stories: "People carry with them and bring into conversation a wide range of self-stories, and these stories are nested in larger and overlapping stories, creating ultimately a kind of *anthology of the self*".[37] The center can hold if individuals takes their responsibility seriously to be at least good editors of their many stories, a task akin to James's self-assigned intellectual problem solving. Individual lives and social communities will be enhanced by such making of meanings.

"From a life-story standpoint, lives are like evolving narrated texts, known and read as stories, framed through discourse, told in culture, and couched within a particular historical moment. . ."[38] Like Augustine, Gusdorf, and Olney, McAdams recognized that the construction and then the editing of a life story requires the selection of episodes and then the interpretation of their meanings. Cognitive neuroscience research on autobiographical memory further supports his assertion that this process is not distortion. Self-defining memories are, indeed, matters of choice, the fruits of developmental changes and adaptations. His psychological perspective can support not only Gusdorf's notions about autobiography as a second reading of experience, but Smith and other feminist scholars' commentaries that life narrative texts are self-conscious performances, occasions to "talk back", "autobiographical pacts" with defined and undefined audiences. "Human intentionality is at the heart of narrative. . ."[39] In post-millennial America, McAdams interpreted the theme of redemption to be at the heart of his respondents' stories. This theme emerged in living color in most narratives composed for popular consumption as well.

For an anthology on self-construction written by psychologists, McAdams wrote an autobiographical reflection in 2005: "A Psychologist without a Country or Living Two Lives in the Same Story" [40] His comments serve as an apt conclusion to my review of his work.

> Let me confess: I live a double life, split between empiricism and
> hermeneutics. I do so publicly with little shame but more than a little
> awkwardness. . . .The truth is this: I would love to live as a full-fledged
> patriot for both countries, loyal to their respective creeds and constitutions.
> But my dual citizenship never seems to achieve the comfortable fit
> for which I long. Nonetheless, my double life is not without its rewards.
> And I have even managed to make a story out of it.[41]

McAdams is a researcher, and with the assistance of successive generations of his graduate students, has become a co-author of his respondents' life story, told within the protocols and parameters of psychological science. Listening to his autobiographical reflection, I was reminded of our explorations of collaborative autobiographical works in Chapter Three. Other scientists may, like John Neihardt, argue that their agendas do not intrude on the telling of the story or its final print version. Some scientists, more like Alex Haley, strive to be faithful scribes of a powerful story, then compose epilogue discussions in which their personal interpretations are revealed. McAdams drew the parallel between poring over the stories of his respondents with the same excitement and appreciation as he read Dostoevsky and Kierkegaard. The efficacy of using his lenses to study this literary genre can be summarized by this following insight.

> Not only were life stories constructed through social interaction, as I acknowledged from the get-go, but they were also performed with respect to particular audiences, told with respect to certain discursive aims and traditions, and tailored for short-term strategic ends. Not only did stories integrate lives and provide some semblance of unity and purpose, as I argued in my first book, but they could also disrupt lives, express discontinuity and incoherence, contradict themselves and confuse their audiences, and fulfill a wide range of other functions—psychological, social, economic, and political. . . .[42]

Few, if any, other psychologists could offer a more systematic and appreciative framework within which to evaluate a serial autobiography—a continuing anthology of the self. Using McAdams's compass, we can now map the controversial, lyrical, and always thought-provoking essays from the life terrain of Richard Rodriguez.

ASSESSING RICHARD RODRIGUEZ

Biographical Notes

Richard Rodriguez was born in San Francisco on July 31, 1944. His father, Leopoldo, was a dental technician, and his mother, Victoria Moran, a clerk typist. Both parents emigrated from Mexico, met, and married in the United States. Rodriguez described his father as melancholic and Mexican by temperament, although he hated that country after his experiences with violence during the revolution. In contrast, his Mexican-loving mother always was more optimistic and Californian-American. The family moved to Sacramento when he was three for his asthmatic older brother's health; the family then moved from house to bigger house, or as he said once, up the socioeconomic ladder. When Richard began first grade at Sacred Heart Catholic School, his English vocabulary was about fifty words. The Irish nuns who taught him addressed his reticence in the classroom, then made a home visit and chided his parents for speaking Spanish. They stopped. Language—old family and newly schooled, private and public discourse—became a preoccupation. He understands spoken Spanish, but does not speak it.

Rodriguez graduated from Christian Brothers High School and completed his B.A. in English at Stanford University in 1967. He received an M.A. in religious studies from Columbia University (taking most of his courses at Union Theological Seminary) in 1969, and pursued doctoral studies in English Renaissance literature at the University of California at Berkeley from 1969 to 1972, and again from 1974 to 1975. He was a Fulbright Fellow at the Warburg Institute in London, from 1972 to 1973, and received a National Endowment for the Humanities Fellowship. He decided not to finish doctoral studies and not to pursue an academic career. The personal choices and public stances he took during this time were a source of constant turmoil— about the academic profession and study of literature, Affirmative Action policies in higher education, bilingual education in primary schools, and the tensions between his passion for writing and his anxiety about language. He took menial jobs to support himself while writing, and published three critically reviewed essays between 1974 and 1980: "Going Home Again: The New American Scholarship Boy", "The Achievement of Desire: Personal Reflections on Learning 'Basics'", and "Aria: A Memoir of a Bilingual Childhood", and wove these pieces into his first book-length work. *Hunger of Memory: The Education of Richard Rodriguez. An Autobiography* [43] was rejected by eight publishers until a small Boston house, Godine, accepted it and the memoir ended up being reviewed on the front pages of the *Los Angeles Times* and the *New York Times*.

Rodriguez moved to Los Angeles after the success of *Hunger of Memory* and a celebrity status it brought him. His companions were intellectuals and writers who were thriving in Hollywood's environment doing screenplays, transforming their characters and plots into television sitcoms. Rodriguez encountered much loneliness amidst the garish wealth and lifestyle of what many Americans considered to be the beautiful people. He moved to San Francisco to live more privately, but also became more publicly recognized by virtue of his televised essays.

In 1982, Rodriguez received the Christopher Award for autobiography, a gold medal from the Commonwealth Club, and the Anisfield-Wolfe Award for Race Relations. He won an Emmy Award for a historical piece in 1992, "Pearl Harbor Anniversary." *Days of Obligation: An Argument with My Mexican Father* [44] was a finalist for the Pulitzer Prize in 1993. He received the George Foster Peabody Award for his essays on the PBS *MacNeil-Lehrer NewsHour*, with ninety pieces televised between 1997 and 2005. He received the Frankel Award from the National Endowment for the Humanities and the International Journalism Award from the World Affairs Council of California.

After "The New American Scholarship Boy" in the *American Scholar* in 1974, his work appeared in national publications with a wide readership including: *American Enterprise, Forbes, Harper's, Mother Jones, New Republic, The Chronicle of Higher Education, The Los Angeles Times, The New York Times, The Wall Street Journal, Time, and U.S. News and World Report.* He is an editor for the Pacific News Service and remains in constant demand as a guest speaker for educational, community, and political forums around the globe, using television, print journalism, and lectures as his public intellectual's podium-canvas.

In elementary school, Richard lugged ten books at a time home from the public library. He read William Saroyan who wrote about Fresno and California's Central Valley, and, years later, he read a Joan Didion essay about disappearing Sacramento. Like Merton, he discovered personal geography was a topic worth examining, and became a writer when he realized that he had something to say. With *Hunger of Memory*, he found a national popular audience while steadfastly remaining anchored in the literary tradition's composition values.

Rodriguez does not consider his books to be sociological. Unlike the social sciences, literature breaks down categories, it does not construct them. When he goes into a bookstore and finds them clumped with "gay and lesbian writers" or "Latino writers", he feels the urge to scoop them up and restack them on the "opera" or "performing arts" shelves. Echoing McAdams's autobiographical dilemma about finding meaning via paradigms versus narratives, Rodriguez characterized social science research as trying to discover the common denominators of a phenomenon via careful examination of two hundred lives and then drawing conclusions about central tendencies. In contrast, a writer captures a single character and life challenges—let's say how a Mexican American young man feels anxious about his body. Some in the culture with which the author or character is identified will say: "That does not represent us. It is not how our people teach our young men." Rodriguez finds authors most powerful when their descriptions of that Mexican American boy can touch the mind and the heart of a White kid living in rural Mississippi or a Black kid in urban Harlem. They can identify with that same anxiety and how it distances them from their peers; classification and predictability by pigmentation are less salient.

Judith Ortiz Cofer, author of *The Latin Deli*, was criticized because she was not more "political" in her writing, for not being more overtly caustic about gender and ethnic prejudices. She replied that she was a storyteller, not a sociologist and not a political activist. Stories touch the imagination. Those told by her grandmother continued to offer her inspiration and sustenance. AND with them, she unsettles our stereotypes about women, especially those who share her cultural heritage. Leslie Marmon Silko made the same observations about her oral traditions and how she communicated her values by translating those traditions into her writing. Rodriguez took a similar position as Maxine Hong Kingston. Writers are neither representative of their ethnic communities nor should they be identified as exemplars of how to live. He used the case of Virginia Woolf to make his point. It would be problematic to view as exemplary how she led and ended her life. Yet, he found in her syntax and in her sentences, written during some of her deepest depressions, much to emulate and cherish for his own work.

At the end of his graduate career, Rodriguez began reading D.H. Lawrence and discovered in that English writer a voice that spoke to him. There was passion. There was sexual ambiguity. There was the appeal of an author who came from a family of one class trying to get by and to succeed by using the language of another class. Rodriguez described the gardener Meilers' and Lady Chatterley's solution as a bilingual one—bridging the gap of cultural class as well as the private-public prohibitions for talking about intimate sexuality. He read Vladimir Nabokov and marveled at his capacity to write in four languages—Russian, German, French, and then American English. More recently, he reads brown-skinned writers who compose in the English language, like Salman Rushdie and V.S. Naipaul. Octavio Paz greatly admired *Days of Obligation*; Rodriguez loved his poetry and prose and considered him a great teacher, acknowledging Paz's recognition of him as his blessing from Mexico. In *Brown,* he celebrated James Baldwin's style and how important his essays were to learning his craft.

Hunger of Memory exorcised the demons of *The Education of Richard Rodriguez*. He described himself as no longer angry after writing that book. In *Days of Obligation,* Rodriguez turned his attention to the landscape of California and the topographies of being Mexican and Indian. Anger changed to melancholic reflection. He published *Brown: The Last Discovery of America* [45] in 2002, describing it as the final book in his autobiographical trilogy on American public life. The third installment is laced with paradox, a creative synthesis of the argumentation used in his journalistic essays and the lyrical style of his memoirs. Globalization, religious pluralism, discoveries of new compasses for political landscapes and their rocky terrains, the anxious vulnerability of the American people after 911—these have been the continuing themes of his PBS *NewsHour* essays before and after the millennium changed. In *Brown,* Rodriguez filled in the gaps of his autobiographical narrative that he chose not to disclose in the two prior books. The result was what he described as a Crayola box left out in the summer sun. In a PBS interview with Margaret Warner after the book was published, he said he composed it as a literacy performance, searching for a way to write brownly. It was a robust metaphor. Like Augustine's *Confessions*, the book is a transcript of a religious man thinking out loud, probing personal contradictions, seeking private unity in the midst of public complexity. Unlike the autobiographical characters revealed in Augustine's *Confessions* or Merton's *Seven Storey Mountain*, Rodriguez seemed more reconciled with confusion and ambiguity in his life. Perhaps composing *Brown* as he approached the seventh decade milestone of his life was the difference.

In 2006, Bill Moyers interviewed him for a PBS series on *Faith and Reason*. As preamble to this conversation about making commitments to the sacred, he described his encounter with death after renal cancer and surgery. The conversation was replete with the struggles and contradictions voiced in *Brown*, but with a profound tranquility. His experience of grace came with being identified with a community of the wounded. Transcendence found him.

Richard Rodriguez introduced his first memoir, *Hunger of Memory*, as an American story, but it he called it an impersonation of an autobiography, a six-essay fugue. In its entirety, the trilogy is made up of twenty-five essays with preamble statements to introduce each volume. In the following sections, we will examine this thrice-reflected life narrative working as McAdams suggested—evaluating a montage-like text. The author composed the essays at changing developmental points in his spiritual, literary, psychological, and public intellectual journey. He edited already published compositions, transforming them into a continuing anthology of the self. It is a postmodern story, rife with conflicts woven into the fabric of narrative skeins, and all colored quite "brownly".

Maps and Metaphors

Similar to my analyses of Maxine Hong Kingston's *The Woman Warrior: Memoirs of a Girlhood among Ghosts,* Rodriguez's book titles can be evaluated as metaphors carefully chosen to capture our imaginations. What does each word in the three parts of his first title—*Hunger of Memory: The Education of Richard Rodriguez. An Autobiography*—mean to you? Or the two elements before and after the colon in *Days of Obligation: An Argument with My Mexican Father*? How is he trying to provoke our responses with *Brown: The Last Discovery of America?*

We could use the theories we discussed previously to examine all three books as a set. For example, an Eriksonian emphasis on ages and stages begins with the assumption that each title may reflect the developmental crises experienced by thirty-eight, forty-eight, and fifty-eight year old men in American society. Using this lens, identity, intimacy, generativity, and ego integrity themes should be evident in the three memoirs. However, the Eriksonian review we constructed of the titles and of the episodes reported in Saint Augustine's *The Confessions* or Thomas Merton's *The Seven Storey Mountain* will not work, here, for several reasons. First, the earlier two books detail Augustine and Merton's experiences for only the first three decades of their lives. A serial autobiography in three parts covers a wider and more complex landscape. Second, Rodriguez disclosed issues about earlier parts of his life only in the final installment. Third, there is much more than a journey towards understanding divine providence as a source of unity—circling Mount Purgatory—being performed in these three life narratives.

McAdams's life story model of identity seems more apt because it recognizes the continuous editing processes of memory and story-making. All three book titles are about Rodriguez's inquiry into the complex phenomenon of identity development within the context of multiple cultures.

Hunger of Memory: The Education of Richard Rodriguez. An Autobiography was about his family and their social class and how education enables us to construct a sense of self, to understand to what we can legitimately aspire, and how we will be judged on what we accomplish. The title, *Hunger of Memory,* parsed, is a compelling desire or craving for remembered experiences. *The Education of Richard Rodriguez* brashly recalls an earlier paragon of the genre, *The Education of Henry Adams*, also composed during a time of national transition and values turmoil in American education and society. Just in case his audience did not understand, he added *An Autobiography*—but it was his uniquely sad fugue, impersonating the genre that extolled exemplary lives of virtue.

Days of Obligation: An Argument with My Mexican Father explored the terrain of ethnic identity using geographical, religious, and once more, family compasses. The *Days of Obligation* metaphor derives from the Catholic Church's liturgical practice of setting aside Sunday as a first day of rest and reflection, and then celebrating common feast days (e.g. Christmas, All Saints Day) that oblige us to affirm a religious heritage and its responsibilities. The Church encourages individual countries to tailor the common celebration to their particular traditions and cultures. *Argument* is defined as a connected series of statements designed to make clear or assert one's position; *with my Mexican Father* establishes that he will explore the vital relationship between family and ethnicity, not against, but together "with".

Brown: The Last Discovery of America recapitulated the identity themes of the first two books, and asserted that discovery must recognize its pluralistic past, present, and future. Rodriguez strives not for a psychological autonomy grounded in individualism, but an identity with historical and multi-ethnic perspectives, that acknowledges the impurities of our existence, and accepts the challenges of paradox. Recall how Maxine Hong Kingston appreciated how her mother's talk stories gave her a mind large enough for paradox.

Analyses of the chapter titles for all three books offer further insights.

In *Hunger of Memory,* on the very first page of "Middle Class Pastoral", he identified himself as a dark-skinned, part-time writer who stole books and became assimilated. He returned home one summer from college to discover a silence between him and his family, fostered by his newly acquired learning. He was a scholarship boy become middle class by virtue of a prestigious university degree. Being poor held no romantic charm and trying to walk among the rich revealed himself to himself as an imposter, a comedic victim of American culture. "Aria" (One) reminisced about Spanish family language and the intimacies of its sounds, chronicling his teachers' and his self-imposed expectations to leave it behind. "The Achievement of Desire" (Two) dissected education and class and the origins of "the scholarship boy" concept. The more he learned, the less confident he felt; the more he got what he wanted, the more he left behind what he loved. "Credo" (Three) was the chapter and the faith at the center of *The Education of Richard Rodriguez.* Its Latin language and rituals effectively mediated between the public and private spheres of his life. "Complexion" (Four) was an essay with rich interpretations. Over the years, Rodriguez returned to its textual and sub-textual meanings many times. Being brown-skinned made him non-White; the darker the brown, the more menial was one's daily work. In this chapter, he disclosed his shyness and discomfort around girls. He may not have known what to say to them, but he could quote *Lady Chatterley's Lover's* methodology with ease. In "Profession" (Five), he confessed his guilt over being labeled a "minority student", taking the place of those whose economic status absented them from higher education. Finally, "Mr. Secrets" (Six) returned readers to the Rodriguez hearth and to the pain he caused his family by revealing the intimacies of their lives in this intellectual autobiography.

On the first page of *Days of Obligation,* in "My Parents' Village" (Introduction), our hero is on his knees, overcome by nausea and Mexico City, heaving from the unsettling mixture of tragic and comedic elements of his life. Irresolution was judged the best solution to this tension; wisdom was the shaky claim of pursuing either or both. He juxtaposed images of Bobby Brown California taped music with a tolling Mexican church bell at a village funeral. His worldly BBC television crew was confronted by a crippled village idiot who demanded their respect and silence. To make readers privy to *An Argument with My Mexican Father,* he told us his narrative was composed in reverse. If the most recent comes first and then he delved into his past, was this a map for a psychological examination back to the complex origins of the relationship between him and his father?

Europeans sailed over the edge of the earth to find "India" (One); they found Indians and Mexico and a New World. In this chapter, Rodriguez defined himself as Indian, Catholic, English-speaking, and American, with roots deep into the sixteenth century. He looked in the mirror and saw a brown Indian. He lived in a house of the "Late Victorians" (Two), where tragedy and winter were cardinal, in a city where being homosexual required men to live within secrets. A friend dying of AIDS told Richard that he would be spared because he was too circumspect, revealing to him that Catholics' grace comes from embracing life, not just avoiding Augustine's catalogue of evils. "Mexico's Children" (Three) explored how his father and many others came north and were disappeared into America, sinning against memory. "In Athens Once" (Four) was a parable about belonging and discipleship in city life, contrasting two Catholic men's commitments with Tijuana and San Diego as their sites of sin and grace. People live in cities separately and simultaneously; they mourn in unison in the villages. "The Missions" (Five) was a travelogue to unravel two theologies that tug at California. Catholics came north and hoped to establish communities of memory while Protestants came west with deliberate amnesia so that every individual life could be birthed anew. "Sand" (Seven) was more overtly autobiographical; it began with the Sacramento achievement of selling subscriptions for a Catholic periodical and winning a red bicycle and a trip to Disneyland. Richard moved to Protestant Los Angeles at twenty-eight to assimilate with those pursuing vulgar escapes from tragedy. When he looked in the mirror and didn't know the person bent on pursuing the glamorous life, he returned to his parents' San Francisco basement apartment to complete a book. "Asians" (Eight) told the story of immigrant children who must learn to live on a hyphen, until they understand the common language and culture lessons of their grammar school teachers. The best, but most debilitating metaphor of American life may the "melting pot". "The Latin American Novel" (Nine) was another autobiographical pastiche with vignettes from parochial high school, graduate studies, and lectures to community groups; he lamented that Catholics struggle in America to practice a communal faith in a culture that celebrates individualism at every turn. His audience may not want to listen to this educated schoolboy extolling some Catholic dream—respect for authority, embrace of community, safety of continuity in its traditions—born of the Middle Ages. Finally, in "Nothing Lasts a Hundred Years" (Ten), Richard tenderly recalled his father's smile, introspection, and sobriety that were at the heart of his memories of growing up Mexican in Sacramento. He was prepared by the nuns to be an adult in comic America; they never saw a need to mute either comedy or tragedy.

In a 1994 interview, Rodriguez observed that *Hunger of Memory* was more Protestant than *Days of Obligation* because it railed against popular ideologies of its time, and went against his mother's wishes by making the private, public to the *gringos*. He saw the second book as more Catholic and more troubling in its sensibilities. After his younger man's anger had been released in the first life narrative text, he could disclose the more tragic elements of his and others' lives in the second text. It was constructed with ten more years of revising memory's episodes. One of his pursuits was doggedly trying to stay faithful to Catholic faith while its teachings on sexuality seemed increasingly distant and disdainful. Rodriguez mused once that the Vatican took a long time to listen to Galileo; Freud may take them longer, still.

Ten years after *Days of Obligation*, he told us in the Preface to *Brown: The Last Discovery of America* that this was a text filled with paradox, and if readers could not handle such tension, then they must look elsewhere to find more purity in another author. The book was a thrice-constructed review of the themes of class, ethnicity, and race in his life. This third text in his trilogy was a cultural documentary on race and the browning of America. Embedded within his commentary was Richard's continuing memoir about his education, his arguments with many fathers who he esteemed, and his discoveries as a writer. He used the many connotative meanings and images of "brown"—impure, mixed, muddied, unclear—to express the narrative's colored commentaries.

"The Triad of Alexis De Tocqueville" (One) began with the scene from *Democracy in America* where the French scholar encountered a White European child being taken care of by an Indian woman and a Negress slave. The chapter acknowledged the African American voices who inspired Rodriguez's soul early on and on whom he based his craft after working through the histories of their arguments. In "In the Brown Study" (Two), he declared his synoptic identity as a queer, Spaniard, Indian, Catholic who lives in a post-Protestant nation (America), a fading blond state (California), and is most at home in his Chinese city (San Francisco). "The Prince and I" (Three) was a riff on public performances in American life, from Gertrude Lawrence to Malcolm X to the Stanford Indian and back to De Tocqueville's Triad. In "Poor Richard" (Four), he described how the Benjamin Franklin archetype lived on in Richard Nixon and Malcolm X who both wore ill-fitting black suits. He too wore one as an ardent young man who never fit in, trying so hard to do so, but never could, just as the two famous historical figures never could. The young man in the black suit grew up to be "Hispanic" (Five). That noun/adjective/pejorative title described "them" as "here" before the Mayflower, caricatured as the Latin Lover, and reified by the 1973 O.M.B. Statistical Directive 15 that created the equal opportunity categories of: Black, White, Asian/Pacific Islander, Native American/Eskimo, and Hispanic (a term that begat Chicano that begat Latino who will begat one in three Americans in 2040). Laying down another track on top of race and ethnicity, in "The Third

Man" (Six) he acknowledged his identity was a browned composite of the historical influences of Hispanic, African Americans, Irish Catholics, American Jews, and the Chinese of California. He concluded this book with "Peter's Avocado" (Nine) and a statement akin to his 2006 report to Moyers about discovering tranquility. For Rodriguez, brown means love, like a Sermon on the Mount homily filled with paradox and challenge for all of us. It was a splendid admixture of religious and cultural metaphors.

Composition Strategies

"Essay" has its origin in the French verb, *essayer*, to weigh. Its definitions include, in order: a trial, test, experiment; a sample, example, rehearsal; short prose composition on any subject; first tentative attempt at learning, composition, etc., first draft. Richard Rodriguez is a highly polished essayist—on television, at the podium, and in all three installments of his trilogy. He is no longer the person who felt in 1982 that at his best, he just wrote graffiti.

When you read Augustine or Merton or Malcolm, you have a sense of their certainty about how and why they are thinking out loud and to whom they are confessing. Augustine liked what he read in *The Confessions* when he evaluated it at the end of his life. Merton and Malcolm said they did not remember or know the author who began their books when they reviewed their prose, later. Within the oral traditions of Maxine Hong Kingston, Leslie Marmon Silko, or Judith Ortiz Cofer, you know that the story changed each time it was told and will continue to do so. If talk-story did not change, it would not be "true". The psychological processes of composing written essays—whether as Richard's fugue or argument or browning—and recollecting stories from memory are what Dan McAdams explicated, especially when he incorporated post-modern voices into his understanding of life narrative identity.

Rodriguez's essays are intellectual talk-stories rich in literary and psychological qualities. The discontinuities and gaps in the three narratives, the constant grappling with language, the construing of writing as a performance—all are characteristics that align his works with Sidonie Smith's feminist perspective and her poetics of autobiography and everyday life. *Hunger of Memory, Days of Obligation,* and *Brown* have "weighing" passages about his body, its tensions and imposed social constructions. All three have passages that "talk back", "from the margins", to "challenge master narrative standards". The composing voice in the memoir essays, like the audio and video tracks of his PBS pieces, is crystal clear, but never certain. They come across as intellectual "trials" or "rehearsals" of ideas, empathic inquiries into others' stories, using the tone of "first drafts" where tentativeness engages our close consideration and response.

He writes early in the morning when he can listen more carefully to what he is trying to say. Writing is like prayer. Rodriguez's writing life balances essays for print and for the media. He construes journalistic pieces like the sketches or drawings made by a visual artist. After getting down on paper the first impression, they need to percolate, be refined, crafted; brilliant inspiration may emerge from a conversation with a good group dynamic or in association with something read or seen or touched. He once noted that rewriting was important so he could discover what he always intended to say. He was making an observation about the prose at hand, but McAdams would interpret this as the cognitive processes of memory and imagination, as well. Writing is listening, then performing, and then listening again to audience response. Hong Kingston, Marmon Silko, and Ortiz Cofer believed the same and wrote with this in mind. As a rhetoric teacher and pulpit preacher, Augustine probably did, too.

In interviews after *Brown* was published, Rodriguez said that the majority of letters he received came from high school Chinese girls, kids from India and Pakistan, and working class English kids. He always understood, like Erikson, that elementary and secondary school was the scene for so much of our identity development. In a 1994 interview, he noted how education teaches us that we are related not just to our parents, but to slaves and women fighting for the vote and even to the Puritans. Ideas flow forward and education is not about self-esteem, but it is about teaching students to understand the ideas expressed in the language of other peoples. He also receives appreciative comments from older workers who know the differences between the languages they learned in their ethnic homes and what they spoke in society.

Commentaries on the substance of his arguments have been angry and conflicted, and I will introduce those voices in the next section on Gathering Memory's Episodes. Critical reviews of Rodriguez's writing style in the trilogy have been mixed, as well. Newspaper reviewers compared his prose to Albert Camus' and James Baldwin's best works. All three authors deftly, and passionately, illuminated the intersections between personal history, society, and politics. Yet, while some reviewers celebrated his sustained ironies, constant dualities, or a writing style without guile, others castigated his essays as ornamental as a tiered wedding cake, slick, or as forgettable as MTV. Descriptors like passionate, poetic, meditative, and wise have been offset by negative appraisals of elliptical, contradictory, moody, and curmudgeonly. Some of my students have, over the years, described the voice they heard in *Hunger of Memory* as preachy, in *Days of Obligation* as depressed, and in *Brown* as cynical or sarcastic. Others heard genuinely torn and sad, mystical or enigmatic, and playful-in-your-face, respectively.

Finally, in considering the composition strategies used in the three installments, it is important to consider the choices he made about what to disclose.

Recall Michael Mott's epigraph in his biography, quoting Merton, that his seemingly deepest revelations are when he is disclosing the least. There are normative parallels in the Trappist monk-writer in Gethsemani and the Catholic layperson-essayist in San Francisco. Modesty dictated that some topics ought not be disclosed. Recall Merton's journal entry about the battles with his moral and literary censor and how undefined audiences predicted that recounting some events could be a source of scandal. When Rodriguez wrote *Hunger of Memory*, he assumed his audience would be people he never intended to meet, much less to interact with. Essays that are thinking-out-loud "tests" benefit from such an assumption. Recall how Augustine composed *Confessions* chapter by chapter and it was then read to his Sunday congregation in Hippo.

Knowing that your family would read your writing was something that Merton never had to struggle with. Richard did and, for example, chose not to describe in detail the relationships with his brothers and sisters in *Hunger of Memory*. Their absence was a fiction of his real life. Mourning his loss of family connections and heritage in this book was best told to an assumed audience that his learning of formal language prepared him to address. It was a cerebral audience, not an intimate one. His mother was, indeed, saddened by what he disclosed. She asked him why he never told her of his feelings about her expressed fears of his being darker brown and perceived as laboring class. She did not know who to trust—the son she knew at the family dinner table or the one whose sorrow she heard for the first time in his writings. Rodriguez told her to trust the son she met at the table in their house, not the autobiographical "I" he composed as the character in *Hunger of Memory*. Recall how Merton decided not to make public his private journals until twenty-five years after his death. Biography may be inflicted as tough or tender homicide. Autobiographical disclosure is more like suicide.

In the final section on memory's episodes, we will evaluate how and why the trilogy evoked withering responses in academic and ethnic communities. Newspaper reviewers and interviewers characterized him as the author who Chicanos most love to hate, the Martin Luther of *Chicanismo*.

Gathering Memory's Episodes

Gathering memory's episodes is the activity that fuses psychological and literary processes. Recall a 1991 quote from McAdams cited earlier in this chapter. He composed this early in his building of a paradigm with narrative potential.

We *choose* in the *present* to remember the past in a certain way. In the making of the self, there is no objective bedrock of the past from which to fashion the myth. The past is malleable, changing, ever synthesized and re-synthesized by present life choices. . . . History and the self are not total fabrications of the imagination; nor are they pure discoveries of fact. The self as story is *both* "made" and "found out".[46]

Hunger of Memory created a firestorm and his subsequent public lectures, during the conservative 1980s Reagan era, added more fuel. Most of the vitriol was aimed at how Rodriguez interpreted his memories about ethnic identity experiences. His mother predicted the consequences when she regretted his disclosures to the *gringos*. Let's start with some of the commentaries on the first book of the trilogy to appreciate how remembered episodes are projective tests both for the author and for the communities who considered him as "one of their own" when he made those memories public.

I offer several positive readings about what Rodriguez accomplished. One literary scholar, Paul John Eakin, analyzed models of identity and theories of self as orienting positions. He explored autogynography (i.e., how women's many different approaches to self-exploration yielded many different texts), the politics of identity (i.e., how majority culture forms predisposed minority writers to certain textual identities), and indigenous psychologies (i.e., discovering self in a variety of unique cultural contexts). Comparing Rodriguez's *Hunger of Memory* to Hong Kingston's *The Woman Warrior*, he illustrated how ethnic writers must navigate self, language, and culture in their autobiographical speech texts. Rodriguez and Hong Kingston wrote poignant expositions of going to school in America, of learning the voices of what Rodriguez labeled as "scholarship boy" or "minority student". Hong Kingston had the added burden of having to learn the socially prescribed American feminine voice. Both authors discovered that their identities were intimately connected with the oral traditions of their cultural pasts, but that their futures would be measured by acculturation via Euro-American literary traditions. Hong Kingston defied her mother's "tell no one" to begin her life narrative story. Rodriguez had to do the same and he described the resulting loneliness of "Mr. Secrets".[47]

Antonio Marquez reviewed the controversies and offered this synopsis:

Rodriguez's life-story is a querulous assessment of his heritage. In recasting his life and his educational experiences, Rodriguez raises central issues in relation to Mexican and Mexican American cultural history. The most controversial aspect of Rodriguez's book turns on his assertion that his education led to his separation from family and Hispanic cultural roots and that it was a necessary and beneficial separation. He contends that the assimilation into Anglo American culture and the mainstream of the United States is necessary to attain a public identity and to achieve success within that society. Both praised and vilified, *Hunger of Memory* has become the eye of the ideological storm.[48]

As we learned in reviewing the criticism of Maxine Hong Kingston by some in the Asian-Chinese American academic literary communities, Chicanos responded to *Hunger of Memory* differently than Anglo readers. The negative responses were triggered after popular press reviewers identified both authors as "true representatives of their people". In Rodriguez's case, Anglo literary accolades were complemented by fawning comments from conservative political groups who supported his opposition to Affirmative Action and bilingual education programs. Conservatives believed they discovered a minority person who was just like them.

Tomas Rivera, a respected scholar of Chicano literature, contested the subtext of many Anglo supporters, that of the homogenization of Latino authors:

> They are as heterogeneous a kindred group as any that exists
> in our present society. . . . Richard Rodriguez' book is a personal
> expression, an autobiography, and it must be understood as that in
> its singularity. It should not be used as a single way or method of
> understanding the bilingual, bicultural phenomenon of the Hispanic
> group.[49]

Rivera challenged what he understood as *Hunger of Memory's* basic conclusion: "Richard Rodriguez seems to indicate that the personal Spanish voice lacks the intelligence and ability to communicate beyond the sensibilities of the personal interactions of public family life. This is intolerable."[50] Rivera scolded him for not learning (or forgetting) the best lesson of the humanities, that the human condition is universal, not culturally specific. Ethnic heritage and its consequent differences illuminate in special ways. Different angles of vision will not disassociate us from our common yearnings and struggles, which he suggested that Rodriguez concluded. Rivera's essay was composed just before his untimely death and published posthumously. His concluding reactions mingled appreciation with disappointment and sadness:

> What *Hunger of Memory* therefore reveals is one more step
> in the intellectual emancipation of the Mexican-American. It
> represents a significant intellectual step because such views are
> so clearly articulated. His parents knew who they were, and who
> the gringos were. They didn't stop talking to him because they
> didn't understand him, but because he no longer saw the significance
> of their life. Richard Rodriguez lost the memory of all the
> philosophical questions they had helped him face and answer
> long before he walked into the English-speaking world. A writer

is lonely only if he has lost the sense of his community's aspirations
and the integrative values. . . . Richard Rodriguez apparently decolonizes
himself by seeking to free himself from a personal voice, but in so
trying he will likely enter another colony of despair.[51]

Raymond Paredes was less appreciative. He placed *Hunger of Memory* within the classic American form of the conversion narrative with its author embracing the socioeconomic and political religion of ethnic assimilation. Malcolm X attempted fitting-in behaviors, only to contest the White man's oppressive restrictions on freedom, and then to adopt the separation required of conversion to an ethnic pride, whereas Rodriguez dove head first into the melting pot.

Hunger of Memory, like traditional autobiographical narratives
of conversion, accepts the process of transformation without
hesitation. Ultimately, Rodriguez's claim for his middle-class
pastoral is best understood as an attempt to magnify his literary
accomplishment and to obscure the regressiveness of his political
and cultural views behind a pretense of formal innovation. . . .
Hunger of Memory is a self-consciously academic work, replete
with sophisticated literary and cultural references and eager to
establish its intellectual respectability.[52]

He criticized the disparaging remarks about ethnic activism, Mexican-American culture, and minority university students, pointed out Rodriguez's failure to conform to the genre's guidelines about telling more personal stories, and lectured him about using more advanced interpretations of the literary allusions (e.g., Shakespeare's Caliban) and the conditions of colonialism he ignored. Paredes concluded his review thus:

Hunger of Memory is not a work of proselytization; it exists to
confirm traditional American notions about ethnic loyalty,
and in so doing, to validate and strengthen Rodriguez's public
identity. And because of its animating political purposes, Rodriguez
has constructed a remarkably uncritical autobiographical persona. . .
full of contradictions and garbled polemics.[53]

Tomas Rivera reported that he had read *Hunger of Memory* three times, that it had much to say, and became richer with each reading. Raymond Paredes responded differently.

Perhaps we could compare Paredes's critique to those leveled against Maxine Hong Kingston by Frank Chin. Both men were recognized scholars of their ethnic literary traditions and advocates for its recognition and advancement. Both appealed to classic literary standards as well as to more avant-garde interpretive theories. They challenged the perpetuation of ethnic stereotypes. Rodriguez sinned by being the dolorous assimilated Hispanic, with pretensions to a composition style of English literary sophistication. Hong Kingston sinned by being the exotic magical realist who perpetuated historically and culturally inaccurate Chinese stories, especially tales about males. Were both critics actually being too conservative, chafing against these authors' innovations to the genre, as distinctively different approaches to the ethnic memoir?

Consider two other scholars' take on these issues. First, listen to Antonio Marquez again.

> The new forms of autobiographic writing assess, modify, qualify, transmute, and can also reject what has gone before—what is often called "traditional culture"—and seek new ways to express the sense of difference. In some cases, the certitudes of ethnic identity have given way to confusion or skepticism. 'Ethnicity is only a public metaphor,' Rodriguez muses, 'like sexuality or age, for a knowledge that bewilders us.' ("An American Writer," 8). Rodriguez's work, for better or for worse, is a harbinger of new directions in ethnic autobiography.[54]

Sidonie Smith suggested that there was opportunity and danger for women and ethnic writers in taking this new direction of talking back to accepted conventions and a working at the margins. The polished literary style used by both authors was a ruse to have us considering them as mainstream. Consistent with what Rodriguez stated time and time again about not being sociological, Marquez noted that the act of rebellion included his not wanting to be seen as a representative voice. Ghandi did truth and wanted to convert others to a non-violent way of life; Augustine had similar intentions. Rodriguez and Hong Kingston had no such agendas for the adoption of a way of life revealed in their own experiences.

In Chapter Three, I introduced G. Thomas Couser, the literary scholar whose "forked-tongue" analyses of *Black Elk Speaks* and its bicultural authorship was so thought-provoking. In the same book, *Altered Egos*, he compared the works of Richard Rodriguez and Maxine Hong Kingston, characterizing their first memoirs as "bicultural autobiographies in the sense that they recount lives that originated in distinctive minority subcultures but did not end there."[55] Unlike Black Elk, neither of these authors needed a translator for their representations of self. What differentiates the two more contemporary authors, however, were their parents' strategies for being in America. The Rodriguez family moved into Anglo neighborhoods and acquiesced to

Richard's elementary school nuns' request about not speaking their native tongue at home. The Hong family settled into a Chinese-American community in Stockton populated by people from their original village, even dreaming of one-day leaving Gold Mountain and returning "home". Recalling McAdams's insights that "the self as story is *both* "made" and "found out" helps us understand how their respective narratives were crafted differently.

These two celebrated authors used stories to communicate to wider audiences than the family circle, and both studied the canon of stories well. Both were renegades, "outlaw knot-makers", as Hong Kingston proudly proclaimed. Recall how her publisher had to decide among several labels to categorize *The Woman Warrior* because it crashed the boundaries between "fact" and "fiction". Rodriguez accomplished similar fence-busting with his sad fugue impersonating an autobiography. Couser rightly observed, that "For Rodriguez, then, autobiography is not merely the most democratic of genres, but a literary melting pot. In effect, *Hunger of Memory* seems to declare the end or non-existence of minority autobiography—the impossibility of bicultural autobiography".[56] *Ricardo* became Richard; the first installment of the trilogy was an extended epitaph for his earliest memories. His New York editor appealed for more stories and less essays, more Grandma and less politics, but he remained steadfast in its composition strategy and how he chose to interpret memory's episodes for the *gringos*. Couser concluded:

> *Hunger of Memory*, therefore, is a curious and somewhat contradictory
> text: an autobiography that celebrates the education that transformed
> its author, but whose dominant tone is one of yearning for a world as
> secure as the one from which English uprooted him. The real heresy
> of the book lies not in its controversial views on minority issues—which,
> after all, are shared by many—but in its expression of dissatisfaction
> with a society so tolerant of diversity that it not only accepts but
> celebrates ethnic distinctions and idiosyncrasy. [57]

Recall another previously cited quote from McAdams's 2005 autobiographical reflections.

> Not only were life stories constructed through social interaction, as
> I acknowledged from the get-go, but they were also performed
> with respect to particular audiences, told with respect to certain
> discursive aims and traditions, and tailored for short-term strategic
> ends. Not only did stories integrate lives and provide some semblance
> of unity and purpose, as I argued in my first book, but they could also
> disrupt lives, express discontinuity and incoherence, contradict
> themselves and confuse their audiences, and fulfill a wide range of
> other functions—psychological, social, economic, and political. . . . [58]

After all the *sturm und drang* from *Hunger of Memory* and the public statements in response to its supporters and detractors, the author turned southward to reflect on the roots of his ethnicity. The harsh commentators were almost mute in response to his *Argument with My Mexican Father*. Couser capped off his analysis on biculturalism with this statement: "The poignancy of *Hunger of Memory* is that Rodriguez seems genuinely attracted to two worlds that he cannot finally reconcile."[59] *Days of Obligation* was a gathering of memory's episodes about the two worlds that *Hunger of Memory* needed to divorce.

Rosaura Sanchez summarized *Days* in this way: "Rodriguez's text offers a cross between the discourses of the confessional and the travelogue: disparate memories of a gay Catholic man of Mexican origin in search of icons and signs, posts to tell him who and where he is."[60] Her difficulties with him were predictable by the two phrases of her title of "calculated musings: metaphysics of difference". Sanchez discerned his true intentions in the second book of the trilogy as not only wrong—examining metaphysical versus real diversity—but calculated to foster his continuing support from politically conservative groups and the affections of television media who cast him as the public face of Mexican-Americans. To her, his calculations were so manipulative that he used this book as a sly rebuttal to critics of his blatant criticisms of governmentally-sponsored minority programs articulated ten years earlier:

> In a work that raises a number of polemical issues, he enjoys
> bantering and contradicting himself continuously as if his primary
> strategy were to escape being pigeonholed (as he was after his
> publication of *Hunger of Memory*). . . .We are, of course, to revel
> in how much Rodriguez has evolved and is coming to grips with his
> 'identities'. [61]

As I suggested about Frank Chin's or Raymond Paredes's negative responses to other books, these may be valid criticisms, based on the theoretical and political perspectives of the author. They are voices at the table that need to be heard to fully appreciate diverse responses to a text.

I want to focus, however, on another facet of Sanchez's evaluation, how Rodriguez recalled memories that seemed always to be in opposition to one another.

> Among his set of binary oppositions positing essentialist distinctions
> are the following: Protestants versus Catholics, feminine versus
> masculine, communal versus individualistic, loyalty versus betrayal,
> matriarchal/maternal versus patriarchal/paternal-uncle, secular time
> versus religious time, past versus future, tragedy versus comedy,

> Europe versus Asia/India, public versus private, reproduction versus
> non-reproduction, gay versus straight, America versus immigrant,
> intimate/formal versus informal, memory versus failure of memory,
> sin versus forgiveness. [62]

This is quite a catalogue of conflicts for any single person to work through. What Sanchez most resented, however, seemed to be: "In each case he privileges one side as American and dominant, the other side as subordinate and Mexican..." [63] Earlier in this chapter, I shared a similar critical stance when I described how psychological research evolved from ignoring women's or ethnic person's participation, then included them as either/or comparisons, and finally appreciated that there were as many differences *within* identified groups as there were *between* them. Sanchez is doing the same by disagreeing with any ascription of "essential" or "core" identity characteristics to a whole group of people based on dichotomous "metaphysical" labels. She interpreted these oppositions as constructions of majority culture versus real attributes that vary widely within and across individuals. I take a somewhat different point of view at the individual case level. In the middle of one's life, at age forty-eight, when Rodriguez published the second book, the reconciliation of polarities (not a resolution by choosing one or the other) became of paramount importance. Jung suggested that it was this very process that enabled us to truly discover our whole personalities.

Laura Fine viewed the two memoirs as "Claiming Personas and Rejecting Other-Imposed Identities: Self-Writing as the Self-Righting in the Autobiographies of Richard Rodriguez." Like Marquez's and Couser's interpretations of *Hunger of Memory,* she proposed that in both books genre-bending was taking place in tandem with a serious inquiry into identity. Memory's episodes were being refracted so that the argument needed two sides to be complete, but always written as essay-drafts of a work in progress.

> Richard Rodriguez dons competing identities in order to shape
> a new subjectivity through the act of self-writing/righting, a
> performance that defies the attempts of others to categorize him.
> The tension between the identities he assumes and those he masks
> or denies produces multilayered self-writing that critics have overlooked
> because of the unpopular political stands he takes. . . . Thus, to assume
> one of the slew of competing personas represents the "real" Richard
> Rodriguez is to ignore his use of the genre of autobiography to shape
> self-inscriptions that capture the complex twists of subjectivity.[64]

Was his a genuine thinking-out-loud about memory's episodes to discover the unity in life, as Augustine and Merton claimed was their objective? Was this a sustained review of life's unfolding, still hesitant to draw any conclusions about its endpoints, both a catharsis and a discovery as Malcolm X and McAdams concluded was the purpose of fashioning a life narrative? Or should we be more skeptical? Was this author exploring complex terrain in front of us or leading us over some social cliffs? Victor Perera concluded the latter. "At least two Richard Rodriguezes are at work here: the cosmopolitan, post-modern author leached of compassion by his terror of sentimentality and the Catholic Rodriguez who flaunts his faith in 'the prophetic role of community'."[65] Or even more caustically, he concluded: "Too many of Rodriguez's clever insights can cut both ways, or can be neutralized by an equally clever riposte. Examples of ephemeral archness abound in his writing and subvert his seriousness of purpose.[66] Ilan Stavans conceptualized both books as a continuing journey and arrived at a more favorable opinion of its navigator. "Inevitably, his contribution stands next to James Baldwin's legacy, perhaps because the two have so much in common: their homosexuality, their deeply felt voyage from the periphery of culture to center stage, their strong religiosity and sense of sacredness."[67]

At the risk of making too-general statements, perhaps returning to Augustine and extracting some comparisons to Rodriguez might help. Both men reported silent fathers and vocal mothers. Both mothers continually commented on their sons' career choices and how they realized their ambitions. Both men had to go against their mothers' wishes in order to pursue their early vocations. They left small towns for the allure of the metropolitan centers of their times, and became experts in the language of the empire. Augustine and Richard struggled with what they considered the opposing polarities in their lives, in particular how to integrate their sexual desires into some larger philosophy of life. Both men had the benefit of close relationships with same sex friends. The psychological processes of adolescence and young adulthood were similar, as was a lifelong condemnation to relentless introspection to find their true selves.

Richard tasted the sweet fruit of knowledge, turned his back on his family and its ethnic, Spanish intimacy, and forever lost Eden. He confessed this original sin in *Hunger of Memory*. *Days of Obligation* was the often inchoate struggle to find what had been lost. His father left Mexico, became a citizen; his was a sin against memory. The Catholicism that Augustine invented and Aquinas fashioned into a moral theology remained Richard's source of conflict. His original faith constantly reminded him about the loss of intimacy. Attending mass during the Christmas season, he witnessed church volunteers to AIDS support groups called forward to receive blessings and support from their community. He described this scene as a meditation on seeing how others learned to love while he, a reader of Saint Augustine, was left alone to fidget on a cold, wooden pew. And then at a gathering of Catholic priests who asked him to speak about multiculturalism, he could not recognize the faith they preached or practiced. They rolled their eyes at Richard's yearning for the community of a common language Mass, They scorned him when he probed their lack of understanding about why evangelical Christianity had become so successful. When they chided him and asked what his agenda was, he could only reply that he had none, just that he felt lonely.

Amidst all of the melancholic and alienated statements in *Days of Obligation*, one passage was a beacon of hope. It was an Augustinian epiphany that would be profoundly articulated ten years later in *Brown*. Catholicism, the faith of his father, with whom he argued, was a way of life that could absorb more than one right or wrong decision. It stands by its belief that humans will fail; that is their nature. A person can sin and remain a Catholic; one must have the consciousness that we are all sinners to remain a good Catholic.

In *Brown*, there are classic *apologia pro vita mea* statements and episodes that bring the book to a close. Rodriguez declared that he now thinks as a brown man. He is fascinated with how theater soliloquy is such an elegant expression of one's private self in public. Contemplation and prayer attempt to do the same, but never quite accomplish this feat as well. If asked, he will state that his being Hispanic is cultural, or at least its illusion and the belief that what is past always haunts the present. The final memory's episode Richard reported in *Brown* was poignant and at the heart of his soul. He awoke one morning and listened to the breathing of the man lying beside him, knew where he was, that he was alive, and perhaps was connected to earth only by a fragile but simple breath. Yet, he was captured by brown paradox. The Church that taught him about love also told him that this experience of intimacy was not love.

The gathering of memory's episodes in the final book of the trilogy was accomplished in a manner that suggested confidence in paradox, belief in the brownness of love, and an abiding faith that we are accountable for our hours on the stage. We may be filled with sound and fury, but our words do signify something, not nothing. Composing life narratives helps us discover and then redeem whatever that something may be.

In the next chapter, we will synthesize the lenses we have explored and the authors we met in the previous chapters. "Transforming Chaos into Hope" will be the theme I propose for the interdisciplinary readings of post-millennium stories.

NOTES

1. Max Schoen, "Elementary Course in Psychology," *Journal of Psychology*, 37 (1926), 596.

2. Thomas V. McGovern and Charles L. Brewer, "Undergraduate Psychology," in *History of Psychology*, ed. Donald K. Freedheim, Volume 1 in *Handbook of Psychology*, Editor-in-Chief Irving B. Weiner, (New York: Wiley, 2003), 465–481.

3. Baron Perlman and Lee I. McCann, "The most frequently listed courses in the undergraduate psychology curriculum," *Teaching of Psychology* 26 (1999), 178.

4. Dan P. McAdams, "A Conceptual History of Personality Psychology" in *Handbook of Personality Psychology*, eds. Robert Hogan, John Johnson, and S. Briggs (San Diego: Academic Press, 1997), 3–39.

5. McAdams, "Conceptual History", 20.

6. Dan P. McAdams, *Power, Intimacy, and the Life Story: Personological Inquiries into Identity* (Homewood, IL: The Dorsey Press, 1985), 28.

7. McAdams, *Power, Intimacy, and the Life Story*, vi.

8. McAdams, *Power, Intimacy, and the Life Story*, 30.

9. Dan P. McAdams, *Intimacy: The Need to Be Close* (New York: Doubleday, 1989). (See pp. 224–226, footnote 3, for an excellent summary of stories as romantic, tragic, comedic, or ironic.)

10. Dan P. McAdams, *The Redemptive Self: Stories American Live By* (Oxford, UK: Oxford University Press), 142.

11. Dan P. McAdams, "Unity and Purpose in Human Lives: The Emergence of Identity as a Life Story," in *Studying Persons and Lives*, eds. Albert I. Rabin, Robert A. Zucker, Robert A. Emmons, and S. Frank (New York: Springer, 1990), 151.

12. McAdams, "Unity and Purpose", 168.

13. McAdams, "Unity and Purpose", 169.

14. McAdams, "Unity and Purpose", 183.

15. McAdams, "Self and Story" in *Perspectives in Personality. Volume 3: Self and Emotion*, eds. D.J. Ozer and J. M. Healy, Jr. (Bristol, PA: Jessica Kingsley Publishers, 1991), 142.

16. Erik Erikson, *Young Man Luther: A Study in Psychoanalysis and History* (New York: Norton, 1958), 111–112.

17. Dan P. McAdams, "Personality, Modernity, and the Storied Self: A Contemporary Framework for Studying Persons," *Psychological Inquiry* 7, (1996), 295.

18. McAdams, "Personality, Modernity, and the Storied Self", 306–307, (italics added for emphasis)

19. Dan P. McAdams, "What This Framework Can and Cannot Do," *Psychological Inquiry* 7 (1996): 378–386.

20. Dan P. McAdams, "Narrating the Self into Adulthood" in *Aging and Biography: Explorations in Adult Development*, eds. James E. Birren, Gary M. Kenyon, J. E. Ruth, J. F. Schroots, and T. Svensson (New York: Springer, 1996), 131–148.

21. Kenneth Gergen, *The Saturated Self: Dilemmas of Identity in Modern Life* (New York: Basic Books, 1992).

22. Edward E. Sampson, "The Challenge of Social Change for Psychology: Globalization and Psychology's Theory of the Person," *American Psychologist* 44 (1989): 914–921.

23. McAdams, "Personality, Modernity, and the Storied Self", 298.

24. Gergen, *The Saturated Self,* 71. McAdams quoted a commentary on Salman Rushdie's *The Satanic Verses* that "celebrates hybridity, impurity, intermingling, the transformation that comes of new and unexpected combinations of human beings, cultures, ideas, politics, movies, songs. It rejoices in the mongrelisation and fears the absolutism of the Pure." In Dan P. McAdams, "The Case for Unity in the (Post)Modern Self: A Modest Proposal," in *Self and Identity: Fundamental Issues,* eds. Richard Ashmore and Lee Jussim (New York: Oxford University Press, 1997), 49. Richard Rodriguez labeled this phenomenon, "brown".

25. McAdams, "Case for Unity", 55.

26. Dan P. McAdams, "Personal Narratives and the Life Story," in *Handbook of Personality: Theory and Research* (2nd Edition), eds. Lawrence A. Pervin and Oliver P. John (New York: Guilford Press, 1999), 478–500.

27. Dan P. McAdams, et al., "Traits and Stories: Links between Dispositional and Narrative Features of Personality." *Journal of Personality* 72 (2004): 762–784.

28. Dan P. McAdams and Jennifer L. Pals, "A New Big Five: Fundamental Principles for an Integrative Science of Personality," *American Psychologist* 61 (2006): 204–217.

29. McAdams and Pals, "New Big Five", 212.

30. McAdams and Pals, "New Big Five", 213.

31. McAdams and Pals, "New Big Five", 212.

32. Dan P. McAdams and Jack J. Bauer, "Gratitude in Modern Life: Its Manifestations and Development," in *The Psychology of Gratitude*, eds. Robert A, Emmons and Michael E. McCullough (Oxford: Oxford University Press, 2004), 81–99. Jack J. Bauer and Dan P. McAdams, "Growth Goals, Maturity and Well-Being," *Developmental Psychology* 40 (2004): 114–127. Jack J. Bauer and Dan P. McAdams, "Personal Growth in Adults' Life Stories of Life Transitions," *Journal of Personality* 72 (2004): 573–602. Jack J. Bauer, Dan P. McAdams, and April R. Sakaeda, "Interpreting the Good Life: Growth Memories in the Lives of Mature, Happy People," *Journal of Personality and Social Psychology* 88 (2005): 203–217.

33. The American Psychological Association published *The Narrative Study of Lives* with McAdams and two colleagues as its editors. *Turns in the Road: The Narrative Study of Lives in Transition*, published in 2001, brought together academic psychologists, sociologists, anthropologists, historians and other scholars to reflect on human behavior using narrative strategies. *Up Close and Personal: The Teaching and Learning of Narrative Research*, published in 2003, was by scholars who investigated phenomena in the sciences and the humanities, and thereby require literary and hermeneutic analyses to reveal their meanings. The editors asked the contributors to use their autobiographical voices and tell the story of how and why they departed from traditional approaches in order to capture the quality of human behavior. *Healing Plots: The Narrative Basis of Psychotherapy*, published in 2004, addressed how clients bring narratives to their therapies, examine them with the help of a practitioner, and understand them and revise them in light of their continuing story. Therapy is about clients and practitioners co-constructing a new, healing narrative—to fashion a new story from a life filled with adversity. The most recent edition of the series, published

in 2006, *Identity and Story: Creating Self in Narrative*, tackled the complexities of divergent lives and texts, and advanced McAdams's work on the psychosocial construction of self via stories.

34. Dan P. McAdams, "The Psychology of Life Stories." *Review of General Psychology* 5 (2001), 101.

35. McAdams, "Psychology of Life Stories", 115.

36. McAdams, "Psychology of Life Stories", 116.

37. McAdams, "Psychology of Life Stories", 117, *italics* added for emphasis.

38. Dan P. McAdams, "The Redemptive Self: Narrative Identity in America Today," in *The Self and Memory*, eds. Denise R. Beike, James M. Lampinen, and Douglas A. Behrend (New York: Psychology Press, 2004), 105.

39. McAdams, "Narrative Identity in America", 101.

40. Dan P. McAdams, "A Psychologist without a Country or Living Two Lives in the Same Story," in *Narrative Identities: Psychologists Engaged in Self-Constructions*, eds. George Yancy and Susan Hadley (London, UK: Jessica Kingsley Publishers, 2005), 114–130.

41. McAdams, "Psychologist without a Country," 114.

42. McAdams, "Psychologist without a Country," 125.

43. Richard Rodriguez, *Hunger of Memory* (New York: Bantam, 1983).

44. Richard Rodriguez, *Days of Obligation* (New York: Penguin, 1992).

45. Richard Rodriguez, *Brown* (New York: Viking, 2003).

46. McAdams, "Self and Story", 142.

47. Paul John Eakin, *Touching the World: Reference in Autobiography* (Princeton, New Jersey: Princeton University Press, 1992).

48. Antonio Marquez, "Richard Rodriguez's *Hunger of Memory* and New Perspectives on Ethnic Autobiography," in *Teaching American Ethnic Literatures,* eds. John R. Maitino and David R. Peck (Albuquerque: University of New Mexico Press, 1996), 237.

49. Tomas Rivera, "Richard Rodriguez' *Hunger of Memory* as Humanistic Antithesis", *MELUS* 11 (Winter 1984), 5.

50. Rivera, "Humanistic Antithesis", 8.

51. Rivera, "Humanistic Antithesis", 12–13.

52. Raymond J. Paredes, "Autobiography and Ethnic Politics," in *Multicultural Autobiography: American Lives*, ed. James Robert Payne (Knoxville, TN: University of Tennessee Press, 1992), 287.

53. Paredes, "Autobiography and Ethnic Politics", 294–295.

54. Marquez, "New Perspectives", 239.

55. G. Thomas Couser, "Biculturalism in Contemporary Autobiography: Richard Rodriguez and Maxine Hong Kingston," in *Altered Egos: Authority in American Autobiography* (New York: Oxford University Press, 1989), 210.

56. Couser, "Biculturalism", 211.

57. Couser, "Biculturalism", 223.

58. McAdams, "Psychologist without a Country", 125.

59. Couser, "Biculturalism", 226.

60. Rosaura Sanchez, "Calculated Musings: Richard Rodriguez's Metaphysics of Difference," in *The Ethnic Canon: Institutions and Interventions*, ed. David Liu Palumbo (Minneapolis, MN, 1995), 157.

61. Sanchez, "Calculated Musings", 158.

62. Sanchez, "Calculated Musings", 160.

63. Sanchez, "Calculated Musings", 160.

64. Laura Fine, "Claiming Personas and Rejecting Other-Imposed Identities: Self-Writing as the Self-Righting in the Autobiographies of Richard Rodriguez," *Biography* 19 (Spring 1996), 135.

65. Victor Perera, "Labyrinth of Solitude", *The Nation* 256 (January 18, 1993), 64.

66. Perera, "Labyrinth of Solitude", 65.

67. Ilan Stavans, "The Journey of Richard Rodriguez," *Commonweal* CXX (March 26, 1993), 22.

Chapter Six

Transforming Chaos into Hope

PRECIS

To appreciate the life narratives of Saint Augustine, Thomas Merton, Nicholas Black Elk, Malcolm X, Maxine Hong Kingston, and Richard Rodriguez, we used a three-part schema in the last five chapters: maps and metaphors, composition strategies, and gathering memory's episodes. What enabled us to complete our interdisciplinary readings of these multicultural authors were the theoretical analyses from scholars in several disciplines, among others, G.Thomas Couser, Paul John Eakin, Erik Erikson, Georges Gusdorf, William James, Dan McAdams, James Olney, Sidonie Smith and Julia Watson.

In this final chapter, I want to consolidate this platform of theorists and autobiographical texts. You will meet, again, Dan McAdams and Paul John Eakin, a narrative psychologist and a literary theorist, as interpretive voices about the construction of stories. Both of these scholars extended the research on autobiographical memory that I introduced in the first chapter. I will pick up this research where both of them left off, and synthesize critical findings.

Our final, original text to evaluate will be James McBride's The Color of Water: A Black Man's Tribute to His White Mother. *McBride is an award-winning journalist and composer-musician. His mother was raised in an Orthodox Jewish family in the rural South and later embraced by his father's and stepfather's Black Christian families in the urban North. Their interdependent stories are bicultural and continue to inspire readers on many levels. Life narratives require the gathering of memories from increasingly multicultural relationships, reflecting the predictable chaos and the redemptive hope of stories that we have studied thus far, as well as those yet to be told in the new millennium.*

Jill Ker Conway is a social historian of women's lives and their memoirs, as well as the author of three memoirs.[1] Teaching my first undergraduate class on life narratives sixteen years ago, I used her anthology of women's autobiographies, *Written by Herself: Autobiographies by American Women*.[2] Students appreciated Conway's social history perspective and her edited excerpts of twenty-five women grouped as freedom stories by women of color, pioneer scientists and physicians, women in the arts and letters, and social reformers. Conway's social history approach to the genre is an apt framework to draw together the ideas from previous chapters that you have read.

The previous five chapters of this book were organized as a timeline anthology both about how authors composed their personal stories for diverse audiences, and about how interdisciplinary scholars developed strategies to evaluate these texts. In Chapter One, you learned about a three-part schema for examining life narratives and analyzed the very first autobiography written by Saint Augustine over fifteen hundred years ago. Erik Erikson's psychosocial development theory was central to Chapter Two and the examining conscience of Thomas Merton, published immediately following World War II. In Chapter Three, we focused on collaborative relationships as a composition strategy for the religious conversion narratives of Black Elk and Malcolm X. Sidonie Smith's feminist, literary analyses of life narrative texts were central to Chapter Four as we spotlighted female voices and the women of color who emerged in the 1970s, in particular Maxine Hong Kingston. In Chapter Five, we used Dan McAdams's life story model of identity to evaluate the three serial autobiographies composed by Richard Rodriguez.

So, "where are we" in our study of this interesting genre at the beginning of a new century? Can we synthesize the maps and metaphors, composition strategies, and the gathering of memory's episodes that carry-over from the past and may inspire new texts in the coming years? Life narratives have continued to populate *The New York Times* and Pulitzer Prize finalist in non-fiction lists since 2000. They generate robust audiences and they have been seriously reviewed for their ever-changing composition strategies. In subsequent offerings of my course on , "Multicultural Autobiographies", we also read Conway's critical review of life narrative texts, *When Memory Speaks: Exploring the Art of Autobiography* to capstone the last century's work and look to the future.[3]

Her chapter titles in that book communicated recognizable themes that you should be familiar with, now, that she saw after learning more about the gendered history and literary analyses of the genre: "Memory's Plots", "The Secular Hero", "Romantic Heroine", "Feminist Plots", and "Assertive Women". "Different Stories" takes a look at gay men's, lesbians', and transsexuals' life stories as another set of voices in the increasing diversification of how we constructed identity in contemporary culture. "Grim Tales" brought Conway's social history to the end of the millennium. The authors she reviewed in that chapter composed post-modern stories that challenged our notions that we could discover maps for a unified and coherent life's journey or that scientific progress and psychological development necessarily yielded growth and its civilizing effects.

The 1990s produced a flood of memoirs. They were not of the "master narrative" ilk. They were not authored by wise, retiring persons composing their stories in the autumn or winter seasons of a life. Rather, the genre is now being advanced by women and men in their thirties and forties for whom family, love, work, and identity struggles capture the darker, power-based dynamics of our times. Abusive relationships too often characterize these lives and their texts. While some "Grim Tales" may be called survivor narratives (as Smith and Watson labeled them), their broad appeal came from protagonists who had overcome obstacles of all kinds. These were not about exemplary lives for which we erect pedestals, but they portrayed individuals who transformed chaos into hope. I believe that this transformation theme is a contemporary paradigm for achieving, then making public, a virtuous life. Although many of these narratives are non-linear, discontinuous, and heterogeneous, there may be common denominators and signposts that exist amidst such an array of best-selling authors.

Using the three part schema from earlier chapters, I will illuminate these new directions that stand on the shoulders of the authors and texts that went before them. With this interdisciplinary synthesis, new readings of multicultural life narratives may be possible. The final text to be evaluated will be an innovative, *New York Times* best-seller published at the end of the twentieth century—James McBride's bicultural auto/biography, *The Color of Water: A Black Man's Tribute to His White Mother.* [4] Conway examined this book as one of her exemplary "grim tales". I think it captured the transformation of chaos into hope—an emerging strategy, globally, for new century lives.

REDEMPTION STORIES

In tandem with his research program on the life story model of identity, Dan McAdams investigated the adult conflicts that Erik Erikson labeled as "generativity versus stagnation". After resolving identity challenges during adolescence and intimacy crises during early adulthood, individuals may ask: "what matters in the long run?" or "what am I leaving behind for future generations beyond the achievement of purely personal success or status?" These questions become more salient during one's thirties, forties, and fifties, although identity and intimacy considerations always are being addressed in epigenetic fashion. The virtue of caring is the positive outcome of these challenges. Erikson noted that

> . . .if developmental considerations lead us to speak of *hope*,
> *fidelity* and *care* as the human strengths or ego qualities emerging
> from such strategic stages as infancy, adolescence, and adulthood,
> it should not surprise us (though it did when we became aware of
> it) that they correspond to such major creedal values as *hope, faith,*
> and *charity*.[5]

Erikson's conclusions on the psychosocial stages after identity were based on anecdotal clinical evidence and interpretations of literary texts. McAdams compared and contrasted the life stories he elicited from research samples of adults in multicultural urban communities.

The Redemptive Self: Stories Americans Live By [6]

Generativity may be the central moral and psychological challenge of the decades after we become thirty: "Generative adults tend to see their lives as redemptive stories that emphasize related themes such as early advantage, the suffering of others, moral clarity, the conflict between power and love, and leaving a legacy of growth".[7] These stories have great value for psychological health and well-being and model for others a pattern of responsible caring versus the more typical rugged individualism espoused by success stories of the last century. McAdams extended this discovery from psychological research by asserting that these stories derive their broader appeal from themes embedded in American history and its most memorable episodes.

He recognized that social, cultural, and historical tensions surround such stories. Our country's struggle with problems like slavery and racial oppression yielded heroic redemption sagas, but at great costs to the individuals who bore witness and composed them. McAdams was sanguine about motivation: "You can sometimes detect an entitled 'true believer' quality in the life stories of many highly generative American adults—an assuredness regarding the goodness and power of the individual self that may seem off-putting and can sometimes prove destructive." [8]

He found a common plot in these stories. Autobiographers perceived themselves as being favored or special, having received a special blessing or gift or status early in life that set them apart. They had a profound awareness that others had not been so fortunate, disclosing a particular sensitivity to others' sufferings. Out of the crucible of identity formation during adolescence, they described themselves as motivated to make a difference in some as yet undetermined way in others' lives. As the narrative unfolds, the autobiographer was faced with obstacles and suffered setbacks, but although they encountered adversity, the episodes typically led to positive outcomes and significant lessons learned. (Recall Augustine's homilies that we examined in Chapter One about how his sinful episodes revealed a providential plan.) Life's balance sheet demonstrated this favored person's triumph over adversity, of achievement more often than loss. McAdams added a psychological twist to this classic literary story by his assertion that the main character struggled with persistent conflicts about power and freedom set against their callings to love and building community. Plots demonstrated a new found legacy that advanced future generations' prosperity.

Fusing literary traditions with psychologists' expertise in creating classification schema, he created "six languages of redemption" evident in telling such stories.[9] McAdams's "languages" parallel the concept of maps and metaphors that I have used since Chapter One. "Atonement" stories are spiritual autobiographies or conversion narratives, where the authors move from sin to forgiveness and salvation. "Emancipation" stories spring from political sources; in African American slave or abuse survivor narratives, the authors move from slavery to freedom. "Upward mobility" stories are economic tales with Benjamin Franklin's *Autobiography* the prototype for rags-to-riches, immigrant, and motivational programs' testimonials. "Recovery" stories have medical and psychological origins and authors change their lives via therapeutic and self-help interventions. "Enlightenment" stories can be rooted in education and science, demonstrating the passage from ignorance to knowledge via curiosity, discovery, and insight. "Development" stories emanate from parenting and psychology sources as the person moves from immaturity to actualization via their experiences that enhance moral development and character strength.

McAdams took great pains to describe how these languages came from authors who were not one-dimensional or pervasively happy. Existential crises with tragic consequences permeated his respondents' narratives. In fact, he discovered that optimistic stories were not significantly related to measured levels of life satisfaction and a sense of coherence. What distinguished individuals with high generativity scores were their capacities to transform chaos into hope and its redemptive fruits.

McAdams found quite different patterns in the stories of midlife adults who reported that they were not having a positive effect on future generations, or low scorers on the generativity dimension. These individuals' stories reflected "contaminated plots" that devolved into "vicious circles", typically with an early psychological injury with repeating consequences. They were surrounded from youth into adulthood by neglecting or abusive characters, by players and persistent scenes that began well but degraded into bad outcomes. This succession of contaminated experiences motivated them to live only for the moment, settling for short-term satisfactions, encountering more setbacks and adapting to their sense of failure. Psychologists who specialize in the treatment of depression use the term "learned helplessness" to describe this pattern. Yet, McAdams found that even contaminated plots may be transformed into "recovery" or "enlightenment" stories with the right combination of fortunate circumstances.

McAdams was genuinely circumspect in his chapter on "When Redemption Fails". He recognized that the impulse to transform experience into a redemptive lesson often plays into the rugged individualism patterns of the American hero. Succeeding at such transformations repeatedly may breed an arrogant, entitled brand of American exceptionalism, so characteristic of our celebrity or icon culture. The achievement of redemption reinforces power, sometimes at the expense of the self-negating and sacrificing qualities of love and community.

Conway's social history analyses yielded a similar conclusion; post-modernists keep reminding us of the same dynamic. After the Jewish Holocaust and the late twentieth century's repetitive genocides in Cambodia, Bosnia, Rwanda, and Darfurs, after scientists' creation of the capacity to destroy the earth by the proliferation of this power across the globe—all bets are off. Some episodes may be unredeemable. Tragedy and suffering permeate contemporary lives. Elie Wiesel's memoir, *Night*, about spending his adolescence in Auschwitz, losing father and mother and younger sister in the gas chambers, portrayed the limits of our capacity to find redemption in the midst of horror. Yet, as I tell my students when I teach *Night* in my classes, we have to plumb the possibilities revealed by the authors of the Hebrew Scriptures. Our experience of chaos in the darkness of night, so evident in the books of Exodus, the prophets, and the Psalms, teaches us that hope grows out of the night, to be lived in the light of day. Fire was a beacon and its light a presence of the divine, but it could also consume and burn out possibility.

McAdams synthesized his psycho-cultural-literary portrait in this way:

> . . .the redemptive self is a problematic story. It is a story that
> reflects the cultural and psychological tensions with which Americans
> have struggled for a very long time. And we continue to struggle with
> them. But we should not forget that there is no good story that is
> free of struggle and tension. There is no perfect life narrative, just
> as there is no perfect society. Every narrative identity is like a
> double-edged sword. It cuts both ways.[10]

McAdams's illumination of redemption stories offers us insightful maps and metaphors for post-millennium life narratives. Constructing a psychological self via narrative requires a plot with identifiable obstacles, told by narrators who disclose their good and not so good choices, and who are able to discover a continuity that is plausible but not predictable. They make mistakes, and worry when they cannot make sense out of what happened. What makes this psychological self's text a "good read" continues to be explored by literary theorists. I turn now to perspectives on composition strategies by a literary theorist who became increasingly psychological in his turn-of-the-century interpretations.

COMPOSING RELATIONSHIPS

Since 1980, G. Thomas Couser, Paul John Eakin, James Olney, and Sidonie Smith have been among the major literary theorists of autobiographical writing. Recall how Smith and Watson's *Reading Autobiography: A Guide for Interpreting Live Narratives* described the literary criticism as unfolding in waves. The emphasis on *bios* or an historical self-reporting of one's time in the public eye characterized early twentieth century texts and their commentaries. A shift to emphasizing *autos* began with Georges Gusdorf's essay which appeared in translation in the James Olney edited volume in 1980. Smith and Watson marked this change in emphasis as a second wave. The third wave came as a complex synthesis of perspectives that poured forth by emphasizing the *graphe* element. Theorists challenged the tidy assumptions we held about selfhood and how we represent the concept in language and narrative. Ethnic and feminist theorists offered theoretical strategies to appreciate different voices that emerged from the margin and with their identities constructed in a broad array of cultural contexts.

Time will tell if we are now in a post-millennium "fourth wave" of literary criticism on the composition strategies for life narratives. For example, Sidonie Smith was part of the third wave, illuminating as well as predicting new frontiers that we covered in Chapter Four. Her 1990s commentaries with Julia Watson expanded feminist interpretations of texts and of authors' performances of the self and story. She also deepened our consciousness about diverse voices and their unique expression with her emphases on global life narratives. Smith and Watson placed Paul John Eakin in their third wave. I will spotlight his insightful syntheses in this final chapter because of his interdisciplinary use of materials from the cognitive neurosciences.

Paul John Eakin and the Storied Self

In Chapter Three, I reviewed Paul John Eakin's essay on Malcolm X that he wrote for the Olney volume. In subsequent scholarly work on the defining characteristics of autobiographies, he blended literary analyses of specific authors' texts with neuroscience research on memory. As we explored in the last chapter, Dan McAdams built his life story model of identity on a developmental-personality psychology platform, then interpreted the changes that took place in an individual's story using narrative psychology and cognitive psychology research. Paul John Eakin built his platform from literary criticism of autobiographical texts and then interpreted changes in stories of the self using feminist theory and neuroscience research.

In *Fictions in Autobiography: Studies in the Art of Self-Invention,* [11] Eakin described autobiography as a continuing process of creating oneself. The edited volume, *American Autobiography,* [12] was a gathering of scholars to create an historical framework for evaluating four centuries of American works of this genre. *Touching the World: Reference in Autobiography,* [13] demonstrated an interdisciplinary approach to examining issues like autobiography and biography, self, culture, models of identity, language, history, narrative theory, and metaphor. It was in this work that he first introduced his concept of a neurology of identity. He drew on the works of the clinical neurologist, Oliver Sacks, who had generated a broad public audience at that time through his accessible prose about diagnosis and treatment stories, further enhanced by the popular movie, *Awakenings,* with Robin Williams and Robert DeNiro as the psychiatrist and his patient. Eakin began *How Our Lives Become Stories: Making Selves* [14] with an examination of brain and behavior research as the basis for what he termed "registers of self". He broadened his interdisciplinary understandings of self-constructions with chapters on relational selves, storied selves, and the contemporary invasions of private selves, suggesting a need for an ethics of life writing. Eakin brought together another roundtable of interdisciplinary scholars to probe life writing as a form of ethical inquiry, publishing their colloquium papers as *The Ethics of Life Writing.* [15] The plethora of grim tales, as labeled by Jill Ker Conway and published at the end of the century, suggested to this group that ethics may be the sub-text for most contemporary life narrative works.

One of Eakin's principal themes is that composing memory's stories is all about the construction of relational selves. Authors recollect a long story of daily life as well as interpret the meanings of all those details gathered from memory. Choices are made how to conceptualize one's narrative—discovering an evolving self presented as a chronology (e.g., Saint Augustine, Thomas Merton, Malcolm X) or constructing a self as an anthology of thematic episodes (e.g., Maxine Hong Kingston, Richard Rodriguez). He made this connection between memory, language, and that all identity was grounded in relationships by evaluating Maxine Hong Kingston's talk-story in *The Woman Warrior.* Beginning with the maternal silencing passage—"tell no one"—Hong Kingston described the multiple layers of her discovery of voice that we examined in detail in Chapter Four. Strong words and strong selves were attached to the historical figure of Fa Mu Lan, to Brave Orchid her mother, and finally in Maxine as she struggled to find a distinct gendered and ethnic voice with which to relate to American society. Her aunt, Moon Orchid, attempted to cross the cultural bridge to America, but found no voice and devolved into a never-ending mental purgatory without memory and without different stories to tell. Maxine harangued a withdrawn middle school classmate and became ill and mute in the aftermath, but, after hurling her identity tirades at her mother, she ended this narrative with a sense of her own power to create talk-story from many recollected memories initiated and sustained by powerful relationships.

By the end of the 1990s, brain and behavior research progressed to the point where neurological processes and their linkages to memory and identity, and thus to people's narratives had become more accessible. Eakin prefaced *How Our Lives Become Stories: Making Selves* in this way:

> This is a book about autobiography. Even more, though, it is
> a book about how we come to be the people we say we are
> when we write—if we ever do—the stories of our lives. Thus,
> my concerns are both literary and experiential, for the selves we
> display in autobiographies are doubly constructed, not only in
> the act of writing a life story but also in a lifelong process of
> identity formation of which the writing is usually a comparatively
> late phase.[16]

He recalled his analyses of Malcolm X's autobiography from twenty years earlier, captivated still by that author's acute awareness of composing a story in the midst of a rapidly changing social situations. Rethinking memory, self-experience, and its expression in language, however, Eakin was the beneficiary of new research in neuroscience, cognitive and developmental psychology, and memory studies. He understood that the construction of a self required moment-by-moment appreciation of one's biological inheritances and processes. "How much of what autobiographers say they experience is equivalent to what they really experience, and how much of it is merely what they know how to say?"[17] With this query, he opened up whole new avenues for our explorations of self-awareness and its expressions in texts. His interpretations are so appealing because he leaves behind the old questions about individualism and autonomy and about purely psychological qualities of identity. In this book, he synthesized feminist insights about biology with literary insights about the social nature of performance, audience, and the composition of a self.

His theme for the chapter titled "Relational selves, relational lives" was:

Why do we so easily forget that the first person in autobiography is truly plural in its origins and subsequent formation? Because autobiography promotes the illusion of self-determination: *I* write my story; *I* say who I am; *I* create myself. The myth of autonomy dies hard, and autobiography criticism has not yet fully addressed the extent to which the self is defined by—and lives in terms of—its relations with others.[18]

He attributed our changed perspectives on autonomy to the feminist scholars we reviewed in Chapter Four (e.g., Mary Mason, Susan Stanford Friedman, Francoise Lionnet, and Sidonie Smith). "The critique of the Gusdorf model of selfhood and the positing of a female alternative paved the way for the serious and sustained study of women's autobiography—the single most important achievement of autobiography studies in the last decade."[19] The heart of an alternative model of selfhood in life writing rested in his challenges to the binary oppositions of male versus female and how they were woven into scholars' commentaries about individualistic versus relational characteristics of an author. His new paradigm was that all selfhood is relational, and individual differences are based on age, gender, class, ethnicity, and many other socially constructed characteristics.

For Eakin, Leslie Marmon Silko's *Storyteller* illustrated this point so well—she stands out by virtue of her multilayered relationships with family, tribe, myth, and even the landscape. Silko's identity derived from her placement within a line of family storytellers who preceded her in the Laguna Pueblo tradition; "the deep lesson is that everything is part of everything else: everything and everyone in *Storyteller* is story."[20] Oral tradition is collective memory. Recalling stories in a web of interactive participants involves recalling memories not only of oneself, but of all the relationships to which one belongs. It is this process that brings Silko's literary understanding of memory right in line with the cognitive interpretations that began with Book X in Saint Augustine's *Confessions* and continued until *Storyteller.* Eakin asserted that the life narrative author is an ethnographer because identity emerged after being immersed in social relationships and not just by being true, over time, to some unified, autonomous self. He concluded: "The lesson these identity narratives are teaching, again and again, is that the self is dynamic, changing, and plural."[21]

In another chapter in this volume, Eakin examined privacy and the ethics of life writing. Acknowledging that there were almost no taboo topics anymore in autobiography, he raised questions about manipulative self-disclosures, mostly in terms of its social effects on significant others. Have we taken the notion of public, truth-telling too far? Performance in print has become as titillating as the myriad exhibitionistic television talk shows. Eakin asked key questions for our continuing study of autobiography. What price memoirs to the value of privacy for ourselves and those related to us? What are the moral consequences of autobiographical compositions? Have our needs to read about others' pain, not necessarily their triumphs over that pain, further advanced the commodification of individuals? (Recall Sidonie Smith's concern over this phenomenon that we explored in Chapter Four.) Do we have exemplars of the collaborative autobiographical work where empathy in the actual composition process was paramount? He concluded this chapter with a sobering quotation from Philippe Lejeune from whose work, like Olney's, Eakin drew much inspiration: "In confessing our selves we inevitably confess those who have shared our life intimately. . . .The attack on private life, which the law condemns, is the very basis of autobiographical writing."[22]

I think that the following passage merges Eakin's ideas adapted from neuroscientific research with McAdams's life story model of identity and his synthesis material from cognitive psychology, as well:

What is arresting about this radical equation between narrative
and identity is the notion that narrative here is not merely
about the self but rather in some profound way a constituent
part *of* the self. . .the writing of autobiography is properly
understood as an integral part of a lifelong process of identity
formation in which acts of self-narration play a major part.[23]

This literary scholar was led to the interdisciplinary conclusion that our memories are biological, psychological, and literary constructions: "one of autobiography's great themes is the child's awakening to the call of stories as they are performed within the family circle and the larger community."[24]

I now turn to psychological research on autobiographical memory, from scientists whose data come from that family circle, and whose findings appeared after Eakin's book was published. These findings will provide a final synthesis of interdisciplinary perspectives to evaluate life narratives.

EPISODES

Among the first tasks of the life narrative author is to collect vivid episodes from the past that have a story to tell. One scene leads to a second and to a third until the author steps back and attempts to understand, with fresh eyes, how they relate to one another. Psychological researchers gather data to investigate how we form, forget, recall, and articulate memories. Basic neuroscience researchers, who were the primary platform for

Eakin's literary theory, examine the person's biological systems, but typically not the social environment factors which enable memory acquisition and its articulation.

Developmental psychologists interpret data about memory as it unfolds across the lifespan. They may use cross-sectional research studies with samples of five year olds, ten year olds, and twenty year olds to discover what they remember. In contrast, longitudinal research studies gather data from a much larger sample of five year olds and then the scientists follow the same children until they become ten years old, and then twenty years old, comparing how their bank of memories grew or how their recollections of the same memories changed. A third developmental research strategy is to collect data from a sample of adults by asking them, in retrospect, to identify what they remember from as far back as they can, and then to recall episodes from ages five, ten, twenty and so forth. The aggregated data in all of these research designs will have preliminary analyses completed on how the random sample respondents differ based on their gender, ethnicity, age, class, level of education, and a host of other personal characteristics; these variables will then be controlled in accounting for differences in the overall findings.

Cognitive psychology researchers study differences in the acquisition, retention, and reporting of memories in and of themselves, focusing less on developmental changes, but, like neuroscientists, on the biological factors that assist or constrict these processes. The study of memory, and, more specifically, the study of autobiographical memory, has mushroomed since the late 1980s. Once again, as I described in Chapter One when talking about narratives, the study of autobiographical memory and its relationships to language and the presentation of self have gone down parallel tracks in literature and in psychology, with only recent crossovers by interdisciplinary scholars.

Building an Autobiographical Memory Bank

Integrating twenty years of research on this topic, Katherine Nelson and Robyn Fivush drew the following conclusions:

> *Autobiographical memory* is defined here as an explicit memory of an event that occurred in a specific time and place in one's personal past. . .The components that contribute to the emergence of autobiographical memory include basic memory systems, the acquisition of complex spoken or signed language, narrative comprehension and production, memory talk with parents and others, style of parent talk, temporal understanding, representation of self, person perspective, and psychological understanding (i.e., theory of mind).[25]

Let's unpackage this dense summary. What I am trying to illustrate is how scientific research done by psychologists may be integrated with the qualitative understanding of the life narrative processes explored by literary scholars and those in other disciplines, as well.

First, there are different types of memory (e.g., about words, about procedures for solving problems, or about how things work), but autobiographical memory seems to be related most to experiential episodes that we construe as personally meaningful. There are specific neural pathways and brain regions that serve its functions.

Second, the social-cultural-developmental qualities of autobiographical memory means that it emerges gradually across the pre-school years, with language as a key component in its increasing complexity, and that cultural, gendered, and individual differences produce rich variation in its content and expression. Thus, autobiographical memories derive from many internal processes but just as many external influences.

Third, whereas the physiological brain structures required for general memory grow in the first year of life, research suggests that adults' autobiographical memories generally begin around the ages of three to four years. Nelson and Fivush evaluated what has been called the "childhood amnesia" problem, suggesting that there really is no single moment or age when amnesia falls away and we become able to remember personally meaningful episodes. There is too much variability in the obtained data. Their social-cultural-developmental theory and its assertion of gradual emergence accounts for this variability more effectively.

Fourth, many of the broad descriptions used by Erikson for how parents and their children interact and how the young person accomplishes a growing sense of self and identity are now being identified more precisely in experimental studies. Parents begin to talk about past and future events with their language-using toddlers, laying the groundwork for a concept of time and early senses of the child's personal place in a flow of events. Such talk shifts to actual conversations and the telling of stories about the family and specifically about the child. Hearing these tales about precocious moments and verbal expressions or mischievous behavior's consequences teaches the youngster both the nature and structure of story and begins to establish a time-line of autobiographical memory.

Fifth, Nelson and Fivush ascribed considerable importance to learning the function of narrative as predictive of enhanced autobiographical memory.

> Narrative adds layers of comprehensibility to events above
> and beyond what is available from direct experience by linking
> events together through causal, conditional, and temporal markers.
> Narratives are structured around meanings, emphasizing goals and

plans, motivations and emotions, successful and failed outcomes, and their meaningful relation to the teller as well as to the other players. . .narratives provide for the expression of and reflection on personal meaning and significance that in turn allows for a more complex understanding of psychological motivation and causation.[26]

This summary of laboratory-based findings obtained from children and their parents captures the future adult processes that the life narrative author engages in for the gathering of memory's episodes and then finding an effective composition strategy to articulate them.

Sixth, in a section on "adult memory talk", Nelson and Fivush offer persuasive explanations of how the reminiscing style used especially by mothers—how often they talk about the past, how they elaborate, and how they probe their children to verbalize added details about a past event—directly influences a child's skills for constructing their own narrative history. This powerful effect has been demonstrated in both cross-sectional (one age only) and in longitudinal (one group of children studied over time) research findings.

Seventh, through all these interactions, the learning of narrative grows. One's autobiographical memory bank grows and the youngster discovers also that disagreements about memories are to be expected. They concluded: "research conducted over the past decade has established that children acquire memory and narrative skills through participating in adult-scaffolded social interactions."[27]

Memories are representations of events, and our recollections of them may be unique and not shared by others. This is the empirically validated roots of the literary "autobiographical I" that I discussed in Chapter One. There is an "I" who does the remembering and composes, and an "I" who is the created character in the narrative, and an "I" who actually lived the events that were witnessed and can be evaluated by others. These empirical findings may be reasonably extrapolated to the vital importance of oral tradition in the formation of autobiographical memory. Oral tradition's processes, cherished by different cultures and families, and especially by mothers, are the heart of autobiographical memory formation and the development of one's own narrative style for its telling. Nelson and Fivush concluded from the accumulated research by psychological scientists that "in general, adult women have longer, more detailed, more vivid, and more emotionally laden autobiographical memories than adult men of events from both adulthood and childhood."[28] Cross-cultural psychological research is a new frontier in the examination of reminiscing styles, their purposes, and its effects on both the story teller and the younger listener. How do we move beyond defining the individual self by memory to the creation of communities with shared pasts via shared cultural narratives?

Psychologists discovered in their research what authors whose work derived from oral traditions have long known and written about. The self emerges from collaborative interactions and constructive social processes. As we discussed in Chapter Two on Erikson's psychosocial developmental theory, adolescence is a critical time when a person's identity takes shape from often inchoate mixtures of biological, cognitive, affective, and behavioral factors. And, as we discussed in Chapter Five, McAdams built on Erikson's notion of adolescent identity formation to propose a life story model of identity. We become constant editors of an anthology of stories that presents who we were, are, and hope to become.

Other cognitive researchers added to our understanding of how a life story emerges at this time. In their critical review, Tilmann Habermas and Susan Bluck proposed the following:

> . . . we focus on the subjective versions of one's life and
> reserve the term life story for the life as told, remembered, or
> thought about by the individual. . .we differentiate two major
> manifestations: *life narratives* (full products of the life story) and
> *autobiographical reasoning* (the process by which the life story
> is formed and used).[29]

Children remember events and they learn about stories, but adolescents first embed those events in personal narratives as an important way to make sense of them. They develop autobiographical reasoning as a reflective strategy for creating themselves as persons with pasts, presents, and futures. Developmental histories are framed in the context of rich social-cultural interactions, a myriad of conversations about conflicts over gender, sexual orientation, ethnicity, educational pursuits, vocational aspirations, and values. Using cross-cultural survey data, these researchers identified how adolescents and young adults must create and practice their newly emerging stories on applications for school or work, on family histories for comprehensive medical examinations, and in the more routine tasks of keeping a personal diary or composing a graduating yearbook's entries or a personal website/space. Recognizing this boiling stew of motivations, achievements, and disappointments, it is easy to understand why other cognitive researchers found a "reminiscence bump" in the reports of adults over age thirty-five in the number and vividness of their memories from adolescence.

Habermas and Bluck published a second review in 2001 in which they advocated taking a life-span developmental perspective on autobiographical memory. Their research demonstrated that individuals changed their recollections and evaluations of specific episodes as time went by, and often as adaptive strategies to face present-day conflicts.[30] Once again, Erikson seems to have gotten it right. Understanding the individual and interpreting their story requires us to ask: at what age and stage did the author write, in what historical epoch, and in response to what psycho-social-cultural events taking place at the time. McAdams concluded the following in the same special issue on autobiographical memory in which the Bluck and Habermas paper appeared:

> The idea that identity is an internalized and evolving life story ties together a number of important and theoretical trends in developmental, cognitive, personality, and cultural psychology. . . . As psychosocial constructions, life stories reflect the values, norms, power differentials inherent in the societies wherein they have their constitutive meanings. The construction of coherent life stories is an especially challenging problem for adults living in contemporary modern (and postmodern) societies, wherein selves are viewed as reflexive projects imbued with complexity and depth, ever-changing and yet demanding a coherent framing.[31]

This reflexive project underlies the maps and metaphors concept that I have used throughout this book. We begin thinking about a unifying thematic during adolescence, but the task becomes increasingly difficult with more and more memory's episodes to integrate as we grow into adulthood. Psychological research continues to offer supporting evidence for the literary tradition's appreciation of "coming-of-age" stories. We truly begin rehearsing and composing who we may become, at so many levels, during adolescence. As we gather memory's episodes from this developmental period, it makes for a very good story.

Most importantly, as I observed in previous chapters, the ever-expanding number of multicultural narratives, voices, and composition strategies enriches all of our projects and our lives with memory's stories. I turn now to a memoir that spent nearly two years on *The New York Times* best-seller list at the end of the millennium.

JAMES MCBRIDE AND THE COLORING OF IDENTITY

James McBride was born in 1957, the son of Rachel Deborah Shilsky and Andrew McBride, who married in 1942. His Black minister father died of cancer before he was born and James was raised by his White mother and Hunter Jordan, a furnace fireman, who died in 1972. Rachel, who grew up in rural Suffolk, Virginia, as the daughter of a Polish Orthodox Jewish rabbi, found refuge in the Black Christian community in Harlem after leaving home, and was renounced and declared dead by her family. Rachel Shilsky died and Ruth McBride was born. James was her eighth child with eleven brothers and sisters; his siblings became university professors, physicians and nurse administrators, therapists, teachers, and business people. His mother completed her B.A. at Temple University after her children finished their studies.

James was the artist, a jazz saxophonist and writer, among the McBride-Jordans. He received his B.A. in music composition from the Oberlin Conservatory of Music and an M.S.J. in journalism from Columbia University at age 22. He worked on the staffs of *The Washington Post, Boston Globe, Rolling Stone*, and *People Magazine* for eight years until he returned to creating music. He wrote songs (music and lyrics) for Anita Baker, Grover Washington Jr., Gary Burton, Everett Harp, Rachelle Farell, and PuraFe, and children's song for Silver Burdett Textbooks and for PBS television shows like "Barney". He composed the scores for the musicals "All Roads Lead Home" and "Harlem Kids Symphony", and his award-winning jazz, hip-hop musical, "Bobos", premiered in 1993. His musical theater composition honors included the American Music Theater Festival's Stephen Sondheim Award, the American Arts and Letters Richard Rodgers Award, and the ASCAP Richard Rodgers Horizons Award.

His life changed with the publication of *The Color of Water* [33]. The book was listed on *The New York Times* bestseller list for two years and he received the 1997 Anisfield Wolf Book Award (as had Maxine Hong Kingston and Richard Rodriguez). He published a novel in 2002, *Miracle at Saint Anna*, a redemption story about the Black American "Buffalo Soldiers" during World War II, fighting in' Italy. It is a mosaic of narratives to which McBride brought his journalism investigative skills and his storytelling talents. When the jazz musician Quincy Jones published his autobiography, *Q*, James was the ghostwriter on that project, having been selected by the author for his rare mix of musical and literary skills. He now mines both creative veins on a full-time, self-employed basis, writing in the morning and composing music in the afternoons.

The Color of Water began as a Mother's Day feature story that McBride wrote for the *Boston Globe* in 1982, and that was published simultaneously in the *Philadelphia Inquirer* where his mother lived at the time while studying for her baccalaureate. The piece received favorable response and motivated him to dig deeper than what he knew and the very few stories he had been told by his mother over the years. She tempted him with bits and pieces of her life narrative. He returned to the scenes of his grandfather's abuses in Virginia for detective-like interviews with those who still remembered his mother, to flesh out the story into a book-length memoir.

Redeeming a Grim Tale

James once asked Mommy why she cried in church on Sundays. She told him that God made her happy. His adult memory recalled having had intuitions that there was more behind this response. He bugged her by asking whether she cried because she wanted to be Black like everyone else in that Baptist church. Was God Black or White? Which color folks did God like better? She responded that God is a spirit and loves all people. He pressed. What color is God's spirit? Ruth stopped the young boy's persistent inquiries by telling him that God does not have a color. God is the color of water. Kids may believe that water has no color. When we grow up, however, adults know that water can be found in many places and can often reveal to us its many colors. Young James was quelled for the moment, but it was a story that lived a long time in his memory.

McBride used yoked, thematic chapter titles as a map for this auto/biography. Mother's and son's stories unfold in a linear chronology, weaving in and out of each other. The titles in italics were about Ruth's, his mother's story followed by James's: *Dead* / Bicycle; *Kosher* / Black Power; *The Old Testament* /The New Testament; *Sam* / Brothers and Sisters; *Shul* / School; *Boys* / Daddy; *New York* / Chicken Man; *Graduation* / Driving; *Lost in Harlem* / Lost in Delaware; *The Promise* / Old Man Shilsky; *A Bird Who Flies* / A Jew Discovered; *Dennis* / New Brown. He titled the last chapter "Finding Ruthie" and brought the story to its contemporary conclusion as lives lived in tandem. In the Epilogue, he described bringing her to his friend's wedding, a Jewish marriage in a synagogue. Ruth's story and James's biracial and bicultural identity came full circle back to their genesis.

James was thirty-nine and Ruth was seventy-five when *The Color of Water* was published. In the Eriksons' ages and stages model, James was in the midst of the generativity concerns of adulthood and Ruth in the despair versus integrity elder stage with wisdom as its principally accomplished virtue.

> ...we claim that wisdom rests in the capacity to see, look, remember,
> as well as to listen, hear, and remember. Integrity, we maintain,
> demands tact, contact, and touch. This is a serious demand on the
> senses of elders. It takes a lifetime to learn to be tactful and demands
> both patience and skill; it is all too easy to become weary and
> discouraged.[32]

The Eriksonian virtues of hope, fidelity, and caring sing from the pages of James's part of the memoir. The text reveals how McBride construed his life in McAdams's redemptive terms. Despite having never known his father, having lived a hard scrabble economic existence in a family of twelve, with a mother of murky origins and exhibiting rather strange daily behaviors, he recognized his special advantage and blessing from being in this family. He was deeply aware of the suffering of others in the midst of the Civil Rights era and the constant struggles among his family and Black people to balance power and communion as the sources of their freedom.

This story, both James's and Ruth's, illuminates McAdams's languages of redemption. The *Old Testament* / New Testament chapters, especially, are about atonement. Emancipation characterizes *Kosher* / Black Power and later *A Bird Who Flies* / A Jew Discovered. McBride weaves all the languages of recovery, enlightenment, and development throughout the narrative as he navigates the pain of Ruth's life in Virginia leading to nurturance among Black Christians in New York City and her maternal power. He articulated his story as a classic American tale that led from confusion about ethnic identity to being lost to being found and growing to appreciate his bicultural and dual religious roots. Ruth's story demonstrated how a contaminated plot from an early psychological injury could lead to either a succession of repeated failings OR, in her life, to a redemptive, inspirational story where hope, faith, and love are discovered and celebrated. James's ultimate generative act was the composition of a memoir that so many found to be a "good read" as the millennium drew to a close.

Composing Stories as a Relationship Strategy

Eakin connected language, memory, and identity and his analyses help us understand this story at deeper levels. Like Hong Kingston's mother's admonition that began Maxine's story, "Tell no one", Ruth established a similarly stark beginning for her son, James. In the early stages of his exploring stories with his mother, Ruth told James to hurry up and get the interviews over with. Like the "No Name Woman", she declared that she was dead as the very first lines of the book. James wanted to listen to stories about her family, but she had been erased from their lives for over fifty years when he began his exploratory conversations. She wanted no part of them because they had made it clear that they wanted no memory, no story from her life, at all. Composing memories of broken or erased relationships were the resurrection strategies used by both Maxine and by James to celebrate their mothers and to discover themselves.

Ruchel Dwarja Zylska was born in Poland on April Fool's Day. Her parents changed her name to Rachel Deborah Shilsky when they came to America, and she changed it again to Ruth when she left Virginia in 1941. Each time, one life died so that another could begin. Tateh (father in Yiddish) was an itinerant Orthodox rabbi who kept getting terminated by his congregations. He ran a general store in rural Virginia when Ruth was nine years old. He abused his wife, hated his predominantly Black customers, cheated them at every turn, and they hated him. During one of her interviews with James, she wrote on a piece of paper the word, "molest", and finally let out this childhood secret. Her sorrow and anger poured forth with this disclosure, fearing that a reading public would interpret that she stooped low to marry a Black man only because of having been abused. In plain-speaking terms, she told James that it was his Black father who changed her life, lifting her up in profoundly emotional and spiritual ways.

Mameh (mother in Yiddish) was temperamentally the opposite of the father. Ruth described her as meek and gentle, paralyzed on one side of her body from polio, and nearly blind in one eye. She mourned the fact that she had not done right by her mother, had not been grateful enough for all she had been given by this woman who herself was silenced at every turn. Ruth fell in love in Virginia with the only boy who befriended her, a young Black who risked his life to be seen with her, either by Tateh or in a town filled with Ku Klux Klan members. Mameh never said a word when she became pregnant at fifteen, and sent her to relatives in New York City, where she had an abortion. She left Virginia, again, the night after high school graduation.

The elder Ruth told her son how she felt starved for love and affection, receiving none from her father and not knowing how her mother survived all the while. In the passages describing when Ruth met her first childhood love in Virginia, McBride inserted the following reminiscence. She recalled that Peter was not judgmental and that this attitude was probably what attracted her most to Black folks all her life. In 1939, she met Andrew Dennis McBride, a worker at her aunt's leather factory, who had come from High Point, North Carolina, graduating from the same high school as John Coltrane. Her first husband was a singer and a violinist who composed music and songs and played gigs in halls and churches whenever he could get them. Ruth remembered fondly his basic Christian values and how immediately understood and respected she felt by him. She returned one last time to Virginia to take care of her ailing mother. Tateh had divorced her; he pleaded with Ruth to stay home, run the store, and to care of Mameh. When she balked, her father delivered his final blow. He knew that she was going to marry a Black man, and told her that if she did so, to never come home again. Ruth went back to New York with Mameh's Polish passport as her parting gift in hand, and never saw her mother again. She married Dennis who brought her out of the depression into which she plunged when her mother died and her family declared Ruth dead to them as well. Ruth told James that the Jew in her had been dying a slow death, but its final moment came with the death of her mother, and Christianity's embrace via her husband, James's father. Their family grew. They moved to Brooklyn, founded a Church together, and had seven children. Dennis died but in the same year, 1957, James McBride, their eighth, was born.

After McBride sent the manuscript to the publisher, his editor suggested that he restructure the mother's and son's continuing stories as alternate chapters. This revision was such an effective composition strategy, advancing the genre stylistically and symbolically. Auto/biography became dialogic performance in this text. Moreover, the yoked story lines demonstrated Eakin's understandings of self as constructed by a pattern of relationships. McBride served as auto-ethnographer for life as a member of a bicultural family growing up during the times of Malcolm X and Martin Luther King, Jr., benefiting from the continuing commitment of the New York City public school system to educate first generation triumphs, and American higher education's fledgling attempts to balance access and excellence for its new populations. Eakin's conclusion seems apt: "the writing of autobiography is properly understood as an integral part of a lifelong process of identity formation in which acts of self-narration play a major part." [33]

In the final section, I turn to James's memories in the final chapters, "A Jew Discovered" and "Finding Ruthie".

Revising the Anthology of Memory's Stories

McBride recalled that as a boy, he knew nothing about where his mother came from, about her birth and her parents. He asked her often to tell him stories. She blunted his curiosity by telling him that God made her and He made him, too. He remembered asking Mommy whether she was white. She described herself as light-skinned, and then changed the topic. After the original Mother's Day story was published, it still took him many years to pry the stories out of her memory. The book became the story of her life as told to him, and James's life was woven into the pages of the text as well.

McBride began his first chapter with an autobiographical memory of being a fourteen year old. His coloring of identity was its theme. His stepfather, the only dad he knew, had just died. James dropped out of high school, stole, smoked marijuana, and became painfully aware of his strange White mother pedaling her bicycle around an all Black neighborhood. She seemed oblivious to the outside world and ran their household like a drill sergeant. He ended the opening chapter with an episode about leaving home on the school bus to go to kindergarten. He recalled that he understood for the first time that his mother was not the same color as the other parents. The discovery led to the predictable round of questions to Mommy. She told him that he asked too many personal questions and the story was not important. What was important was school and educating his mind about more important things than skin color or her past life. Thus, McBride began the chapters of his life by confessing the sins of his adolescence and his redemption by the grace of an incredible woman. His story is a many times revised and layered set of memories.

James returned to his thematic, autobiographical memory in the chapter on "Black Power". As he grew older, he felt an ache that grew stronger. His mother refused to confess her whiteness and he remembered that he never knew why. His teachers knew; at PTA meetings they asked early every academic year whether he was adopted. This is McBride talking, the adult editor of the revised anthology. One central memory for James was staring out the school bus window, in dread, at his white mother standing next to a Black Panther father of a classmate. He tried to warn her, but the bus pulled away, and so he did the next best thing to control his fears and give voice to his anxieties as an elementary school kid. He punched the son squarely in the mouth. Every year, my students name that memory's episode as one of their most memorable.

McBride constructed his identity out of his dialogues with Ruth. The web of relationships, however, went beyond this dyadic pairing. Autobiographical memories of his brothers and sisters were key ingredients in his construction. The Church community members had their part to play as well. The Christian and Jewish threads, as well as the Black and White fibers needed to be woven together into some workable garment. McBride, composer of this anthology of stories could finally say that as a grown man he became more appreciative of his origins in two worlds. The adult author of this story became a Black man with a Jewish soul.

In a chapter with the title, "Old Man Shilsky", James crystallized this identity. In 1982, with the first Mother's Day story published, and with a crude map of Suffolk, pieced together from Ruth's stubborn withholdings, he returned to his grandparents' home town. He knocked on a door and met a sixty-six year old Black man who could not contain his laughter when he introduced himself as Old Man Shilsky's grandson. James heard his mother's childhood name, Rachel, the kind-hearted one, for the very first time (still later to discover her as Ruchel). A diplomatic recounting of Shilsky's qualities gave way to a less sanitized one at James's urgings. McBride reported conversations he had with other men from the extant Jewish community. They were as incredulous about his color as the first Black man. While with one of his story-tellers, James had him telephone his mother. He told her how glad he was to meet Rachel's son, how proud she should feel about this nice young man, and to come back home if ever she could, because her original Jewish community would welcome her, and wished the best for her.

Ten more years elapsed in this continuing anthology that McBride was creating. He was now married and the father of two. After considerable investigative probing to flesh out the details of his family's diaspora, he returned to Suffolk and stood in front of the synagogue. Then, he went to the Nansemond River where murdered Black men had been entombed for so many years of the racist South. Walking along its banks, he felt the spirit of his Jewish grandmother, remembering her in a chapter titled "A Jew Discovered". He mused about how lonely she must have felt, separated from her extended family, a Polish immigrant to America, not knowing the English language, and with a physical disability. Her hateful husband and her family seemed to be without much of a future. Yet, her spirit filled James. Her reality dissipated his uncertainty about from where and from whom he had come. The ache of the young boy diminished. The adult man returned to New York, now confident that his life reflected the strength of her life. His grandmother's story was no longer silent. It washed into his soul, coloring it with complex hues.

A Concluding Reflection

In "Finding Ruthie", James McBride captured what psychologists and scientists continue to map in their empirical research, what story tellers always knew.

Augustine created memory's stories first. He sustained our efforts ever since.

Erikson and Merton probed the moral fabrics of critical episodes. Their developmental maps and pilgrim journey metaphors continue to inspire.

Haley cherished his composing relationship with Malcolm and Neihardt extolled Black Elk's story to inspire others. The fruits of their lives and what they revealed linger; the scribes' earthy relationships with their muses served us well.

Hong Kingston learned to talk-story just like her mother taught her. She composed a magical reality to which we can all go to find a heroine, then return home to discover that we often live with one.

Rodriguez colored in brown how we disclose our selves to ourselves, and then eloquently essay our lives out loud to others.

McBride remembered what happened as Ruth gathered her memories in front of his eyes. As she remembered, she was stunned until the episodes flowed forth like lava and like water. She died again and again with the retold story. Her resurrection via stories, gave birth to her son James's adult identity.

We too may do the same, if we read with empathy others' multicultural stories, often so different from our own. Remember that we have been constructing our identities and composing our texts for many years, already. It may be time to begin writing, too.

NOTES

1. Jill Ker Conway, *The Road from Coorain* (New York: Knopf, 1989); *True North* (New York: Knopf, 1994); *A Woman's Education* (New York: Knopf, 2001).

2. Jill Ker Conway, ed., *Written by Herself: Autobiographies of American Women* (New York: Vintage, 1992).

3. Jill Ker Conway, *When Memory Speaks: Exploring the Art of Autobiography* (New York: Vintage, 1999).

4. James McBride, *The Color of Water: A Black Man's Tribute to His White Mother* (New York: Riverhead Books, 1997).

5. Erik H. Erikson and Joan M. Erikson, *The Life Cycle Completed. Extended Version with New Chapters on the Ninth Stage of Development* (New York: Norton, 1997), 58.

6. Dan P. McAdams, *The Redemptive Self: Stories Americans Live By* (New York: Oxford University Press, 2006).

7. McAdams, *Redemptive Self*, 11.

8. McAdams, *Redemptive Self,* 12.

9. The material on the languages of self is more fully illustrated in Chapter One "Redemption and the American Soul", especially Table 1.1.

10. McAdams, *Redemptive Self*, 269.

11. Paul John Eakin, *Fictions in Autobiography: Studies in the Art of Self-Invention* (Princeton: Princeton University Press, 1985).

12. Paul John Eakin, ed., *American Autobiography* (Madison: University of Wisconsin Press, 1991).

13. Paul John Eakin, *Touching the World: Reference in Autobiography* (Princeton, NJ: Princeton University Press, 1992).

14. Paul John Eakin, *How Our Lives Become Stories: Making Selves* (Ithaca, NY: Cornel University Press, 1999).

15. Paul John Eakin, *The Ethics of Life Writing* (Ithaca, NY: Cornell University Press, 2004), 6.

16. Eakin, *Lives Become Stories*, ix.

17. Eakin, *Lives Become Stories*, 4.

18. Eakin, *Lives Become Stories*, 43.

19. Eakin, *Lives Become Stories*, 48.

20. Eakin, *Lives Become Stories*, 70.

21. Eakin, *Lives Become Stories*, 98.

22. Eakin, *Lives Become Stories*, 185.

23. Eakin, *Lives Become Stories,* 101 (emphases in original).

24. Eakin, *Lives Become Stories,* 118.

25. Katherine Nelson and Robyn Fivush, "The Emergence of Autobiographical Memory: A Social Cultural Developmental Theory", *Psychological Review* 111 (2004), 486.

26. Nelson and Fivush, "Emergence of Autobiographical Memory", 494.

27. Nelson and Fivush, "Emergence of Autobiographical Memory", 499.

28. Nelson and Fivush, "Emergence of Autobiographical Memory", 505.

29. Tilmann Habermas and Susan Bluck, "Getting a Life: The Emergence of the Life Story in Adolescence", *Psychological Bulletin* 126 (2000), 748–749.

30. Susan Bluck and Tilmann Habermas, "Extending the Study of Autobiographical Memory: Thinking Back about Life across the Life Span", *Review of General Psychology* 5 (2001): 135–147.

31. Dan P. McAdams, "The Psychology of Life Stories", *Review of General Psychology* 5 (2001), 117–118.

32. Erikson and Erikson, *The Life Cycle Completed*, 112.

33. Eakin, *Lives Become Stories,* 101.

Index

Alighieri, Dante, 38–39, 41, 46, 48–49;
  Inferno, 38, 46; *Paradiso,* 38;
  Purgatorio, 18, 38–40, 52n29
Allport, Gordon, 130, 132, 135
Ambrose, Saint, 11–12, 15–16, 47
American Indian Religious Freedom
  Act, 86, 92–93n47
Angelou, Maya, 18n9, 100; *I Know Why
  the Caged Bird Sings,* 9, 26, 110
audience, 2, 6, 8, 15, 60, 95, 138–39,
  142–43, 159, 169, 176; Augustine,
  15; Erikson, 36; Hong Kingston, 112,
  121; McBride, 187; Merton, 37, 41,
  53n35; Rodriguez, 148, 153–54;
  Smith, 98–99, 101–3, 107
Augustine, Saint: Adeodatus (son),
  10–12, 16, 47; Brown, Peter, 10–11,
  14, 22n33, 22n40; *The Confessions,*
  5, 10, 12–15, 18, 21n28, 22n37,
  22n40, 26–27, 34, 36–37, 39–40, 46,
  96, 119, 147–48, 152, 154; memory,
  10, 12, 16–17, 21n24, 21n25, 27, 43,
  49, 120, 135, 177, 190; Monica
  (mother), 10–12, 16, 18, 47;
  O'Donnell, James, 11, 13–14, 18,
  21n25, 22n37, 22n46
autobiography, 8, 18n1, 19n3, 76,
  90n15, 111, 147, 156, 159, 161,
175–76, 178; autobiographical "I", 4,
  6, 37, 45, 49, 102, 112, 114, 136,
  154, 177, 181; autobiographical pact,
  95, 142; *autos,* 4, 6, 27, 37,
  50–51n11, 60, 72, 81, 95, 100, 106,
  111, 174; *bios,* 4, 7, 27, 37,
  50–51n11, 60, 72, 81, 95, 100, 106,
  111, 174; *graphe,* 4, 50–51n11, 60,
  72, 95, 100, 106, 174
The Autobiography of Malcolm X. See
  Malcolm X

Barbour, John, 4, 19n4, 57, 89n8
Benstock, Shari, 98, 107
Black Elk, Nicholas, 21n24, 32, 37, 47,
  57, 61–65, 67–73, 79–80, 84–85, 87,
  109, 112, 119, 158, 169, 190; *Black
  Elk Speaks,* 5, 26, 61–65, 67–73,
  79–80, 84–87, 111, 158; DeMallie,
  Raymond, 64, 67, 69, 84–85, 90n18;
  Ghost Dance, 63–64, 70, 80, 84. *See
  also* John G. Neihardt
Brown, Joseph Epes, 65, 119
Brown, Peter. *See* Augustine

Cheung, King-kok. *See* Maxine Hong
  Kingston
Childhood and Society. See Erik Erikson

Chin, Frank. *See* Maxine Hong
    Kingston
class, 4, 52n27, 77, 81, 98–99, 101, 103,
    113, 115, 123n13, 130, 141, 146,
    148–49, 151, 153–54, 157, 177, 179
cognitive psychology. *See* neuroscience
    and cognitive psychology
composition strategies, 2, 5–7, 36,
    98–99, 102, 107, 134, 140, 174–78;
    Augustine, 15–16; Black Elk, 67–73;
    Hong Kingston, 110–13, 119–20;
    Malcolm X, 67–68, 73–78, 81;
    McBride, 186–88; Merton, 39–41;
    Rodriguez, 152–54, 159
The Confessions. See Augustine
continuity and unity of self, 7, 9, 18,
    26–27, 29, 31–33, 45, 97, 100, 112,
    133–37, 139, 143, 147, 159, 161,
    170, 174; discontinuity, 96–97, 143,
    152, 159
conversion, 12, 15, 18, 39, 47–48,
    55–59, 63, 66, 70, 75, 83–86, 88
Conway, Jill Ker: *When Memory
    Speaks,* 20n20, 169–70, 173, 175;
    Written by Herself, 19n7, 121, 169
Couser, G. Thomas, 60, 62, 69–71,
    90n15, 91n29, 91n35, 111, 158–61,
    174

DeMallie, Raymond. *See* Black Elk
Dorsey, Peter, 58, 89n9
DuBois, W.E.B.: double consciousness,
    19n7, 82, 88; *Souls of Black Folks,*
    19n7, 19n9

Eakin, Paul John, 26, 75–76, 92n37,
    113–14, 155, 174–79, 186, 188
Elijah Muhammad, 66, 68, 74–77, 80,
    83, 87. *See also* Nation of Islam
empathy, 6, 9, 55, 87, 96, 99, 104, 112,
    178, 190
Erikson, Erik, 8, 14, 18, 29, 32, 34, 41,
    77, 101, 139, 153, 170–71, 180, 182,
    190; *Childhood and Society,* 30;
    epigenesis, 8, 35–36, 41, 43, 45, 49,

79, 133; *Gandhi's Truth,* 20n12, 32,
    34–36; *homo religiosus,* 20n12,
    21n24, 33, 37, 41, 49; identity, 29,
    118; *The Life Cycle Completed,*
    20n12, 34–35; life cycle
    psychosocial theory, 8, 18, 30–35,
    41, 49, 79, 132, 134, 147, 169, 182,
    185; *Young Man Luther,* 20n12,
    32–34, 135
Erikson, Joan Serson, 20n12, 30, 32, 35
essay, 152–54, 161, 190
ethnicity, 4, 52n27, 99, 102–3, 108,
    112–13, 119, 123n13, 125n53, 130,
    145, 148, 151, 158, 160, 176–77,
    179, 182

feminist scholarship, 6, 8, 96, 98–99,
    103, 107–9, 112, 114, 129, 142, 169,
    174–77
Franklin, Benjamin, 7, 75, 91n35; *The
    Autobiography of,* 1, 65, 95, 172
Freud, Sigmund, 8, 28–29, 32, 34, 129

Gandhi, Mahatma, 49, 58, 77; *The Story
    of My Experiments with Truth,* 17, 34
Gandhi's Truth. See Erik Erikson
Gates, Jr., Henry Louis: *Bearing
    Witness,* 19n7, 55
gender, 4, 9, 34, 52n27, 96, 98,
    100–103, 105, 108–10, 112–13, 115,
    119–21, 123n13, 124n34, 125n53,
    129, 141, 145, 169, 176–77, 179–80,
    182
generativity, 6, 14, 30, 32, 41, 44, 49,
    59, 80–81, 85, 89n12, 132, 134,
    139–40, 147, 170, 172, 185–86
Gergen, Kenneth, 9, 20n15, 51n16, 101,
    137, 140–41; *The Saturated Self,* 7,
    9, 137
Gilmore, Leigh, 98, 123n13
grace, 11, 26–27, 33, 38, 45, 49, 55–60,
    147, 150, 189
Gusdorf, Georges, 8, 27–28, 45, 49,
    50n9, 50n10, 50n11, 72, 76, 95,
    97–98, 123n21, 142, 174, 177

Habermas, Tilman, 23n44, 182–83
Haley, Alex, 57, 62, 66–67, 73–77,
    81–82, 119, 143, 190. *See also*
    Malcolm X
Hong Kingston, Maxine, 22n33, 61,
    102, 110, 112–21, 146, 149, 152–53,
    155–58, 175, 184, 186, 190; Brave
    Orchid (mother), 113–18, 121, 176,
    186; Cheung, King-kok, 112,
    125n50, 125n53, 125n54; Chin,
    Frank, 111, 157, 160; *China Men,*
    111, 119–20, 125n53; Fa Mu Lan,
    109–10, 113–17, 176; father, 111;
    The Fifth Book of Peace, 119; Moon
    Orchid (aunt), 109, 113, 116–17,
    176; No Name Woman (aunt),
    109–10, 113–15, 117, 120–21, 186;
    Tripmaster Monkey, 119, 121; Ts'ai
    Yen, 109, 113, 118; *The Woman
    Warrior,* 3, 6, 9, 14, 108–10, 113–14,
    118–21, 125n53, 157, 159, 175;
    Wong, Cynthia Sau-ling, 111,
    125n53, 125n54
hope, 38, 49, 59, 68, 70, 79, 85, 104,
    106, 109, 139, 163, 171–73, 182,
    185–86

identity, 23n44, 27, 52n27, 96, 98–99,
    129, 131, 147, 170, 174–76; Black
    Elk, 61, 78–80; crisis, 33–35, 47, 170;
    Erikson, 31–33, 180, 182; ethnic,
    19n9, 72, 82, 87, 113, 148, 155,
    157–58, 160, 183–86, 188–89; Hong
    Kingston, 109, 115–17, 120; Malcolm
    X, 76–77, 80–83; McAdams, 48, 132,
    136, 139, 141, 172–73; Merton,
    41–42, 44, 46, 48–49; Rodriguez,
    148, 152, 155, 160–61; Smith, 102–3,
    106, 108, 125n48
intentions. *See* motivations
interdisciplinary perspectives, 3, 26, 29,
    32, 49, 56, 72, 95, 99, 107–8, 128,
    130, 133, 137, 163, 169–70, 175,
    178–79
Irwin, Lee, 87, 92n46, 93n47

James, William, 9, 84–85, 128, 136–37,
    142; definition of religion, 56, 89n4,
    89n7; *The Varieties of Religious
    Experience,* 20n17, 47, 52n28, 55–57
Jelinek, Estelle, 97, 107, 122n10
Juhasz, Suzanne, 110

King, Jr. Martin Luther, 34, 77, 88, 188
Krupat, Arnold, 61, 71–73, 101;
    ethnocriticism, 72

Lee, Spike, 67, 78, 92n42
The Life Cycle Completed. See Erik
    Erikson
life narratives, 4, 15, 18, 19n5, 26, 36,
    86, 95, 108, 111, 113, 117–19, 128,
    136, 139, 141–42, 146–47, 151, 155,
    159, 163, 169, 173, 177–78, 180,
    182; collaborative, 5, 67–78, 143,
    169, 178; conversion, 5, 66, 76, 157,
    169, 172; "grim tales", 20n10; ethnic
    or immigration, 6, 19n7, 23, 104,
    108, 111, 190n54, 139, 158–59;
    serial autobiographies, 6, 121, 148,
    169; spiritual autobiographies, 9, 16,
    20n16, 27, 57, 60, 75, 88, 96, 172;
    therapeutic and survivor narratives,
    6, 20n10, 170, 172
literary criticism, 3, 7, 26, 62, 71, 75,
    97–98, 139, 174

maps and metaphors, 2, 7–9, 102, 107,
    131, 190; Augustine, 13–14; Black
    Elk, 61–65; Hong Kingston, 108–10,
    119; Malcolm X, 65–67; McAdams,
    170–74, 183; McBride, 184–86;
    Merton, 38–39; Rodriguez, 147–52
Malcolm X, 16, 21n24, 32, 37, 47, 57,
    60, 65–68, 73–78, 80–84, 87–88,
    100, 112, 119, 151–52, 157, 162,
    169, 175, 188, 190; *The
    Autobiography of Malcolm X,* 5, 26,
    65–67, 75–78, 80–81, 87–88, 176;
    Betty (wife), 74–75; Ella (half-
    sister), 82–83; father, 65, 81; mother,

65, 74, 77, 81–82; Ostroski incident, 82, 87

Mason, Mary, 27, 89n9, 96–97, 107, 177

master narratives, 27, 50n6, 75, 99, 124n29, 152, 170

McAdams, Dan P., 26, 29, 102, 130–43, 145, 153–55, 159, 170–74, 183; anthology of self and stories, 6, 48, 106, 139, 142, 147, 175, 182, 188–90; life story model of identity, 6, 48–49, 122, 131–43, 148, 152, 169–70, 175, 178, 182; redemption, 14, 59, 89n12, 132, 142, 170–74, 185–86; *The Redemptive Self,* 171–74

McBride, James: Andrew (father), 183, 187; *The Color of Water,* 6, 9, 26, 184–90; Hunter Jordan (stepfather), 183, 188; Mameh (grandmother), 187, 190; Ruth (mother), 183–90; Tateh (grandfather), 186–87, 189

McCluskey, Sally, 62, 68–70

McGovern, Thomas, 50n4, 128

memory, 3, 7, 38, 95, 179–81; Augustine, 10, 12, 16–17, 21n24, 21n25, 22n39, 27, 135; autobiographical, 4, 17, 23n42, 23n43, 23n44, 26, 102, 134, 141–42, 176, 178–83, 188–89; Black Elk, 67, 79; childhood amnesia, 23n43, 180; Eakin, 175–77, 186; Hong Kingston, 113–14, 116–17, 120–22; Malcolm X, 65, 74, 76–78; 80; 82; McAdams, 59; McBride, 184–85; 188; Merton, 39, 43–44, 49; Rodriguez, 150, 153, 155–56; 160, 162; reminiscence bump, 17, 23n44, 182; Smith, 99–100, 103, 108

memory's episodes, 2–4, 58–59, 78–79, 178–83; Augustine, 16–18; Black Elk, 78–80; 84–86; Hong Kingston, 109, 113–19, 121; Malcolm X, 76–77, 81–84, 87; McAdams, 138, 140, 142; Merton, 36, 41–49; Rodriguez, 151, 154–63; Smith, 100, 102, 107

men's stories, 8, 26, 96–98, 120, 158, 181

Merton, Thomas, 16, 18, 21n24, 36–37, 57, 59, 76, 84, 86–87, 112, 125n50, 145, 152, 154, 161, 169, 175, 190; *The Labyrinth,* 40–41; 52n30; Maud (aunt), 44, 46; Mott, Michael, 40, 42, 46–47, 50n10, 52n26, 154; Owen (father), 43, 45; Ruth (mother), 42–43; *The Seven Storey Mountain,* 5, 17–18, 36–41, 76, 119, 147–48; Trappists, 36–40, 44, 48

Misch, George, 27, 95, 97, 123n21

motivations, 2, 4, 15, 37, 111, 130–31, 133, 142, 160, 171, 182

Mott, Michael. *See* Thomas Merton

Murray, Henry, 28–29, 49, 66, 130, 132–33

Nation of Islam, 66–68, 73, 75, 77, 80, 83. *See also* Elijah Muhammad

Neihardt, John G. ("Flaming Rainbow"), 61–64, 67–72, 78–80, 84–85, 119, 143, 190; Enid (daughter), 62, 67, 90n18; Hilda (daughter), 62, 67, 90n20. *See also* Black Elk

Nelson, Katherine, 179–81

neuroscience and cognitive psychology, 3–4, 17, 26, 102, 108, 117, 129, 142, 175–79

O'Donnell, James. *See* Augustine

Olney, James, 4, 17, 19n3, 21n24, 22n39, 26, 51n11, 95, 98, 135, 142, 174, 178

oral tradition and story telling, 61–62, 70–72, 96, 101, 104, 109–12, 117–21, 145, 155, 177, 181, 190

Ortiz Cofer, Judith, 19n9, 120, 152–53; *The Latin Deli,* 9, 145

performance, 15, 69, 72, 95, 102, 142, 152, 161, 163, 174, 176–78 post-modern perspective, 6, 31n15, 72, 97, 105, 107, 110, 113, 132, 137, 140–41, 147, 152, 162, 170, 173, 183

prophecy, 5, 21n24, 55, 60, 63, 69, 84, 86–88, 90n15, 162

psychobiography, 28–29

psychology: academic discipline, 128–29; cognitive perspective, 129, 131, 134, 175, 178–79, 183; humanistic perspective, 129; narrative, 132–33, 137–41, 165n33, 180–81; neuropsychological perspective, 129; paradigms, 26, 132, 137–38, 141, 154; personality, 130–39, 175, 183; psychodynamic perspective, 129; sociocultural perspective, 197; traits, 131, 135–36, 138–39

race, 34, 65, 81–82, 98, 101, 103, 123n13, 128, 141, 151

redemption, 5–6, 8, 10, 14, 27, 55, 58–59, 70, 80, 85, 88, 170–74, 184, 188

The Redemptive Self. See Dan McAdams

Rodriguez, Richard, 19n9, 112, 121, 143–63, 169, 175, 184, 190; Baldwin, James, 146, 153, 162; *Brown,* 6, 9, 146–49, 151–53, 163; California, 143–44, 146, 149–52; Catholicism, 143–44, 148–52, 154, 160, 162–63; class issues, 146, 149, 151–54, 157; critical commentary, 154–62; *Days of Obligation,* 6, 9, 26, 144, 146–53, 160, 162–63; gay identity, 145, 150–51, 160–62; *Hunger of Memory,* 6, 9, 112, 144–50, 152–57, 159–62; language, 144, 152, 154–55, 162; Latino community, 145, 149–51, 155–56, 158; Lawrence, D.H., 146, 149; Leopoldo, (father), 143, 150, 162; Mexico, 143, 149–50, 155–57,

160–62; PBS NewsHour essays, 144, 146, 152; Victoria (mother), 143, 151, 154–55, 162

Sayre, Robert, 2, 7, 18–19n1, 69, 95, 97, 105, 122n2

The Seven Storey Mountain. See Thomas Merton

sexuality, 96, 101, 103, 117, 146, 152, 158, 162

silencing, 96, 103–4, 109, 112–14, 149, 175, 190

Shakespeare, William, 28, 30–31, 157

Silko, Leslie Marmon, 71, 109–10, 121, 146, 152; *Storyteller,* 3, 9, 110, 116–17, 177; Yellow Woman, 110, 116, 123–24n28

Smith, Sidonie, 89n9, 142, 158, 169, 174, 177–78; *Moving Lives,* 103–5; *Poetics,* 100–101, 109–10, 113, 152; *Subjectivity, Identity, and the Body,* 98, 102; *Where I'm Bound,* 99–100, 123n17

Smith, Sidonie and Julia Watson: *De/Colonizing the Subject,* 103, 124n34; *Getting a Life,* 105–6; *Human Rights,* 103–4; *Indigenous Australian Voices,* 103; *Reading Autobiography,* 4, 20n10, 27, 95, 99, 107–8, 139, 174; *Women, Autobiography: A Reader,* 6, 97–99; 106–7, 123n15; *Writing New Identities,* 103

Snow, Jade Wong, 121

Stanford Friedman, Susan, 98

Stone, Albert, 19n1, 77

story telling. *See* oral tradition and story telling

subjectivity, 6, 99, 102, 106–7, 109, 141

text, 4, 17, 24n46, 96; linear chronology of events, 15, 20n14, 37, 79, 112, 175; structure, 15–16, 96–97

truth-telling, 4, 17, 36, 49, 57–58, 77, 89n8, 111–12, 152, 158 unity. *See* continuity and unity

Van Doren, Mark, 37, 40, 47, 86
The Varieties of Religious Experience.
　See William James

Wideman, John Edgar, 18n9, 88
Wiesel, Elie: *Night,* 26, 173
Wolfenstein, Eugene, 77–78
Women: of color, 6, 16, 96, 99, 101–2,
　105–6, 109, 111, 117, 169; identity,
96–98, 115, 120; stories, 6, 8, 16,
19n7, 26–28, 61, 88, 96–97,
100–101, 105, 108–9, 113, 145–46,
169, 177, 181; "talking back" /
from the margins, 98, 101–2,
106, 109–12, 120, 142, 152, 158,
174
Wong, Cynthia Sau-ling. *See* Maxine
　Hong Kingston

Young Man Luther. See Erik Erikson